San Diego Christian College
2100 Greenfield Drive
El Cajon, CA 92019

More Praise for *Extreme Facilitation*

"In *Extreme Facilitation* Suzanne Ghais has generously shared her significant experience and insights facilitating difficult situations, to give us a rich resource that every facilitator will want to have on hand."

—Ingrid Bens, author, *Facilitating with Ease!*

"After years of courtship, facilitation and conflict resolution are finally getting married. This deep and thorough book describes their relationship and shows why they are meant for each other."

—Mark Gerzon, author, *Leading Beyond Borders: Tools for Transforming Conflict into Synergy*

Extreme Facilitation

Suzanne Ghais

Extreme Facilitation

Guiding Groups Through Controversy and Complexity

JOSSEY-BASS
A Wiley Imprint
www.josseybass.com

Published by Jossey-Bass
A Wiley Imprint
989 Market Street, San Francisco, CA 94103-1741   www.josseybass.com

Jossey-Bass books and products are available through most bookstores. To contact Jossey-Bass directly, call our Customer Care Department within the U.S. at 800-956-7739 or outside the U.S. at 317-572-3986, or fax to 317-572-4002.

Jossey-Bass also publishes its books in a variety of electronic formats. Some content that appears in print may not be available in electronic books.

Library of Congress Cataloging-in-Publication Data

Ghais, Suzanne, date.
  Extreme facilitation : guiding groups through controversy and complexity / Suzanne Ghais.
     p.   cm.
  Includes bibliographical references and index.
  ISBN 0-7879-7593-1 (alk. paper)
  1. Group facilitation. I. Title.
  HM751.G48 2005
  302.3'5—dc22   2004021979

Printed in the United States of America
FIRST EDITION
HB Printing   10 9 8 7 6 5 4 3 2 1

Contents

Acknowledgments

I extend my heartfelt gratitude to all those who have enabled me to write this book. I never would have mustered the courage were it not for Bernie Mayer, who urged me years ago to consider putting my thoughts to paper and has continued to support my effort, most recently by providing thoughtful feedback on my manuscript. I also thank my other two reviewers—Robbi Makely, friend, fan, and moral supporter; and Bruce Naylor, friend and spiritual mentor—for their caring, time, and wisdom.

I feel as though the author line should include the names of all those I have learned from, especially past and present colleagues at CDR Associates: Mary Margaret Golten, Bernie Mayer, Chris Moore, Susan Wildau, Louise Smart, Peter Woodrow, Mike Hughes, Judy Mares-Dixon, J. Michael Harty, Amy Miller, Julie McKay, and Jonathan Bartsch. I am indebted to my editor at Jossey-Bass, Alan Rinzler, whose willingness to take a chance on me I'll never forget and whose forthright feedback made me a better writer. I also thank Carol Hartland, Dave Horne, Sarah Miller, David Greco, Seth Schwartz, and all others involved at Jossey-Bass.

I offer deep and loving gratitude to my husband, Omar Jabara. He helped me with this project in innumerable ways, from covering for me in parenting duties to offering intangible support to which words can't do justice. He has offered consistent, selfless, and wholehearted support.

Finally, how do I thank my daughter Yasmeen Jabara, who is three years old as I write this, and was an infant when the inspiration to write this book first hit? I've learned more from her than she'll ever know. She is perhaps just beginning to understand what I've been doing when I've picked up my laptop computer, kissed her good-bye, and left the house to write. While this book has robbed her of some of my attention and energy, I hope it will serve her as a source of pride and an inspiration for her own accomplishments.

Suzanne Ghais
Arvada, Colorado

To Omar and Yasmeen

Extreme Facilitation

Introduction

Several government agencies and local interest groups in a medium-size Western city are sharply divided over whether to complete the last segment of a beltway around their metropolitan area. The governor, leaders of two of the suburbs, and several developers see it as crucial to making this a prosperous, world-class city; the leaders of one suburb and a coalition of citizens' and environmental groups see it as a major threat to their quality of life and to the environment. The issue involves not only impassioned emotions but endless amounts of technical data, from threatened species habitats to forecasts for increased traffic to the engineering challenges of using various alternate routes. You have been hired by the state's Department of Transportation to convene representatives of the major stakeholders on this issue—including mayors and county commissioners as well as environmental and economic-development interest groups—and to facilitate the resolution of this controversial proposal. Some participants question your ability to remain impartial when you are being paid by the agency who has made public their goal of completing the beltway, and they attack you personally, saying the Department of Transportation is just using you to create the illusion that public input mattered.

You have been hired to convene the executive team of a mid-size software company, which is doing well financially but coming apart at the seams internally. They have cycled through three CEOs in four years, and the current one (the former chief operating officer) acquired the role after waging a stealth campaign to discredit the prior CEO. Now some allies of the prior CEO are writing letters to the board of directors criticizing the current CEO. Some executives see no need to do anything but forget these "ego wars" and get on with their work. Others believe it's only a matter of time before the mounting disgruntlement and distrust translate into increased turnover and decreased productivity. There are already signs—a couple of valuable managers have resigned in disgust, and those who remain are beginning to take sides. One executive, a friend of both the current and the recent-past CEO, has been on sick leave with severe back pain. You have been hired by the chairman to turn this ship around. If you're unable to accomplish some constructive resolution within the next three days, the board of directors will have to "take action"—and that, executives suspect, means heads will roll.

Facilitation is not for wimps. You may have read other books about how to facilitate group processes or taken facilitation training. Perhaps you're a seasoned facilitator but looking to stretch your capabilities further. Perhaps you've been thrown into the role of facilitator with no instruction at all. Or perhaps this book is your first introduction to facilitation. In any case, you may have had little trouble with the basic skills of managing a group process and helping people make decisions or improve their functioning as a group. Yet when you are confronted with difficult scenarios like the ones above, you get sweaty palms or a queasy stomach, feeling ill prepared for such crisis intervention.

This book will help you change that. It presents a method called *extreme facilitation*, which is about how to facilitate in the most challenging situations—ones that are controversial, complex, large-scale, emotional, or otherwise exceptionally difficult.

The concept of the facilitator—a person who focuses on the process of meetings, as distinct from the person who makes the substantive decisions—was popularized in the late 1970s by the book *How to Make Meetings Work!*[1] Since then, dozens of books have been written on the subject.

Why then write yet another book about facilitation? The main answer is that tough situations require facilitation with more depth, more adaptability, and more strategy than is reflected in most of the existing literature.

Another answer is that many books on facilitation focus on a particular arena, such as self-directed work teams in organizations or land-use planning processes, whereas my work as a facilitator and mediator has allowed me to gain an unusual diversity of experience. I've done organizational work with large and small corporations, nonprofits, and government agencies. I've dealt with public-policy issues involving all levels of government, industry and business associations, private individuals, and citizens' groups ranging from large international advocacy groups to local volunteer groups. Every case has involved different issues and subject matter. I've learned that what works like a charm in one of these settings would draw jeers and rolled eyes in another.

Another distinction between me and some other facilitators is that my colleagues and I at CDR Associates, because of our background in conflict resolution, are often called in when things have gotten ugly. Whereas many books on facilitation treat conflict as an occasional snafu, I consider it a given. Conflict resolution is infused throughout this book. If there is no conflict, then the job will be easier. When there *is* conflict, I am ready and eager to dive in, and you can be too.

This book, then, picks up where others leave off—with an approach that's flexible enough to adapt to a wide variety of settings, and with strategies for handling the most frightening challenges.

Facilitation can be so much more than just keeping a group on its meeting agenda, keeping order, and taking notes. It can be an intervention that transforms how group members interact with each other and view the issues. It can help large publics work through a complex array of issues efficiently. It can allow organizations to conceive and implement major change or to conquer severe morale or communication problems. It often can enable resolution of the most divisive organizational or public-policy conflicts. It can provide a way for strong emotions to be channeled into productive decision making or improved relationships. To do all this, however, the facilitator must be equipped with a broader, deeper set of skills than is commonly assumed. This richer, more high-impact approach is what extreme facilitation is all about.

An Overview of Extreme Facilitation

Extreme facilitation is a creative endeavor, so the specific process is different for each group and each situation. Still, there are some core elements:

- The extreme facilitator is an *architect of a custom process*—one designed to suit the group and the situation.
- Customization requires a *deep understanding of the group*—its goals, needs, culture, and external conditions (pressures, requirements, and constraints).
- Customization also requires *knowledge of a wide range of possible techniques*. I'm using the term *techniques* broadly, to include, for example, things you might say to steer the discussion, questions you might ask to deepen mutual understanding, tasks to assign to participants, sequences of steps to get to a decision, or small-group activities. This does not mean that facilitation is all about techniques. The process design should be driven by the group and its needs, not by the techniques. Still, just as an architect needs knowledge of a range of typical floor plans and materials, the extreme facilitator needs a large selection of techniques in order to pick one—or invent one—that will be just right at a particular moment.
- The extreme facilitator must have a *strong personal presence*— the "right stuff." So much of a facilitator's success lies in the intangible impression she makes. Is she credible? Is she in control? Does she care about us? Can we trust her? Does she

remain centered as the going gets tough? Creativity is also critical. The right stuff is not a matter of technique—but it can be cultivated.

- The facilitator must *draw on all of the group's capacities—physical, intellectual, emotional, intuitive, creative*, and even *spiritual*. Each of these is a need that the facilitator must help fulfill, as well as a capability participants can lend. For example, if someone's emotions can be expressed and understood, he can offer the ability to be receptive to others' strong emotions. If someone's need for logical analysis and clear information is met, she can put her intellect to use in helping solve a tough problem.

Key Phases and Skills of Extreme Facilitation

Extreme facilitation can be understood as a mixture of basic phases, skills for drawing on the five capacities, and skills for responding to particular challenges.

1. The first phase in extreme facilitation is in-depth *assessment*, allowing the facilitator to gain an intimate understanding of the group and its culture, goals, and external pressures. Unless the facilitator is already a member of the group he's facilitating, he must usually do much more than meet with the group's leader or liaison, if he is going to take on a challenging group task.

2. In many situations, the facilitator also must conduct *convening*—that is, determining who the stakeholders are and how they should be represented. Sometimes it's obvious who should be at the table. In many situations, however, there is a vast public and multiple entities who are affected by the issue at hand, or a large organization with thousands of employees or members. In such situations, identifying stakeholders and determining representation are crucial.

3. During these early stages, the facilitator is also actively *contracting* with the group—gradually building both formal and informal agreements on what results the group members can expect from the facilitation and what resources and energy they need to commit in order to achieve that success. Contracting is a much overlooked part of facilitation, yet crucial to success, particularly in extreme cases.

4. Extreme facilitation requires careful *process design*—devising a custom process to suit the unique characteristics of the group and its situation, drawing from a wide range of techniques and activities. Of course, the facilitator must adapt to the changing dynamics of the group in the moment. Just as the design of a custom home will evolve during construction, so the process design will change as it unfolds.

5. Finally, there are the full-group meetings themselves. There are some broad stages to these: opening, building understanding, achieving the task, and closing. We can also look at group meetings through the lens of the "capacities" named in the previous section.

Here, then, is what I mean by the five capacities:

- *Physical*—the energy and physical comfort of participants. Physical discomfort or fatigue can undermine the most brilliant process design and the most well-executed facilitator techniques. Good mental and emotional functioning require a good physical state.

- *Emotional*—the productive expression of emotion. Ideally, emotions are handled such that (a) participants can express and relieve their emotional tension, (b) others can understand the reasons for the emotions, and (c) the expression of emotion does not make others feel threatened or uncomfortable. The extreme facilitator welcomes strong emotions and knows how to channel them toward the resolution of the underlying issues.

- *Intellectual*—the information content and logical problem-solving approaches. (Some books on facilitation focus on this realm almost exclusively.) This dimension includes not only classic problem solving, but how to manage technically complex information, as well as how to find solutions to competing interests.

- *Intuitive*—intuitive insights and creative ideas. The facilitator helps participants access their intuition and creativity through less-traditional modes of interaction and discussion. This dimension can help produce breakthroughs to difficult dilemmas or deadlocks, and can help turn around unhealthy relationships and organizations.

- *Spiritual*—the capacity to transcend narrow self-interest, extend compassion, and rise above base instincts; to maintain hope in the face of adversity; to feel gratitude rather than bitterness; to be truthful. The most difficult of all the dimensions, it does not require the facilitator to bring in either religion or "new age" concepts. Rather, it entails establishing the conditions—in comfortable, almost invisible ways—that draw out the best side of human nature. The spiritual dimension can help overcome the most deep-rooted conflicts.

Finally, the extreme facilitator must be able to confidently handle the challenges we most fear, such as

- Individuals who dominate the discussion
- Efforts to undermine the facilitator's authority or the process
- Hidden agendas
- Cultural clashes

- Angry outbursts
- Altercations between participants
- Physical aggression

An Overview of This Book

The chapters of this book roughly follow the components of this method as described above.

Part One lays the groundwork. It includes an exploration of "the right stuff"—key elements of self for the extreme facilitator. It also includes an overview of the concept of the facilitator as architect of a custom process, including a discussion of creativity as applied to facilitation, and a critical discussion of consensus and alternatives to it.

Part Two covers the all-important preparatory phases—assessment, convening, and contracting. (Of course, process design is also preparatory, but it is difficult to describe process design before describing the kinds of meeting content one might design, so this topic comes in Chapter Twelve.)

Part Three covers first some basics for the novice facilitator, followed by chapters on each of the five capacities—physical, emotional, intellectual, intuitive, and spiritual. It culminates in a chapter on pulling it all together through process design and handling particular challenges that many facilitators fear.

If you are new to facilitation, you will find that this book will provide a solid beginning to your learning and practice. If you are already a trained and experienced facilitator, it will stretch you further. You may notice that I reject some conventional wisdom about facilitation. For example, I believe that

- Consensus is often *not* the best group process.
- Creativity is largely about thinking *inside* the box.
- The facilitator's most important work is done *before*, not during, group meetings.

- Facilitators should *not* always confront someone who violates a ground rule.
- Facilitators should *not* always expect participants to state their views openly in front of the rest of the group.

You may also find that although I identify broad phases of the extreme facilitation process, I do not provide easy, step-by-step recipes for success. While such formulas are comforting, they don't allow for the creativity, flexibility, and customization that are so crucial for extreme facilitation.

Whether you are a professional facilitator or your professional or volunteer role simply calls on you to be savvy about group process, you will find yourself much more confident and competent to face the most daunting challenges by the time you finish this book. *Bon courage*, and happy facilitating!

Note

1. Doyle and Straus, *How to Make Meetings Work!*

Part One

Foundations

Chapter One

The Right Stuff

What It Takes to Be an Extreme Facilitator

A young woman was facilitating a dialogue on gangs, under the auspices of the city's mayor. The group included citizens, officials, and several gang members. Early in the first meeting, she referred to the flip chart. One Filipino gang member angrily told her that the word "flip" is used as an ethnic slur against Filipinos and that she had no business leading this group if she didn't know that. According to one participant, "The facilitator agreed in what could have been construed as a condescending tone, and apologized profusely. Not only did the ensuing discussion have nothing to do with the issues the group had originally gathered to discuss, the facilitator lost control."

What was going on here? This story was told to me by the participant quoted, Israel Davis.[1] He and I debated about what she might have said or done differently. As I imagined the scenario, though, I suspected the real problem was less what the facilitator said or did and more what was going on for her internally: perhaps she was afraid of the gang members. Perhaps she feared she lacked the competence to be working with ethnic minorities. Perhaps she really did look down on them. Perhaps she became overly self-conscious about the incident, worrying about her credibility with the group, consequently losing her focus on the group's needs and—ironically— the very credibility she was scrambling to prove.

Most of this book will be about the overt skills of facilitation. Yet this incident illustrates that your internal state can make all your brilliant skills and techniques irrelevant. In my opinion, the facilitator was not wrong to use the term "flip." Nor was it inappropriate, in my view, to apologize for having done so once she learned its double meaning. If she had approached the situation with authenticity, confidence, genuine caring for the group members, and the ability to stay centered, she would have been able to calmly and quickly apologize—perhaps after saying "Oh, really?" with curiosity to invite a little more elaboration—and return to the matter at hand.

She also might have asked herself, What's going on for this participant? Is he just aching to share what it's like growing up Filipino in a white-dominated culture? Is he trying to intimidate me? Why? Does he feel insecure in this forum? Does he doubt his ability to hold his own with these high-ranking city officials? Does he think this whole process is bogus? What might he need as evidence that it's not bogus? She also might have checked out other participants' reactions: Are they rolling their eyes? Do they look fearful and intimidated? Do they look fascinated, eager to learn more? Are they wondering if this whole effort is going to be a waste of time?

Depending on her "read," she might have acknowledged aloud what was going on, perhaps allotting some later time on the agenda to discuss the matter further (for example, to discuss the city's treatment of ethnic minorities). The point is, she would have been able to keep her focus on serving the group, instead of on preserving her own credibility and control—and thus would not have lost control.

Whether we're aware of it or not, our inner states, moods, attitudes, and thoughts are always on our sleeves. As extreme facilitators, we must be able to bring authenticity, confidence, presence, trustworthiness, and calm into the room. It is much more difficult to explain how to build these inner qualities than to teach skills and techniques. Yet these qualities can be cultivated. This chapter will help you do that.

Authenticity

My first professional job after graduating from college was training arbitrators. I was a twenty-three-year-old woman from an international, multicultural background. Because arbitration is much like judging, it tends to attract people who fit the stereotype of a judge—older, white men.

In my training sessions all around the country, I was often training people twice or even three times my age, and with whom I felt I had nothing in common. My employer was not worried about my lack of experience—the training focused mainly on the rules and procedures of the arbitration program, so the main qualification was that I could competently make a presentation. Nevertheless, I felt like an impostor. I tried to hide my youth, remained mute about my distinctive cultural blend, and pretended that I was comfortable in the homogeneous pockets of the country where I actually felt completely foreign. I was trying to be someone else.

I wonder now, as I look back, What if I had been open about my youth, my awe of the trainees' wisdom and experience, and my unusual cultural background? What if I had begun each training with some mildly self-deprecating humor about how I wasn't the type they expected to see at the front of the room? What if I hadn't censored myself from disclosing my Egyptian-English-Irish ethnic mixture or the years I'd spent overseas? What if I had acknowledged that my role was to teach the arbitration program's rules and procedures, not to presume that I could teach them judgment? I suspect I would have reached the trainees more readily, made the training more credible, and enriched it by drawing out participants' experience and wisdom. I suspect they might have had more respect for me, rather than less, as I feared.

In facilitation, not only do I connect better with groups when I am being authentic, but I have also learned that one of the most effective interventions I can make is to admit when a meeting is not going well and I don't know how to get it back on track.

In one facilitation, I sensed at one point that the discussion was going poorly, but I couldn't get a handle on exactly what was wrong or what I should do about it. Rather than plowing ahead trying to hide my sense of failure (which I'd done in the past), I openly admitted I was unsure what to do, called a break, and invited anyone who had ideas about how to proceed to come speak to me. Five or six people took me up on the invitation, and one in particular had excellent insights about what had gone wrong and solid ideas for how to proceed. After the break, we quickly got back on track. The key was being authentic about both my observations of what was happening and my inability to fix it myself. To admit such a weakness actually takes some strength.

Authenticity does not mean you have to reveal all aspects of your personal life in work settings. It is one feature of American culture that we disclose intimate details quite readily, and occasionally go too far. Some people do build rapport with a group by revealing personal information. Depending on the cultural setting, this could work beautifully, or it could make everyone feel uncomfortable.

Authenticity also does not mean being unprofessional. Just because you might swear, get drunk, or tell dirty jokes in your personal life doesn't mean that you need to do these things in your professional life in order to be authentic.

Authenticity does mean being comfortable with yourself, letting a group know who you really are, having congruence between your work and your values, and being willing to reveal your shortcomings or uncertainties—selectively—when this helps build a group's trust or improve the process or outcomes of facilitation. Authenticity allows people to connect with you more easily, which is crucial to having participants be open to your guidance.

Confidence

Authenticity clearly requires self-confidence. What do you do when you feel you aren't up to the challenge before you? How do you cope when you feel your authority or credibility could be attacked?

The paradox of confidence is that the more you worry about it, the less confident you will be—and the more vulnerable to attacks on your authority or control. I facilitated an internal meeting of our staff at CDR Associates during my first year at the firm, when I was still in an entry-level position. I felt intimidated at the prospect of facilitating a meeting of the people who held the fate of my career in their hands. At one point I suggested we end a particular discussion and take a break, and a senior partner said, "No, we need to finish this," and proceeded right on as if I weren't there. Obviously, I thought at the time, this partner had undercut and undermined me.

As I later recalled this scenario, I realized the underlying problem was not the behavior of that senior partner but my own trepidation. This fear not only may have exuded itself and weakened my presence, but more important, it kept me from continuing to serve the group. Had I focused back on the group rather than on questions of my authority, I could have asked the group members whether they needed a break, looked around for tired body language, listened for whether people sounded energized to continue the discussion, and intervened again if necessary. The point is that challenges to the facilitator's authority are in the eye of the beholder. If you're not worried about such challenges, you will welcome people's complaints or even attacks as valuable information to allow you to serve the group better.

So what can you do about your confidence? First of all, it's important to be honest with yourself up front about when something is truly over your head, even if it means turning down a golden opportunity. Second, needless to say, it is critical to be totally open about your credentials and experience with all prospective clients. Third, it's essential to prepare thoroughly as discussed in Part Two of this book, so that you are not walking in cold.

Then comes the key: after all that—once you've agreed to take an assignment, the group has made an informed decision to retain you, and you've done your prep—it's time to let the worries go. The group is getting exactly the level of competence they bargained for. They could have hired someone with ten more years of experience, but they didn't. They think you are good enough, and so should you.

This doesn't mean you won't have butterflies in your stomach. If you never want to feel nervous, extreme facilitation is not for you! It does mean that you keep your focus on the group and its needs—indeed, the needs of every single participant—rather than on your worries about your competence. You will get absorbed in your task, and magically, people will respect your role.

Presence

Beyond authenticity and confidence, we each must know what kind of presence we bring with us when we walk into a room, and build that into a strong, unique brand. A large part of our effectiveness as facilitators rests on this intangible presence.

Some people immediately exude warmth and compassion, somehow inducing people to open up to them. Some carry an aura of diligence, helping others get down to business and be productive. Some are strong intellectual thinkers, effortlessly leading others through analyzing and solving problems. Some are naturally funny, putting people at ease and helping them think more playfully and creatively. Some are persistently optimistic, helping a group maintain hope in the face of misfortune. These are just a few examples, and any of these strengths can be powerful aids to facilitation.

We probably cannot fundamentally change the basic presence we bring in the room or the effect this has on others. Presence is based largely on personality, which is formed early in life. What we can do is understand and enhance the natural strengths of our own presence, mitigate the negative aspects, and develop a unique, effective individual style. Following are some ideas for doing this.

Knowing Yourself

The first step in creating a signature presence is to know yourself. You cannot enhance your strengths if you don't know what they are; you cannot rein in your weaknesses if you do not realize you have them; you aren't going to develop your personal "brand" if you are unaware of what people already think of you.

Knowing yourself is a lifelong endeavor, but here are some good ways to start.

Get Feedback from Others. It sounds obvious, but many of us rarely ask for feedback. Colleagues and client groups, as well as family and friends, can all be good sources of information about how we come across to others.

Of course, what someone says about you is a function of their personality as much as yours. Particularly if feedback is negative, it's tempting to write it off as stemming from the failings of the other person. The trick is to remain open minded, get feedback from lots of different people, and look for common themes. If there are contradictions, it may help to try to figure out whether these are based on the idiosyncrasies of those giving you feedback, or if there is some other explanation.

For example, I was puzzled to learn that some people find me nurturing, empathetic, and approachable, while others find me aloof and intimidating. Eventually I figured it out: it takes time for me to develop rapport with someone new, for me to open up to them, and for them to feel at ease with me. The people who find me more approachable are generally those who have known me longer. This explanation helped me make sense of apparently contradictory feedback—and further proved the importance of getting feedback.

Take Personality Inventories. Personality inventories are excellent ways to strengthen your self-knowledge. They provide not only a way to look in the mirror but also a vocabulary for describing your personality and the ways it differs from others.

The most widely used and well-researched personality inventory is the Myers-Briggs Type Indicator®.[2] Some other instruments that can be helpful for facilitators include the Thomas-Kilmann Conflict Modes Instrument[3] and the Strength Deployment Inventory®,[4] which measures motivational values and how these change in conflict. Any well-designed inventory can provide insights on somewhat different aspects of personality.

There are two potential drawbacks to such instruments. First, it is easy to get pigeonholed or even stereotyped. (One training participant asked me how I could be in my line of work without being an "extrovert" and a "feeler" in Myers-Briggs terms. Please!) Second, they depend on our ability to answer questions about our own behavior accurately. The danger is that we'll answer the questions based on how we *want* to be.

Still, the inventories can give us some interesting insights. When I first tested as an INTJ (introvert, intuitor, thinker, judger) in the Myers-Briggs, I hated the description, which sounded like that of a boring, over-analytical scientist or engineer. With the help of a Myers-Briggs expert, I came to realize that the type did match the strengths I seem to have been born with. I've come to accept that the INTJ characteristics are part of my strengths and to use them, even though my experience and conditioning have led me to be quite different from a typical (or stereotypical) INTJ.

Observe Yourself.   There is one additional tool for achieving self-knowledge that is at least as effective as the others, but potentially very painful: watching yourself on videotape. If you have ever been through this experience you may remember cringing as you heard yourself stumble over your words or saw yourself looking more awkward than you had imagined. In my most recent experience of this, watching a videotape of myself giving a presentation, I discovered to my horror that I used annoying facial expressions and distracting head movements that I had been completely unaware of previously. Of course, we are our own worst critics. After overcoming my horror, I also saw the possibility of cultivating a personal brand that combines intellect and passion. This method gives us a way of seeing ourselves and our effect on others that is more brutally honest than any other.

Building on Your Strengths

Recent research indicates that outstanding leaders are not, as one might expect, "well rounded." They do not try to build all the skills of their occupation to the same level. Instead, they hone and rely heavily on their strengths, and they work around their weaknesses.[5] This, of course, requires acute awareness of one's strengths and weaknesses.

In extreme facilitation, you will need every resource you have—and the easiest way to maximize your resources is to build on your strengths. It won't help to obsess about your weaknesses. It will be crucial to know what your weaknesses are, so that you can minimize their impact or work around them—in other words, manage them, rather than try to fix them. This doesn't mean we shouldn't learn new skills or try to improve. It means that we will be most success-ful if we enhance and find uses for what we already do best, rather than forcing ourselves to go against our grain.

Trustworthiness

A facilitator who does not earn the trust of the group will fail. Par-ticipants in a facilitated process often feel vulnerable or skeptical. They may look for ways to test us. If they don't trust that our process is fair, honest, and reasonably safe, they will rebel or with-draw, and the process will lose credibility or even fall apart.

It will help you build trust if you are authentic and confident, and you project a signature style that uses your natural strengths—but it requires more than that. One could discuss at length things you could *say* or *do* to build trust, but being trustworthy begins inside, with your values and with how you feel about the partici-pants you are serving.

Values

A key to building trust is to act consistently. Consistently with what? With what some guru or book says you should be doing? If that doesn't jibe with your own most deeply held values, you won't be authentic. It's important to articulate for yourself the values you bring to facilitation, so that when faced with a dilemma or a diffi-cult situation, you will more easily be able to act consistently, explain your actions, and maintain participants' trust.

While some facilitators believe there are certain values that all facilitators must hold,[6] I believe that we each bring our own distinct set of values to facilitation. The task is to make them explicit and hold yourself to them. Following are the values that underlie my facilitation practice and therefore also the ideas presented in this book. You will need to identify what values are most important for you and your practice.

- *Human potential.* People have the potential to achieve great things, rise above animosity and distrust, and make decisions that are both compassionate and wise. Our challenge as facilitators is to help establish the conditions that allow people to achieve that potential.

- *Genuine participation in the collective life of organizations, communities, and the world.* Genuine participation (provided it includes education necessary to understand the issues) often leads to outcomes that are better and also more durable, because they have broad-based support.

- *Respectful engagement with people of different identities and perspectives.* Facilitation invites participants to name the issues that separate them and discuss them openly and respectfully. Such dialogue is essential to resolve contentious issues among people who cannot easily go separate ways.

- *Learning and creativity.* Participants in a truly successful dialogue are curious and open, prepared to change their minds in the face of new information or insights. They are also creative in searching for new solutions. For facilitators, ongoing learning (about the groups we serve, ourselves, and our methods) and creativity have obvious importance.

- *Honesty.* As facilitators, we must be honest about who we are and what we can offer. Honesty is also essential among participants for respectful dialogue and good working relationships. Honesty does not necessarily entail disclosing everything—confidentiality is often important—but honesty means not withholding information if that means deceiving others.

Some other values facilitators might hold include community, individualism, fairness or justice, transparency, courage, excellence, safety or security, harmony or peace, neutrality or objectivity, directness, equality, and so on.

If articulating our values is difficult, it is far more difficult to apply them consistently. We need to invite our clients and colleagues (and, for that matter, our friends and family) to let us know when we are not measuring up to our espoused values. It is humbling to realize how often we fall short, and it makes us more forgiving of others who may not be living up to their values.

Over time, acting consistently with our values helps us earn trust. Obviously, sometimes facilitators make mistakes. From a small mistake such as calling a participant by the wrong name to a major error such as breaking a confidence, our mistakes will diminish participants' trust in us. They will be more forgiving the more we have demonstrated, through our deeds, commitment to our values.

Not all facilitators articulate their values, but as groups become more sophisticated about choosing facilitators, it will become more important for facilitators to make our values known to our prospective clients. Being clear within ourselves about our values will become even more important.

Caring and Respect

Another key component of being trustworthy is genuinely caring about group members and feeling respect for them. It has become fashionable, particularly in dealing with discrimination and harassment in organizations, to say that we can't try to change someone's attitude—that is, we can't convert a racist or a sexist into an egalitarian—but we can set out rules of behavior (such as that supervisors must treat people equally). Maybe that's true in general (I'm skeptical), but for facilitators it is not. If we can't get past our dislike of someone, or if we think they are beneath us, it will show. Our attempts to *act* caring and respectful will come across as condescending or fake.

Of course, lots of people will rub us the wrong way. We will suspect participants of lying and playing games. We will encounter people who seem to act according to no values. We will meet personalities we simply find repulsive. What can we do?

When I encounter such a situation, I remember a story I read when I was traveling in Texas in 1999. There had been a string of murders along a railroad. Law enforcement officials had a suspect but had not captured him. The suspect's sister telephoned a Texas Ranger, Drew Carter. Negotiating through the sister, Carter worked out a deal with the suspect. They met at a pre-agreed location. The Texas Ranger shook the suspect's hand, then calmly handcuffed him.

Authorities were baffled as to why the suspect would return from hiding in Mexico to surrender voluntarily. The key, according to other law enforcement officials, was the rapport and trust established between Carter and the suspect via his sister.[7] If you think some of your participants in facilitation are unsavory, remember, *this was a suspected serial killer.* Somehow the Texas Ranger found a way to treat him with dignity and respect.

Even if we find some people unlikable, we need to still look for their underlying nugget of good, or at least their positive potential. We must try to see the world from their point of view, if only for a moment. We need to truly care about them and to respect them. Only then can we earn their trust—which is a prerequisite for having any influence on them.

Trust is like a house of cards—it can be built only slowly and painstakingly, yet it can be knocked down with one blow. Consistency and genuineness are key to building and maintaining trust, and you'll need to build all the trust you can in extreme facilitation.

Calm

I was once facilitating a series of meetings for a work team that was falling apart with interpersonal conflicts. Things had become so difficult that some team members were communicating only by e-mail, both to avoid blow-ups and to protect themselves against others' distortion of their words. We held a series of short meetings, about two hours each.

I arrived at one meeting feeling tense, overloaded, nervous, and anxious. As the discussion progressed, the tension level in the room seemed to escalate—all of the paranoid and hostile dynamics of the group were on display. The next week, I arrived at the meeting calm and relaxed. While I was no less busy, I had taken some time earlier that day to rest and do some deep-relaxation techniques. I also had thought through my to-do list and set some realistic priorities. This time, the tone of the meeting was focused and calm. Strong feelings were expressed, but in a productive, open-minded way—an impressive accomplishment for this singularly ill-functioning group. Is it possible that my own emotional and physiological state actually rubbed off on the participants?

I believe so. Research shows that our emotions are actually contagious—that others around us pick them up, even if we don't say a word.[8] My experience as a facilitator bears this out.

When issues get complicated, emotions run high, or discussions get jumbled or heated, it is easy to get caught up in it and feel scattered, confused, tense, or caught off guard. We need instead to be able to stay calm, centered, and focused.

There are several ways to do this. I have relied heavily on the use of deep-relaxation techniques, which I first learned as a way of conquering insomnia. I have gained the ability to relax the muscles throughout my body almost instantly, as well as a greater awareness of when I'm becoming tense. When facilitation gets difficult and I find my own tension escalating with that of the group, I consciously reverse it in my body—which in turn helps me bring more calm to the group. (If I have time, I spend a few minutes getting into a deep relaxation before facilitation begins.)

There are numerous techniques for relaxing. One simple way is to first tighten, then relax every muscle group, one at a time. Once you have used that technique several times, you will be able to relax each muscle group without tightening first. Other techniques for relaxation include various breathing techniques (for example, breathe in for four counts, hold for four, exhale for eight) as well as visual imagery such as imagining yourself lying on a beach.

Closely related to relaxation is meditation. Meditation focuses less on muscle relaxation and more on clearing the mind (although the two tend to go together). While there are many meditation techniques, most involve concentrating on something simple, such as an image (a point of light, a flower, a candle), your breath, or a word or phrase repeated over and over. The mind wanders easily (especially when we're worried—about a tough facilitation, for example), and it takes discipline to continually bring it back to the task of meditating. People who meditate often find that they can bring greater clarity, concentration, and focus to their work.

Another technique for learning to be the calm at the eye of the storm is centering.[9] Centering involves focusing on the actual center of gravity of one's body—usually an inch or two below the navel. It can be enhanced by imagining one's weight sinking down toward the floor, with one's legs rooted firmly there. Borrowed from the martial art of aikido, centering helps maintain both literal balance (it has been used, for example, in skiing instruction) and figurative balance—the ability to not be thrown off by unexpected turns of events. It can also help maintain stability in the face of an attack, whether physical or verbal.

There may be other ways you can find to get better at being the calm at the eye of the hurricane. The point is to pick one and get good at it. You'll need to do this outside of facilitation, so that once you are in front of a group, you can call on your calming technique instantaneously—remember, the big pitfall is to worry too much about yourself and forget to focus on what is going on in the group.

Enhancing authenticity, confidence, presence, trustworthiness, and calm is a long-term journey. It's not as if you have to be perfect in these ways before ever facilitating anything—I'm certainly not. I have, however, found my ability to handle extreme situations strengthened as I've made progress in cultivating these personal attributes, and I'm confident you will too.

The next chapter will help you make a quick yet profound change in how you facilitate—approaching each facilitation as an opportunity to be creative in coming up with a process to fit the situation and the group.

Notes

1. Israel Davis, private communication to author, 2004.
2. The Myers-Briggs Type Indicator is available from CPP at 800-624-1765 or custserv@cpp.com.
3. The Thomas-Kilmann Conflict Modes Instrument is also available from CPP, as shown in note 2.
4. The Strength Deployment Inventory is available from Personal Strengths Publishing at 800-624-7347 or www.personal-strengths.com.
5. Buckingham and Clifton, *Now, Discover Your Strengths*, pp. 19–27.
6. See, for example, Schwarz, *The Skilled Facilitator*, p. 8.
7. Thatcher and Kelley, "Slaying Suspect Surrenders," p. A1.
8. Goleman, *Emotional Intelligence*, pp. 114–117.
9. Crum, *The Magic of Conflict*, pp. 53–83.

Chapter Two

The Facilitator as Architect

The average person probably thinks of a facilitator as someone who does more or less the same thing each time—assembling an agenda from a list of topics provided by the group or its leader, standing in front of the group and calling on raised hands, signaling times to change to the next agenda item, and perhaps curbing members who dominate or encouraging the quieter ones.

If you imagine facilitation this way, consider the following scenarios.

• *Small Nonprofit.* I facilitated an annual retreat of about twenty people for a small nonprofit organization. We conducted the retreat with participants sitting in a circle in chairs with no tables. Among the activities we did was a visualization exercise. With the participants' permission, I guided them into a deep relaxation, then asked them to imagine an ideal workplace, one that embodied the values the organization stood for. The participants came up with richly detailed, inspiring descriptions.

Later, I also conducted a "coaching exercise," in which people paired up with someone they liked and were comfortable with, and shared a situation involving a difficult interpersonal relationship or incident at work. With written guidance provided by me, they coached each other on finding ways to resolve or improve the situation.

• *Partnering Workshop.* I facilitated a partnering workshop for a contractor team and client working on a massive construction project. The client team involved two government agencies and two companies; the contractor team included an engineering firm and over a dozen subcontractors. Over fifty people were present, sitting in groups of six to eight at round tables. One task was to identify "critical issues" in the project. To accomplish this, I had each table take two critical issues and identify what competing goals made them critical (for example, the short timeline for the project created a tension between the competing goals of doing the job right and doing it on time). This yielded a clearer picture of the challenges all would have to work together to meet.

Later, we had an hour and a half to build, from scratch, a partnership charter and reach consensus on it. To accomplish this, I had everyone write down on a sticky note what they needed from each other to make the project successful. Then I had them post the notes on the wall so everyone could read them. If anyone disagreed with someone else's note, they were to attach a different-colored note with the reasons for their objection. I took the notes to which no one objected, used an extended break (during which I encouraged participants to get to know each other) to compile and condense the notes into a coherent list of elements of a charter, and we hammered out consensus in the remaining twenty minutes.

• *Fast-Growing Company.* I cofacilitated a meeting of the leadership team of a fast-growing high-tech corporation that had in two years exploded from twenty-two employees to nearly five hundred as it won a series of major government and private contracts. The leaders sought to deal with problems resulting from operating in a constant crisis mode and to try to shift to more of a proactive, planning mode. There were only seven people present, and although they were nominally a leadership "team," they rarely had time to meet.

In designing the agenda, my colleague and I planned no overt "techniques"—no sticky notes, index cards, small-group breakouts, or activities. Instead, we focused on framing good questions for dialogue, and we worked throughout the meeting to ask questions that would prompt participants to go deeper to underlying problems. We also pushed them to keep their focus on the big picture of how the company's different departments worked together and not on individual

or department-specific issues. The result was much greater understanding and appreciation of each other's roles and constraints and a
plan for improving decision making, coordination, and teamwork.

• *Stakeholder Negotiation*. I cofacilitated a stakeholder negotiation to develop a recommendation on how to lower the levels of a
particular contaminant in an important reservoir that supplied
drinking water to a lower-income neighborhood but was also used
for yachting and other high-brow recreation. The controversy pit-
ted the outrage of the community against the funds and political
connections of the yacht owners. There had been street demonstrations that blocked rush-hour traffic for hours, angry letters to
the newspaper, and anonymous threats on the life of a yacht club
leader. High-priced lawyers and high-pitched national advocacy
groups descended on the town to support the opposing sides. We
convened a table of twenty-five people representing the key antagonists (neighborhood groups and the yacht club) as well as other
interested parties, including other recreational groups, companies
with factories near the reservoir, and environmental groups.

While the process took sixteen days' worth of meetings over a
period of eight months, it was an orderly one following a classic
problem-solving model: identify the problem or task, identify criteria for a good solution, brainstorm to discover possible solutions,
then evaluate and narrow the solutions. (A lot of education on the
technical issues took place early in the process as well.) Several different methods were used first to narrow the range of possible solutions and then to evaluate and select from them. The methodical,
rational approach seemed a soothing counterpoint to the fiery,
politicized controversy that had been raging for months.

These stories illustrate how different facilitation can be from one
situation to the next. The four processes bore little resemblance to
one another. Even the tone and atmosphere were different—intense
and personal in the small nonprofit, fast-paced and jovial in the partnering session, earnest and eye opening in the fast-growing corporation, painstaking and businesslike in the stakeholder negotiation.

The differences were not an accident. They were based on the goals and cultures of the different groups. If I had tried to do the visualization exercise, complete with deep relaxation and lying on the floor, in the construction partnering session, the participants would have either rebelled or laughed me out of the room. If we had used the highly-structured activities of the partnering session with the high-tech corporation's leadership team, it would have been a barrier to helping them have the kind of dialogue they needed. If we had let the stakeholder negotiation proceed in the unstructured way we handled the corporation, it would have descended into chaos and anarchy halfway through the first meeting. One size does not fit all in extreme facilitation; each is tailor made.

Designing the Custom Process

The extreme facilitator is much like an architect building a custom home for a family. An architect needs to understand a lot about the family: Do they cook much? Entertain? Do they have small children? Elderly members? Are they pack rats? Architects also have to understand the external environment: How's the climate? The noise level of the area? The slope of the land? Architects also have to know the family's goals in building the house, physically and emotionally: Do they need more space? Want an efficient space for fast-paced lives? Seek a beautiful setting for their art collection? Similarly, the facilitator needs to know a lot about the group. The architect develops a "program" or set of goals to guide the design, just as the facilitator works with the client group to agree on purpose, goals, and outcomes of the facilitated process.

Equipped with this "program," the architect has to tap her knowledge of many different typical floor plans, materials, fixtures, ways of doing wiring and heating and cooling, and so on. Similarly, the facilitator needs to draw on a wide range of possible group activities, techniques, and processes to design the details of the process that will meet the agreed-upon goals.

Then there's the creativity: the architect comes up with the design for *this* house for *this* particular family that has *this* set of goals and *this* set of circumstances. One architect may have some favorite floor plans or fixtures, but if his designs are truly custom, no two of his houses will be exactly alike. Similarly, no two facilitated meetings will be exactly alike.

Finally, design of a custom home is not a once-and-for-all decision. It will morph many times—when the client sees the design, when construction begins, and as it unfolds. Adjustments will be made continually, until the entire house is done. Similarly—and perhaps more so for a facilitator—the initial design is just a point of departure. Numerous changes to the agenda and to the techniques and activities used will be made on the spot.

Customization requires four things:

1. An in-depth understanding of the group and its circumstances
2. Agreement with the group about the purpose and goals of the process
3. Knowledge of a wide range of techniques and activities
4. Creativity

Item 1 will be covered in the next chapter, on assessment; item 2 in Chapter Five, on contracting. Item 3 will be covered throughout the book, beginning in this chapter with a critical look at consensus. First, though, we will focus on item 4, creativity in facilitation.

Tapping and Applying Your Creativity

Creativity is the magic ingredient that takes you from knowing what the group is after to being able to offer it, from having no plan to having the ideal plan. Therefore, creativity is one of the key attributes of the extreme facilitator.

I used to think of myself as quite uncreative. I played classical music, but I was lost without sheet music in front of me, and I found my brief attempt at learning jazz improvisation petrifying. I did some drawing, but always tried to replicate a photograph or a real-world scene, never devising a scene myself or creating anything abstract. I cooked only from recipes.

I'm not sure at what point I realized that a lot of the work I did was creative—not in an artistic way, but in a way that involved developing something that met a particular need at a particular time and that, in the end, was something new. Examples included developing new segments of training programs; coming up with new ways to meet organizational goals at work; setting up an event as a member of an activist group; coming up with the best way to approach someone about a difficult issue; and, I increasingly realized, designing meetings or processes to accomplish goals of particular groups.

We all have creativity. In what follows, I will help you access your creativity and apply it to facilitation. I will attempt to demystify it, though it is somewhat mysterious. Who can explain that moment when an idea comes to you? Creativity—the inception and cultivation and coming-to-fruition of an idea—is like the conception and gestation and birth of a child: we provide the conditions that allow conception to occur and the fetus to grow, but we do not *make* the baby ourselves. It just happens. When a baby is born, it is a miracle. The same is true of an idea.

With that in mind, here are some observations—including some folk wisdom I've found truth in—that will help allow these miracles to occur.

Necessity Is the Mother of Invention

People develop innovative ideas to meet particular needs at particular times. This phenomenon helps explain much technological development—cures for terrible diseases, ways to reduce industrial pollution, and so on. These require creative problem solving. Sometimes there are apparently conflicting needs to be bridged—for example, how can you make a smaller computer without it over-heating while in use? Creativity is needed to resolve such dilemmas.

Even some pure "problems" are really dilemmas if you look more closely. In other words, sometimes it's easy to solve the problem if time, money, and other resources are unlimited. The dilemma, then, is how to solve the problem within resource constraints. For ex-ample, "how to reduce pollution from a power plant" is stated as a problem, but "how to reduce pollution from a power plant without dramatically increasing costs" is stated as a dilemma. Similarly, "how to build consensus in a group of 150 people" is a problem, but "how to build consensus in a group of 150 people without using more than two days' worth of meeting time" is a dilemma.

To lay the groundwork for your creativity, it is important to articulate what problem you are trying to solve. This is often best done by framing it as a dilemma between conflicting needs or goals, and identifying explicitly what those are. For example, when I was new at CDR Associates, I worked with CDR partner Bernie Mayer helping to facilitate a retreat for a government agency. There were three different divisions that the agency's administrator had decided should be merged into one. The directors and managers in these divisions were so opposed to the decision that many were threaten-ing their resignations and a few had written letters to their Con-gressional representatives, but the administrator was clear that it was nonnegotiable (she had several good reasons that had to do with politics and the agency's funding). What was negotiable—and what we were brought in to help with—was *how* these leaders could struc-ture the newly merged division and function well within it.

As Bernie and I were crafting the agenda, we were searching for an opening question that would allow the participants to establish their voice and also express some of their frustration with the deci-sion. However, we also needed to keep the group focused on the "how" question (how the newly merged division would function), and not the "whether" question (whether the merger decision was a good one). Once we articulated these conflicting needs, we thought in silence for a moment, and then Bernie had an "aha" moment. He came up with the question, "What are the opportunities and challenges posed by the new structure?" The "challenges" question would allow some venting of frustration, but it would frame the gripes as challenges to be overcome. The "opportunities" question would help the group think more positively about making the new department work. The articulation of the dilemma—the competing goals—provided the soil from which the creative idea sprouted.

There Is Nothing New Under the Sun

Most "new" ideas are really not entirely new. Instead, they take things that already exist and graft them into a new context. For example, new American cuisine borrows elements of Asian and Mexican cuisines, as well as maintaining earlier influences from Italian and other European cuisines. Rock 'n' roll, a great American invention, emerged from the blending of the folk music of white Americans with the blues of black Americans.

Creative ideas in facilitation can also come from taking something from a different context into facilitation. For example, I began using a laptop computer in 1999. The obvious application for a laptop computer is to do desk work while at home or traveling. In one facilitation that year, it dawned on me that I could make use of it in facilitation. Initially, I used it just for taking notes. Soon, however, I realized I could use it in developing consensus documents by hooking it up to an LCD projector. As areas of consensus began to emerge, I would draft possible consensus language (sometimes during breaks), and project it for all to see. I invited participants to raise any disagreements they had with the language and to offer ways to improve it.

As tentative changes were made, I used the "track changes" function to underline new language and strikeout deleted portions, so others could consider and discuss the changes. Participants found it gratifying to see their proposed changes happen right in front of their eyes, and the method was far easier and faster than any other. Now I can't imagine developing a consensus document without a laptop and projector—even though this use probably never occurred to the inventors. When looking for that perfect idea to use in facilitation, the answer may come from someplace outside the established practice of facilitation.

Think Inside the Box

We are all familiar with the concept of "thinking outside the box." In my experience, being told to think outside the box can be paralyzing—you want to leave the box but don't know where else to go. Less widely recognized is the need to have a "box"—some structure, rules, or constraints within which most creativity can flourish. Then, if needed, the rules can be broken selectively—but you can't go outside the box if there is no box.

Creative writing is an example. Anyone who has written stories—from cartoon strips to novels or film scripts—knows that there is a certain formula that guides almost all storytelling. First the setting is established. Then there is a precipitating incident, followed by rising action (possibly accompanied by reversals), then a climax, then falling action, and finally denouement.[1] This simple formula has spawned thousands of stories throughout history. Far from constraining creativity, it enables it.

In facilitation, we operate within some structures. This book will lay out some broad phases, including assessment, convening, contracting, process design, and the full-group meeting. It will also cover some standard stages within meetings: opening, building understanding, achieving the task, and closing. These structures are boxes, and there is still plenty of room for creativity inside them.

Recreation and Relaxation

We have all experienced making a great deal of effort to solve a problem, getting frustrated, then having the solution pop into our minds later—perhaps in the shower, during a lunch break, or even in a dream. Creativity is housed primarily in the right hemisphere of the brain, which works by intuition and seeing the whole picture, in contrast to the left hemisphere, which works by analysis and logical thinking. Most of our formal education emphasizes left-hemisphere thought, so when we "think hard" in trying to figure out a problem or come up with a new idea, we kill our creativity with analysis. The left brain is also good at criticism (think of "picking things apart"), another creativity killer.[2] For these reasons, the right brain does its best work when we give intentional thought a rest.

One example of this comes from my husband's experience as communications director for a Congresswoman. One Friday, he left work having heard a speech that angered both him and his boss. The speech was made by another member of Congress, the Congresswoman's nemesis. My husband and I took a trip to the beach that weekend. Sunday night, I drove home while he gazed out the window at the farmland and the sunset. He didn't say a word, but when we got home, he whipped out a pad of paper and pen and started scribbling furiously. He wrote a funny yet biting speech, one of the most brilliant of his career. His boss delivered it with delight the next day.

Many of my ideas about process design come to me in a similar way, if not always so dramatically. Typically, when I first contract with a client, the situation sounds manageable. Then as I conduct assessment and convening, learning more of the background and the challenges involved, I feel increasingly overwhelmed, wondering how I can possibly create a process that meets the client's goals. Then, as I near the end of the assessment and convening phases, ideas start to come to me (and I try to capture them in writing along the way). I often get ideas in the morning after ruminating on the challenge the evening before.

When I begin process design in earnest, I often try to find a pleasant, relaxing place to sit and sip a hot drink while I work. A picture starts to emerge of how the facilitation will flow. Once I've connected the dots and put my ideas into a coherent agenda, I can then shift back into left-brain mode and critically review it, making changes as needed. We'll come back to process design in more detail in Chapter Twelve. The key point here is that we need to allow ourselves the time and space for creativity to flow.

Think Outside the Box

While most creativity takes place inside the box, there is also value to the adage of thinking outside the box. What this often means is eliminating constraints or rules that were imagined, not real; conventional, not required.

For example, I facilitated two consecutive annual staff retreats for a consulting firm. This firm was plagued by chronic complaints that came up in retreats year after year. The principals of the firm were frustrated that the staff always seemed to be whining about the same issues—being overworked, needing more opportunities for career growth, and so forth. I, too, observed that while the staff members were brilliant and dedicated, they largely seemed focused on selfish concerns rather than on how they could help make the firm a success.

When the second retreat was over, the firm asked me to write a report with my observations or suggestions about the organization. (This is an unusual request but one that I enjoy fulfilling.) Toward the end of the retreat I had learned something fascinating—that the principals of the firm held strategic planning retreats every few years with an outside, informal advisory board. The rest of the staff were not involved in it. As I relaxed on the plane home and got ready to start my report, something dawned on me: the staff were wrapped up in their self-interests because that's all that was left for them to discuss. The bigger-picture, business strategy discussions were done elsewhere. My report recommended that the staff be involved in the strategic planning in some way, and suggested multiple different ways this could be done.

In this case, the "box" was the idea that strategic planning could only be conducted by the principals and the outside advisers.

This was just a custom, not a rule—or at least, not an unbreakable one. Breaking this custom was key to shifting employees' energy from grumbling and whining into productivity and teamwork.

Using Consensus Strategically

The extreme facilitator must be not only creative, but strategic. The process must be tailored to meet the needs of the particular group at a particular time. For this reason, I disagree with those who argue that consensus is always the best way for a group to work together.[3] Consensus—defined as a collaborative process leading to a decision that all group members can accept—has both advantages and disadvantages. It is one of a range of possible group processes.

Consensus has become more popular as the expectations for participation and influence have increased. For example, Denver Public Schools now has a consensus-based committee at each school comprising faculty (represented by the union), administration, parents, and—in high schools—students. This seems to have been a way to respond to activism by these various groups to influence school decision making. Rather than making decisions and then defending them later against attacks by these stakeholders, it made sense to ensure up front that decisions have their buy-in. This is a positive example of using consensus to respond to increasing demands for participation and the sometimes contradictory pressures that can result.

Consensus has advantages including democratic participation, an opportunity to draw on the knowledge of all group members, and the resolution of disagreement. Consensus allows the group to find ways to satisfy the most important interests of all participants.

On the downside, everyone who has participated in a consensus process on a difficult issue knows that it requires tremendous work! It takes a great deal of time to identify all parties' interests, heal or build relationships, and conduct the kind of creative problem solving that will yield consensus decisions. It can delay action. That is worthwhile if a divided outcome will leave the group members fighting to block implementation or even to get decisions reversed. In other words, in high-stakes or potentially divisive situations, the time spent in consensus building can often save time later. However, not all situations meet this description.

Using consensus when it's not really needed can actually damage relationships, rather than strengthen them as intended. This is because of the frustration that emerges from trying to "make everyone happy." It's the frustration of having a decision blocked by a small minority.

For people with the proclivities to become a facilitator, it can seem terribly important to make sure everyone's interests are satisfied. It has been liberating for me to realize that in many situations, people are content not to have decisions go their way, because they get the procedural satisfaction of knowing that decision making will stay on course and action will not be delayed. Sometimes people are willing to change their destination if it means they can keep moving instead of being stuck in traffic.

I used to share the view that consensus was the superior decision-making process across the board. A big turning point in my views occurred in a situation in which I was a group member, not the facilitator. I was a member of a local activist group advocating for changes in U.S. policy toward the Middle East. The group operated by consensus of all members present. There was a small minority who favored very different activist methods than the majority—they used property destruction, flag burning, and other hostile tactics that I and many others opposed.

Because of consensus, we had to reckon with this minority not only on substantive matters, but on procedural ones too. One way groups can deal with such disagreements is to delegate the issue to the team in charge of a specific event. In this case, however, this same minority opposed letting any subgroups make decisions.

If I had encountered this organization as a professional facilitator, I might have seen such a controversy as an interesting challenge, and I probably would have pushed for continued work toward consensus. As a group member, however, I firmly believed that this subgroup was simply wrong. It annoyed me to have to entertain their opinions. Even if I were to be more open-minded and say that their views were just different and not inferior, they were still in the minority—so if anyone were to leave the group and start a new one, it should have been them. Instead, a number of us in the majority eventually left the group in frustration and founded a new one. We freed ourselves from the tyranny of this minority, but sadly, we also divided the energies of a group of otherwise like-minded activists.

I'm not against consensus. I have been part of many successful consensus processes—some as a participant, some as a facilitator. The point is that consensus is only one choice among many, and the choice should be made strategically.

Types of Processes: A Model

There are many types of group processes. Consensus assumes that the group needs to actually make a decision or a recommendation as a full group. There are other possibilities—input to a decision maker; identification of issues to delegate to a subgroup; a more informal meeting of the minds; or dialogue for the purposes of understanding only, with no decision involved at all. Even if the group is authorized to make or recommend a decision, there is majority and supermajority voting in addition to consensus.

Figure 2.1 shows a diagram of different process outcomes. The horizontal axis is a spectrum of group involvement in decision making. The variable on this axis is to what extent the decision maker elicits input from a broader group—of employees, citizens, or members.

We can mark off six points along this spectrum:

0. *No decision needs to be made.*

1. *Solo decision.* The decision maker needs no group input.

2. *Minimal input.* The decision maker puts out a proposed decision for a quick round of comments.

Figure 2.1. Types of Group Process.

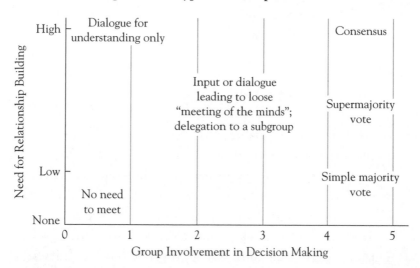

The horizontal axis is adapted from a model on levels of public participation developed by CDR Associates.

3. *Substantial input, or dialogue.* There is an opportunity for two-way communication between the group and the decision maker. This way, the decision maker can digest the initial input and respond to it, and then the group can respond again to the decision maker's concerns. There is more opportunity for a meeting of the minds. Still, the decision maker takes the discussion as input, and retains authority to decide.

4. *Group recommendation.* The group makes a recommendation that the decision maker has agreed in advance to consider seriously.

5. *Group decision.* Either the decision maker has handed over decision-making authority to the group, or (more often) there is no clear decision maker—all participants have a similar level of authority over the issue in question.

Along the vertical axis is the importance of relationship building among the group. At the low end, relationships are of virtually no importance, or they are already so strong there is no need to build them. At the high end, the group is falling apart with strife and needs to put itself back together.

The diagram shows the appropriate process depending on the desired degree of group involvement (horizontal axis) and the need for relationship building (vertical axis):

- If the need for relationship building is low but the group involvement is high, then simple majority voting (50 percent plus one vote wins) is appropriate. An illustration of this is a legislature—most legislators view relationship building with fellow lawmakers as secondary at best. Where the need for relationship-building is higher (further up along the right-hand side of the diagram), the appropriate process shifts to supermajority voting (requiring a larger majority such as 75 percent) and then to consensus. Some boards of directors work by supermajority vote, for instance.

- If the need for relationship building is high and group involvement is at zero (there is no decision to be made), the appropriate process is dialogue for the purpose of under-standing only. An example of this is dialogues held on highly emotional public controversies such as abortion or same-sex marriage, when the goal is not to come to agreement but rather to heal societal divides over these issues (while not asking anyone to change their opinions). As the need for relationship-building decreases (moving downward along the left-hand side of the diagram), there is less and less need to meet at all.

- For the middle of the diagram—some degree of input (on the group involvement axis), and some need for relationship building—it may be appropriate to have a loose meeting of the minds. This is often done in organizational staff retreats—there are discussions that lead to important new understand-ings and perhaps some new ways of doing things, but not concrete decisions. Another possible process is delegation to a

subgroup for decision making. For example, many membership organizations delegate considerable decision making to
working groups or subcommittees.

- The upper right corner of the diagram—where there is high
  need for relationship building and the group has the authority
  to either decide the issue or make a collective recommendation—is where consensus is most suitable. For example,
  members of a corporate executive team who are trying to
  overcome a crisis of leadership, conflict, and morale problems
  would have a strong need for relationship building to restore
  their cohesion and act in unison in leading the organization.
  As the top decision makers of the company, they probably
  have either complete decision-making power or the ability
  to make a recommendation that will be given enormous
  weight by the decision maker, be that the CEO or the board
  of directors. A process to address this executive team's
  problems should almost certainly use consensus.

This model gives some guidance as to when consensus is necessary.

Other Considerations

Of course, making the strategic choice among consensus and other
processes is not as simple as this diagram. Following are some additional considerations:

- *Magnitude of the potential decision.* Decisions that will be far
reaching, long lasting, or resource intensive to implement are more
suitable for consensus. For example, an organization may want to
use consensus for strategic planning—deciding its mission, vision,
values, and key goals. Decisions that are trivial may be suitable for
a vote or for delegation to an individual decision maker, even in a
group that otherwise uses consensus.
- *Culture and values of the group.* Some people are highly
action oriented and have little patience for process. They may be

happy to forego participation in decision making if it means the opportunity to get out of meetings and get on with the task. In contrast, some groups are strongly committed to the nonhierarchical, egalitarian values implicit in consensus. For them, it is just as important for the group to function in a manner that reflects these beliefs as it is for the group to accomplish its substantive tasks.

• *Need for buy-in.* In some situations, the group may need all members to buy in to the decision if it wants them to implement the decision willingly. This is particularly the case if members have the autonomy to implement or not, and to stay in the group or leave. One illustration of the need for buy-in from autonomous members is a coalition—a group of independent groups that wants to take certain actions in unison. The coalition (and particularly weaker members of the coalition whose effectiveness depends on the coalition acting collectively) has a strong case for using consensus to keep member groups from withdrawing and acting unilaterally.

• *Time constraints and deadlines.* Situations when time is tight and the need for action is high are the strongest candidates for authoritative, unilateral decision making. It is no surprise that militaries are strictly hierarchical: they have to act decisively in crises. If the decision maker is a group rather than an individual, a simple-majority vote is the next-fastest alternative.

If the extreme facilitator is to be the architect of a custom process, choosing processes strategically and devising techniques and activities creatively, the first step is to know the group thoroughly. This is the goal of assessment.

Notes

1. Silvester, "Writing Fiction."
2. Edwards, *The New Drawing on the Right Side of the Brain*, pp. 27–47.
3. See for example, Schwarz, *The Skilled Facilitator*, p. 24.

Part Two

Preparation

Chapter Three

Assessment

The Essential First Step

If you're handling a simple, non-extreme facilitation, you may get sufficiently prepared by having a conversation with one person in the client group to learn about the background of the situation and the goals for the process. In extreme facilitation, this is inadequate. You will need a much deeper understanding, and you will need to get at least a sampling of what may be opposite views of contentious issues.

Moreover, extreme facilitation requires customization. If you are going to face the thorniest challenges, one size cannot possibly fit all. The process has to fit the group, its goals, its culture, and its circumstances. Assessment is the process by which you discover those things.

For the sake of clarity, this book presents assessment, convening, and contracting as distinct phases done one at a time. In reality, although they are distinct activities, they take place more or less simultaneously.

Assessment Methods

Each method of gathering information about a group and its situation has strengths and drawbacks. Extreme facilitation usually calls for the intensive method of one-on-one interviews with at least some group members, so I give this topic the greatest emphasis here. Still, other assessment methods—written questionnaires, working with a process advisory group, or doing background reading—are sometimes also needed.

Individual Interviews[1]

Interviews with at least some subset of the group are usually essential in extreme facilitation. I have interviewed all group members in groups as large as forty-five people. In other situations that are not as contentious, I've interviewed a cross section of half a dozen or so.

Advantages.   The individual interview has many advantages:

- *It allows interviewees to be completely candid.* Interviewees can talk about any sensitive information, conflicts, unpopular opinions, and so on, as long as they trust you to keep a confidence. Lots of information comes out in individual interviews that participants would not express in front of anyone else.

- *It allows the interviewee to vent strong feelings in a safe forum.* The interviewee can freely express opinions without leaving anyone else feeling threatened or offended. If you listen actively and empathetically, you can often de-escalate those emotions so that the individual comes to the full-group meeting in a much more calm and reasonable state of mind.

- *It allows you to begin to "coach" the interviewee.* You can help prepare the interviewee to participate in the larger meetings in a way that is both effective in meeting the interviewee's interests and conducive to a good group process. Once the interviewee has given the information you've requested, has expressed her feelings, and has gained some trust in you, then she may be receptive to your gentle suggestions.

These advantages make individual interviews particularly well suited to the kind of extreme facilitation marked by high levels of controversy, conflict, or mistrust.

Disadvantages.   Individual interviews also have some drawbacks:

- *They are time consuming.* Talking to people one at a time is probably the least efficient way of gathering information, especially from a large group of people.
- *The selection of interviewees can get political.* If you interview a subset of the whole group, people often attach prestige to being selected for an interview. One organization, in preparing for a retreat, originally contracted for me to interview a cross-section of six people from a total organization size of thirty. However, two top executives were miffed that they were not chosen. I ended up interviewing them, but it meant I had a more complete view from the top of the organization than from the other levels.
- *There is no opportunity before the first full-group meeting to see the group interact.* This is the only way in which this method is lacking in richness.

Skills for Interviewing.   Several skills can be important in interviewing individuals:

- *Selecting interviewees.* In determining whom to interview, it is helpful to consider the level of conflict, the range of perspectives, and the time and resources available. The greater the level of conflict, the more likely people are emotionally agitated and the more the group will benefit from lots of one-on-one interviews. In one highly conflicted organization I worked with, nearly every interview uncovered some additional issue or distinct set of grievances that had to be considered in the process design.

It is also important to get the full range of perspectives on the issues in question. That might mean selecting representatives of different "camps" or sides of an issue if these exist; of different layers in a hierarchy; of different functional or topical areas or departments; or of different demographic categories (age, gender, race or ethnicity, any other categories)—if these differences are relevant to the issues. In a public-policy process, interviewees may need to represent different types of stakeholders—such as government, industry, and citizens—as well as perhaps different organizational sizes or resource levels, different sides of the issue, different demographics, or different geographic areas.

If there is any uncertainty about whom to talk to, it can be helpful to ask interviewees whom else they think you should interview. (Sometimes the view of your main point of contact on such matters is not the only one you should consider.)

• *Establishing confidentiality guidelines.* The higher the level of distrust within the group, the more important confidentiality will be for ensuring candor. It's critical to get clear with the group leader, your point of contact, or the sponsor of the effort what information they will require you to disclose, and to let interviewees know that up front. Generally, in high-conflict situations, I simply say that all interviews will be confidential, except that I will report themes heard across multiple interviews. I've found that in some situations people feel no need for such protection, but in others they insist on 100 percent confidentiality. The higher need for confidentiality is typically a sign either of high distrust or poor communication within a group.

• *Starting the interview on the right foot.* Before jumping into questions, it's appropriate to start by introducing yourself, giving a little background on why you are conducting the interview, and allowing an opportunity for questions. Your willingness to answer questions about your background, qualifications, or motivations openly will contribute to building trust. You might also want to make the first question a low-pressure one, such as an invitation for the interviewee to say something about her role or position.

• *Using broad, open questions.* Broad, open questions allow interviewees to focus on the issues they see as most important. This is key in identifying issues for group discussion. For example, a question such as "Do you think employees are compensated adequately?" implies that compensation is the most important issue, and invites only a "yes" or "no," prompting interviewees to take sides. Instead, "What are the key issues that need to be discussed?" is appropriately broad and open. If compensation has been established as an important issue, then "What do you think of the compensation system?" is open enough to elicit the most important interests.

• *Active listening.* This skill has been written about and taught widely,[2] and for good reason. It not only draws out information, but also fulfills a need we all have to be heard and understood, especially if we are in any kind of difficult situation or conflict.

Briefly, active listening involves giving the speakers your full attention, showing genuine interest in their perspective, encouraging them to expand on what they have said, and demonstrating that you understand. Specific techniques can include paraphrasing or summarizing what the speaker has said, reflecting back both feeling and content, and using body language or other indications of full attention and receptiveness (such as leaving arms and legs uncrossed, making eye contact, leaning forward, and so on).

The specific techniques are less important than the intent and attention behind them. The techniques will come naturally if you are truly eager to spend some time seeing the world from the speaker's point of view.[3]

• *Holding off on trying to change anyone's mind.* An important part of active listening is knowing what not to do. Offering advice or solutions, questioning the speaker's view of the situation, explaining someone else's point of view, and other well-intentioned interventions detract from the benefits that deep listening offers. It's best to hold off on these things, at least until after the speaker has fully expressed himself, his emotional tension has subsided, and he is convinced you truly understand him. You may have to wait until a future conversation before you can offer any such guidance.

In one large, multiparty process I facilitated, I had trouble dealing with one rather abrasive activist. She tended to make emphatic points at random times, when we were on unrelated agenda topics. Other participants would roll their eyes and tune out, and the activist was frustrated that her points fell flat. I worked and worked to overcome her general distrust of me and the process. Finally, eight months into the process, toward the end of a long phone conversation, she asked for my advice. I gently suggested she might be of greater influence if she thought about timing. "Timing! Right! Timing is key," she enthused, and she was a much more productive participant thereafter. If I'd offered that advice any sooner, when she still distrusted me, it would have been met with only resistance.

• *Coaching.* It can be valuable to offer some coaching when the time is right. Coaching implies criticism, so you need to be delicate—unless the person is, by personality or culture, highly direct and confrontational. You might ask if it would be all right to offer an "observation" or a "suggestion." Then you might gently describe specific behaviors that have been troublesome, offer specific facts that seem to contradict the way the speaker sees the world, or perhaps cite specific statements made by others that contradict the speaker's views of them (without violating any confidences). Better yet, you could ask questions that elicit these.

Alternatively, you might suggest ways of presenting a point that will be more likely to elicit a cooperative response from others. To the extent the group is interdependent, the speaker needs to present his points in a manner that others will be receptive to—a way that asserts his own needs without accusing, threatening, or making ultimatums. It's common, for example, for people to frame their concerns in terms of generalizations about other people's motives, personalities, or psychological characteristics. "He's just jealous of my success and has made me his favorite target" and "She's passive-aggressive" are examples. You need to coach people to describe specific events and actions that were troublesome rather than these generalized explanations that will be taken as character attacks.

All of this coaching will be effective only if your intent is to support the individual, not just to "manage" him or her. The intent will come across.

• *Curbing ramblers and drawing out the succinct.* During interviews, some people talk endlessly, even after they have expressed and relieved their emotions and have conveyed all important information. You may need to put your manners aside and cut the speaker off to ask your next question or to close the discussion. You may also need to avoid paraphrasing and summarizing, as anything you say will prompt a rambler to keep on talking.

It might surprise you to hear that it's even harder to handle the opposite: people who answer with precisely the information that answers the question and no more. You need to encourage such people to expand on the issues they find most important so that you can ascertain what issues will merit group discussion and how contentious they will be.

A key here is to follow up on topics that seem loaded with emotional energy—as indicated by tone of voice, body language, or repeated phrases. Then you can ask what's meant by the phrase, ask for elaboration, or ask for an example—which often brings out *the* example, the real problem.

Written Questionnaires

Written questionnaires are another method of gathering information for assessment. Of course, they have their own advantages and disadvantages. I don't use them often, though when I have they've provided good information to *supplement* the more intensive interaction of one-on-one interviews.

Advantages. Written questionnaires allow the facilitator to get a good deal of information in a condensed period of time, and are therefore cost effective. In addition, some people are more comfortable and candid in writing—they can respond with privacy and anonymity.

Disadvantages. There is a lot of richness lost in limiting communication to the written word. In interviews, you can follow the speaker's energy and emotional emphasis, and spend more time on what the speaker feels is most important. Emotional content is often lost in written responses, and there is no opportunity to follow up on what might be key points. Perhaps more important, there is no opportunity for the facilitator to establish relationships. Finally, return rates tend to be low—some group members may not bother to complete and return the questionnaires.

These drawbacks make written questionnaires, if used alone, inadequate for extreme facilitation. However, they can be an excellent way of supplementing interviews. For example, before a two-day facilitation with an organization to address a number of communication problems, I interviewed a cross-section of six employees, worked with a process advisory group, and used written questionnaires to invite input from all the other employees.

Skills in Using Written Questionnaires. Following are some basic tips for using simple, open-ended questionnaires in assessment. (Any effort to use written questionnaires on a large scale should probably make use of experts on survey research to help design the questionnaire and interpret the results.)

- *Use the same questions as you would for interviews—broad and open.*
- *Be clear about confidentiality guidelines.* A piece of paper can easily make its way around to other people; if you're using an e-mail survey, this is even more true. It's important to be clear and precise about what you are going to do with the completed questionnaires so people can assess how candid they can safely be.
- *Consider urging respondents to provide their names.* You will need to get to know the personalities in the group, and in some settings, comments will only make sense if you know their source. If you can assure a level of confidentiality that group members are comfortable with, you can make a case that names will enable you to do your job best.
- *Try to have a few people from the group work with you.* Have a few group members help either to design the questionnaire or

at least to review it and provide feedback before it's distributed. They may be able to help you determine the kinds of questions that will get the most valuable responses and point out questions that may be misinterpreted.

- *Try to build in some in-person or telephone contact.* For extreme facilitation, you'll need the trust building that occurs with in-person contact. If your only contact with the bulk of the group is through written questionnaires, it will be helpful to set up some opportunity for relationship building with the group. For example, you could briefly attend a key staff meeting and describe what you're doing in the assessment and answer questions. Or you might give respondents an opportunity to contact you by telephone if they wish.

Background Reading

Regardless of methods for obtaining the views of group members, there may also be documents you will need to read to absorb more objective or public information. This is especially true when highly technical or complex issues are on the table.

Group members often suggest reading material for me before I think to ask about it. In other cases, I hear about particular documents during interviews and it becomes clear I should read them. If I'm facilitating discussion of a technical subject I'm unfamiliar with, I ask the client group or knowledgeable colleagues what I can read to get educated (although I'd prefer to cofacilitate with someone who does know the subject matter). In my assessment experiences I've found myself reading everything from newspaper articles to organizational charts, from angry letters to past agreements, from marketing materials to regulations.

Working with a Process Advisory Group

In extreme facilitation, it can be useful to have some subset of the whole group work with you on process matters. They can review agendas and give feedback, provide insights when you're bewildered or stuck, and otherwise guide and advise you. We at CDR Associates often refer to this as a process advisory group. Such a group helps develop the larger group's capacity to steer its own processes. It also may help broaden commitment to the process.

Process advisory groups are more appropriate when the group is larger, when the process is longer-term or complex, when there is a need for broader buy-in to the effort, or when the group wants to develop some stronger internal capacity for managing process.

Here we focus on the possible role of an advisory group in assessment. In organizational facilitation, it's often clear who will participate in the facilitation, and therefore we can select from among that group to form the process advisory group. In other situations, however, we won't know who will constitute the full group until after convening. In that situation, we can't assemble a process advisory group until later.

Possible Roles of an Advisory Group. A process advisory group, if formed at this early stage, could take on any of several possible roles in assessment:

- *Advise you on whom to interview.* If your advisory group represents a good cross section of the full group, they'll be tuned in to the different subgroups and factions that you'll need to connect with.
- *Work with you in developing written questionnaires.* An advisory group can help formulate questions or, at least, review a draft questionnaire and provide feedback.
- *Provide a group interview.* Conducting an assessment interview with the whole process advisory group at once can be a way of saving time over one-on-one interviews, while still providing some important in-person contact. While some of the candor of individual interviews is lost, you might be able to observe a sample of how the group interacts.
- *Interview other group members themselves and give you summaries, either oral or written.* This could be another way to

save time, and it has the added advantage of building process expertise among the advisory group members. The possible drawbacks are, of course, that the opportunity to build your own relationships with the larger group is lost, interviewees may not trust these group members as much as they might trust an outside facilitator, and you may lose specificity of information. Consider whether advisory group members should interview people from inside or outside their own work units, and whether they can be most effective interviewing organizational peers, superiors, or subordinates.

- *Review and analyze written questionnaire responses.* Allow the advisory group to do this if and only if all respondents are aware that this will happen and you are fairly certain that this will not cause respondents to hold back important information.

Possible Challenges. A process advisory group can take additional time. It can also be difficult in some settings to set meeting times that work for all members, so the overall process could be slowed down. If speed is essential, you may choose not to use a process advisory group, opting instead for simply getting process guidance from participants individually.

Skills in Working with a Process Advisory Group. A process advisory group is another group to facilitate and attend to. For this reason, a number of skills are important in maximizing their usefulness.

- *Selecting advisory group members.* The same guidelines that apply to selecting individual interviewees apply here as well—the group should be a cross-section of the full client group with respect to whatever divisions, camps, levels, or demographics are relevant. In addition, advisory group members ideally should be people who seem to have a knack for process (according to their colleagues)—though they needn't have any special expertise.

- *Using the group's time judiciously.* It's important to give process advisory group members your best estimate of the time commitment involved, and to ensure that you have their agreement to serve on the group. Consider when you need to have a meeting, or when a shorter conference call or even individual check-ins might suffice.

- *Making sure they have a role.* Once you've established the process advisory group, don't forget to take advantage of its members' ability and willingness to help, even if only occasionally.

Getting Started

Before beginning assessment, you'll need some form of introduction. Ideally, someone will have told the group members in advance who you are, how you were selected, what's happening, and why. If this is impossible, you will need to have ready an explanation of the facilitated group process and your background. (If distrust is extremely high, participants may need to play a part in selecting the facilitator; otherwise, they may reflexively distrust whomever has been chosen.)

If you're using interviews, it is ideal to distribute the interview questions in advance, so interviewees have time to think about how they will respond. This helps make the responses clearer and more coherent. I learned this through an experience as an interviewee when I was a participant in a facilitated process. I found it very difficult to answer the big, broad questions the facilitator asked, and I felt my answers were muddled and disorganized. My answers would have been much more useful had I been able to mentally prepare for the questions.

In describing the process to participants, remember that the more people have a say in what will happen, the more supportive they will be. Most of us treasure our freedom and resist being told what to do. In other words, the more that can be left open for shaping by the participants, the more buy-in you will get.

For example, suppose you have been asked to facilitate a stakeholder dialogue to develop a consensus master plan for a municipality, and you're just beginning to approach potential participants. People will be more engaged if you can truthfully say, "We are exploring the possibility of holding some kind of citizen-participation process on the City's Master Plan, and we thought you might be interested in this," instead of, "We are planning to have a stakeholder dialogue on the City's Master Plan, and we would like you to be part of it."

Assessment Content

We now turn from assessment methods to assessment content: What kind of information are you trying to gather? The short answer is, whatever you need to know to understand the group, its issues, its culture, and its goals. Following is the longer answer, along with some examples of questions for interviews or questionnaires. They will have to be selected and tailored to the situation. For each interview, you will want just a handful of questions—say, five to ten. With some interviewees, you may only get to two or three of your questions, so you will need to prioritize them. (Convening, when it's necessary, will require its own set of interview questions, as discussed in the next chapter.)

Issues and Problems

Often, a facilitator is brought in to help deal with fairly identifiable problems. We need to uncover what these problems are, from various viewpoints.

Sample Questions

- What are the major issues you need to confront or problems you need to tackle?
- What do you feel are this group's weaknesses?

- What obstacles have made it so difficult to reach your goals?
- What about this situation is the toughest?

Goals and Desired Outcomes

Group members may have a clear sense of what they might achieve through a facilitated process. If so, you need to hear it. If not, they need to start thinking about it.

Sample Questions

- How do you think a facilitator could help with the problems you've mentioned?
- What prompted you to seek a facilitator?
- What are you hoping this process will achieve?
- What are your highest hopes and your greatest fears for this process?
- What would happen if you did not conduct this process?

Key Stories

Questions about goals, problems, and issues will often lead into stories. Any set of people with ongoing interaction is likely to have key stories deeply etched in its collective memory.

The stories are often about alleged or perceived wrongs done by one person or group to another. The lesson often derived is "they can't be trusted." These are trauma stories, and to some degree, the people affected are traumatized. They may act in ways to guard themselves against similar traumas in the future—withholding information, securing a coalition of trusted allies, demanding certain actions from the offending party, making preemptive strikes. (Success stories will be discussed under "strengths" further on.)

Sample Questions

- Can you give me an example of this problem?
- What have been the key turning points for this group (or in your relationship with _____)?

- When did your feelings about _____ start to turn negative? What happened at that time?
- It sounds like there may have been some really bad incidents between you and _____. Can you describe one?

Strengths

A highly effective way of bringing about change is to seek the strengths of the group, identify its successes, and find ways to replicate or expand on that success.[4] For a facilitator walking into an extreme situation, it is important to elicit problems, but this should be balanced with identifying positives. This is encouraging and energizing for participants, and it puts the problems in context. It's natural to direct one's energy toward problems in order to solve them, but this sometimes magnifies them. Instead, we can help the group search for ways to build on successes.

An example of this comes from within my organization, CDR Associates. For years, we had numerous frustrating meetings about "marketing." We all felt we should be better at it, yet the topic seemed both intimidating and distasteful. We finally found a productive way to approach it: we identified our most important clients and traced the story of how our relationship with each client began and continued. This made the "marketing" topic much more manageable—we simply resolved to do more of the strategies that had already worked.

Sample Questions

- What do you feel are the strengths of this group (or this relationship)?
- What have been some of your greatest successes?
- What are you most proud of in this group (or this relationship)?
- What would you *not* want to see change?
- Can you identify a time when this was not a problem? How were things different?
- What is your vision of what this group could be in the future?

External Conditions

Sometimes a big source of a group's trauma or troubles is external. There may be forces placing nearly impossible demands and pressures on a set of players. For example, I once worked with a federal agency that had a challenging mandate to start with. Over time, Congress continually both reduced the agency's funding and increased the expectations of it. All the while, the agency was getting negative press, while its successes seemed to go unnoticed by the media.

External forces could include public opinion and expectations, market forces (demand for the product or service, the competition, economic conditions), laws and regulations, budget changes, and the demands of external groups such as regulators, customers, voters, suppliers, partner organizations, fellow coalition members, parent organizations, organizational superiors or administrators, or boards of directors.

Sample Questions

- What kinds of external pressures are you under?
- What demands are being placed on you from outside?
- What external conditions affect the problems we're discussing?
- What trends and changes do you track, or should you track?

Process Concerns

Many people have some idea of what they do or don't want in a facilitated process. For example, when I worked with one group of agriculture specialists, many said they did not want us to do anything "touchy-feely" or make them "hold hands and sing 'Kumbayah.'"

If the group already exists as a group, it's important to find out how its meetings typically go and how members feel about them. The facilitated process may be an opportunity to begin to change some bad habits. Similarly, if people have had past experience with facilitators, they may have strong feelings about things those facilitators did well or should have done differently.

When you ask about process concerns, some people will not have an answer. They may be puzzled about why you asked, or respond that "you're the expert." That's fine. The important thing is to uncover the procedural concerns if there are any.

Sample Questions

- What concerns or interests do you have about the process we're undertaking?
- Have you worked with a facilitator before? What was that experience like? What was helpful? What was unhelpful?
- What are this group's meetings usually like?
- Are you looking forward to this process or dreading it? Why?
- What advice or suggestions do you have for me in working with this group?
- In an ideal world, how would this process unfold?

Assessing Group Culture

Knowledge of a group's culture is crucial to designing and delivering the kind of custom process needed for extreme facilitation. For example, if group members are highly task-oriented, they'll get frustrated if you hold a full-group discussion about what ground rules would be useful or how to sequence the items on the agenda. Alternatively, members of a more process-oriented group might get suspicious if you denied them the opportunity to discuss such matters.

Cultures vary in innumerable ways. Here I will focus on a few key cultural variables that have the most significant impact on extreme facilitation.[5] Because people are usually unconscious of their culture, asking direct questions about it rarely works. Instead, I offer some clues to look for in discerning a group's culture.

Emotional Expressiveness

You might associate extreme facilitation with dramatic emotional displays, but it depends on culture. You might instead see tense stillness and pursed lips. Emotions are universal, but there is tremendous cultural variation in the degree to which it's acceptable to express them.

Clues to the Degree of Emotional Expressiveness

- *The use of emotion words, such as* scared *or* mad. In emotionally reserved cultures, emotions are referred to (if at all) via metaphor, such as "My neck was on the line" rather than "I felt vulnerable."

- *The strength of emotion words or phrases.* Cultures less comfortable with emotions may tend to understate; cultures more emotionally expressive may tend to overstate: *tired* versus *exhausted, pleased* versus *ecstatic, annoyed* versus *furious*. Expressive cultures may also use more profanity—but this also depends on deference to authority, described later (whether you would swear in front of your boss, for example).

- *The degree of animation in people's speech.* More dramatic facial expressions, hand gestures, and range of volume, pitch, and speed indicate more comfort with emotional expression.

- *Reactions to an emotional outburst.* Do others welcome and embrace an outburst and remain relaxed? Or do they feel threatened or assaulted, and find excuses to leave the room or change the subject?

Implications for Extreme Facilitation. Following are examples of how the degree of emotional expressiveness affects the facilitator's work:

- If a group is emotionally reserved, the facilitator may have to minimize or sideline participants' emotional displays, such as by calling a break, reframing strong statements to more emotion-free language, or suggesting ground rules about how people express themselves. This might sound counterintuitive—one might think such a group would need to be drawn out emotionally. In my experience, however, emotionally reserved participants will be more comfortable if there are constraints on the expression of emotion. This guards against emotional outbursts by the minority in the group who may be more emotionally expressive, which could be terribly upsetting to a mostly reserved group.

- If a group is emotionally expressive, the facilitator will need to fully integrate emotions into the discussion, such as by drawing out participants' feelings and by encouraging exchanges in which strongly held views are aired. Emotionally expressive participants will not feel the meeting has "gotten to the real issues" unless feelings get expressed openly.

Deference to Authority

All cultures have hierarchy, whether formal or informal, acknowledged or denied. The important variable for extreme facilitators is the degree of deference—in other words, how differently people treat others depending on status. Some cultures mask hierarchy by using very little deference: everyone is equally open and direct with everyone; anyone can ask anyone else for a favor.

In most cultures, however, there are many ways in which one treats a status-superior differently from a status-equal and a status-equal differently from a status-subordinate. In one large bureaucracy I worked with, one could draw a line across the organizational chart below which people went by first name and above which they went by Mr. or Ms. plus last name. Other signs of deference are more subtle.

Clues to the Degree of Deference to Authority. The greater the deference to authority, the more marked will be the following:

- Your ability to tell who's the boss (or the higher-ranking official, the higher social class, and so on) before you've been introduced to anyone. An acquaintance of mine often negotiated with automobile companies as part of her job. She said that in the team that represented one of the "big three" American companies, it was obvious who was the boss—he did most of the talking, and the others nodded along, looking at him for approval when they did drum up the nerve to speak. In the team representing a newer, more innovative company, my acquaintance said it was impossible to tell who had what rank—this company had a more egalitarian culture, one with less deference to authority.

- A change in the tone of conversation when higher-status people enter or leave the room.

- A more formal tone when lower-status people speak to higher-status people. This is often accompanied by a more tense physical posture.

- Terseness or abruptness when higher-status people speak to lower-status people, and, by contrast, more qualifiers when lower-status people direct requests, complaints, or other sensitive messages to higher-status people. Consider "Kevin, could you complete that questionnaire today please," versus "Um, Ms. Lewis? I wonder if you have had a chance to—er, if you might have time today to fill out and return that questionnaire that was handed out last week."

- A tendency to give the "floor" to higher-status people when they interrupt or enter the room. If one person enters a room when another two are talking, who makes whom wait?

Implications for Extreme Facilitation. Conventional approaches to facilitation tend to assume minimal deference to authority—the boss or status-superiors are treated just like any other participant. Indeed, many facilitators hold strong values about egalitarianism, and may not be accepting of high-deference cultures. We need to be careful about trying to change any cultural characteristic if that's not what we've been hired to do. Following are some things facilitators may need to do to accommodate deference to authority.

- Structure the process so that participants can express themselves without openly challenging a status-superior. This may be done by, for example, interviewing people individually, splitting the group into subgroups of roughly equal status for some parts of the discussion (at the risk of widening the divide between levels of the hierarchy), or allowing people to post anonymous points on index cards.

- Honor participants' choice not to raise difficult issues with status-superiors, if they've consciously made that choice. We can offer suggestions and encouragement for raising issues in appropriate ways, but we can't force it. We may feel frustrated that the issues are not being put on the table, but the participants are the ones who will suffer the consequences of being seen as "uppity," insubordinate, or not knowing their place.

- Involve participants in developing the agenda, guidelines, purpose statement, and so on, rather than drafting these and offering the group an opportunity to make changes (since some may be reluctant to challenge the facilitator's suggestions).

- Find a way for participants to give evaluation feedback without openly critiquing the facilitator—such as by a written evaluation form.

Directness or Indirectness

Another major cultural variable affecting facilitation is the degree of directness. In a very direct-dealing culture, complaints are addressed directly to the person believed responsible. Because people expect anyone with a concern to state it straight out, they tend not to look for subtle clues about others' feelings. Open confrontation and debate are acceptable (though these may or may not involve emotional expressiveness, which is a separate variable).

By contrast, in a very indirect-dealing culture, avoiding loss of face—one's own and others'—is paramount. Because addressing concerns directly entails some loss of face, people find other ways to raise issues, such as telling stories in which the complaint is implied, or using formal or informal intermediaries. People may choose to avoid confrontation in most circumstances, because the costs of confrontation are seen to outweigh the potential benefits of raising issues directly.

Signs of a Direct Culture

- Open confrontation with the facilitator, such as direct questions about your qualifications or statements of disagreement with your proposed approach.
- Direct confrontation between group members, leaving no one upset. They may even enjoy it, seeing it as something of a sport.
- Oblivion to subtle hints or clues.

Signs of an Indirect Culture

- Significant differences between what people say in interviews and what they say to each other (though that could be because their thinking has evolved and emotions have cooled since the interviews).
- Embarrassment or anger when an even slightly negative comment is made about an individual in front of a group.
- Tendency to accept the facilitator's suggestions and guidance without challenge.
- Facial expressions or body language suggesting consternation, but no open articulation of it.
- Sarcastic mutterings instead of plain statements of opinions.
- An inclination to "read things in" to people's actions or statements (indirect communication requires this kind of deciphering).

- A tendency for people to come up to the facilitator at breaks to say what they really think.

Implications for Extreme Facilitation. The conventional approaches to facilitation tend to presume direct dealing among all participants. For instance, participants are generally expected to speak up if they have a point of view on the topic at hand. In addition, some facilitators enforce ground rules by directly pointing out violations in front of the whole group. This approach assumes a highly direct-dealing culture in which a participant's loss of face is not a concern.

Instead, the extreme facilitator should tailor his or her interventions to the degree of directness participants are comfortable with. Here are some possible ways to adapt facilitation to a more indirect culture:

- Use individual interviews to draw out information about people's concerns, and make an oral or written presentation of the themes or patterns drawn from the interviews.
- Offer coaching to individuals on how to frame complaints and concerns in the most diplomatic way before they attempt direct dealing.
- Use an escalating sequence of interventions to deal with individuals who are behaving unproductively. That is, first try the most subtle, indirect method. If that fails, try something slightly more direct, and so on. To confront an individual directly in front of the whole group is the most direct method and should be used only as a last resort.
- Use small-group breakout sessions in which participants are grouped with those they're most comfortable with. Their concerns can then be presented as the product of the small group.
- Use anonymous written comments on index cards or sticky notes to gather input from the group.

- Honor participants' decision to remain silent and drop an issue if that is their informed choice.

Task-Relationship-Process Orientation

The final major cultural variable affecting facilitation is the value placed on getting the task done versus building and maintaining relationships versus ensuring the best and most thorough process.[6]

This variable is closely related to another cross-cultural variable: orientation toward time. Relationship-oriented cultures tend to have a longer sense of time and a slower pace. Task-oriented cultures tend to be the most fast-paced and immediate-future oriented.

Clues to Task-Relationship-Process Orientation

- *Like or dislike of meetings.* Task-oriented groups hate meetings and will let you know it. Process-oriented groups tend to address every issue by proposing a meeting. Relationship-oriented groups are somewhere in between—meetings are okay, but informal interaction is also important.

- *What the group's natural strengths are.* Strengths may include strong cohesion, goodwill, and morale (relationship oriented); quick decisions, results, and actions (task oriented); or well-thought-out processes for decision making, planning, and interaction (process oriented).

- *Ease of decision making.* Task-oriented groups reach decisions the fastest, as they can let small concerns go in favor of getting to the task. Relationship-oriented groups tend to need some pushing (such as the facilitator stating areas of apparent agreement), but they will respond to it well, as long as there's an effort to address everyone's needs. Process-oriented groups will tend to rework proposed decisions until every detail is satisfactory.

- *Degree of attention to personal sensitivities.* For task-oriented groups, personal feelings and egos must sometimes be sacrificed for results. If someone appears offended, you, the facilitator, may be the only one to notice. Relationship-oriented groups will react the most to hurt feelings. They may want to take a break to console the person individually, or they may want to work through the feelings in the full group. Process-oriented groups take notice of the feelings, but rather than working with the feelings themselves, they take them as a signal that the person's point of view needs to be considered and incorporated into decision making.

Implications for Extreme Facilitation. The group's task-relationship-process orientation will have a great impact on how you facilitate.

Task Oriented

- A task-oriented group will not want to spend time discussing process. The facilitator should come prepared with the purpose statement, agenda, desired outcomes, and recommended ground rules. A review of these with a quick opportunity for changes will suffice.

- If the process hits a rocky point, the task-oriented group will not want to talk in plenary about how to get the process back on track—the facilitator will need to take a break to deal with the process concerns and then reopen with substantive discussion.

- A task-oriented group may be less interested in reaching consensus.

- A task-oriented group will want to keep meetings short.

Relationship Oriented

- A relationship-oriented group will want to devote time to relationship-building activities, such as informal social time between meeting sessions and activities enabling them to learn about individuals' personalities and backgrounds.

- Although a relationship orientation does not necessarily imply more emotional expressiveness (as described above), it does mean that tending to emotions is more important. The facilitator should help set the right emotional tone and help soothe anyone who becomes upset.

Process Oriented

- A process-oriented group can work with the facilitator in establishing the process (purpose statement, agenda, expected outcomes, guidelines).

- If the process hits a snag, a process-oriented group will want to discuss it openly, not only to accomplish the task but also to derive lessons about how to improve its processes.

- A process-oriented group may resist breaking up into small groups because members may prefer to all hear all of each other's comments.

- A process-oriented group may want more detailed meeting summaries or minutes.

- A process-oriented group may plan meetings that are not really necessary.

Putting It All Together

If all this sounds really involved, it is. In extreme facilitation, you can't just appear in front of the group and figure it all out on the spot. Nor can you customize a process to the group if you don't have a rich understanding of that group.

At the same time, it needn't be a complicated process. You pick your assessment method, create a list of questions, and just do it. You keep your antennae up for cultural clues throughout.

It does get somewhat more complicated in situations that involve large enough groups of people that you need to conduct convening, the subject of the next chapter. Then, assessment and convening are done simultaneously. Convening requires additional questions so you

can determine who should be at the table and under what circumstances they'll be willing to take part.

Notes

1. Some of this material was informed by Moore, *The Mediation Process*, pp. 120–139, and Carpenter and Kennedy, *Managing Public Disputes*, pp. 71–85.
2. See, for example, Gordon, *Group-Centered Leadership*, pp. 177–182.
3. Mayer, *The Dynamics of Conflict Resolution*, pp. 120–122.
4. This comes from Appreciative Inquiry, an approach to organizational development. See, for example, Watkins and Mohr, *Appreciative Inquiry*.
5. This set of variables was inspired, in part, by Hofstede's four international differences in work-related values (Hofstede, *Culture's Consequences*). My variables differ from his, though my "deference to authority" is similar to his "power distance."
6. This three-part variable was inspired by Moore's three types of interests—substantive, procedural, and psychological (Moore, *The Mediation Process*, p. 75).

Chapter Four

Convening

Creating a Democratic Table

In some facilitations, it's obvious who the participants should be. For example, if the task is to facilitate an annual staff retreat for a small organization, the participants are obviously the staff members.

In larger, more complex situations, it's not so easy. You may be handed the task of organizing a group process when the affected population includes hundreds of thousands of people. For instance, imagine that a controversy has raged for years—complete with angry letters to newspaper editors and gubernatorial pronouncements—over a state's plan to introduce a school voucher program. From this broad public upheaval, it's up to you to assemble a group that can sit in a room together and end the battle. This kind of extreme facilitation requires the skill of *convening*.[1]

Convening is the process of identifying interested parties ("stakeholders"), inviting—or perhaps persuading—them to come to the table, helping identify individuals to represent them, and determining the structure of the "table." Closely related is determining how the broader general public (or employees or membership) can have input. Convening also involves determining, through discussions with potential participants, whether it will be worthwhile to proceed with a facilitated process or not.

There is, however, a deeper point to convening. A seat at the table means power. Organizational and public-policy issues are too often decided by a small number of power brokers, taking too little account of the views of the people who will be affected. Company executives decide on restructuring plans or strategic initiatives without participation of middle managers or rank-and-file employees.

Government officials decide on new regulations or land-use changes with minimal participation of the regulated entities or the residents and businesses affected.

Good convening ensures the affected people will have voice and influence. Convening is the difference between the proverbial dark, smoky room and a radical approach to democracy—*direct* participation in dialogue and decision making by the people affected by a decision.

Convening is often needed in public policy issues. For example, I once cofacilitated, with my colleague Mike Hughes, a negotiation among thirty-five stakeholder groups about how to reduce levels of air pollution in a metropolitan area. This followed a public outcry over a plan to address pollution by requiring drivers to submit to lengthier and more expensive automobile emission tests. The stakeholders included contributors to air pollution, such as automobile drivers, gas station owners, oil companies, factories, and utilities; health advocates; environmental groups; and local, state, and federal regulators.

Convening can also be required in some organizational facilitations. For example, I once helped a municipal government agency decide on a new slate of health care plans for its employees in the wake of sharp increases in premiums. The human resources department was the subject of lingering anger and mistrust over a compensation study conducted the previous year that led to changes in pay scales—with some people getting paid less as a result. This agency had several unions, and, depending on which union they belonged to, employees paid either nothing toward their premiums, a certain percentage of it, or a fixed dollar amount toward it. There were also non-union employees. We had to determine an appropriate way for these various groups to be represented in order for the human resources department to devise a plan that would gain widespread support, avoiding the angry backlash that followed the compensation study.

Assessment and convening are intertwined. The definition of the purpose—which begins to emerge through assessment—helps determine who should be at the table. At the same time, an important strategy for getting parties to the table is to allow them some influence in shaping the process, including a precise definition of the purpose. For these reasons, assessment and convening happen more or less simultaneously.

How Purpose Drives Convening

The purpose of the group process is an important determinant of who is a stakeholder. The term *purpose* as used here means three things:

1. What issues are on the table?
2. What issues are off the table—that is, not open for discussion or negotiation?
3. What is the desired outcome—a consensus decision, a vote, input, or dialogue?

An example will illustrate the relationship between purpose and convening. In one case facilitated by CDR Associates, a county department of social services needed to find a new site for a home for abused and neglected children. After an in-depth exploration of alternatives, the agency identified a preferred location. However, nearby residents, upon learning of the plan, protested in earnest. They had visions of drug-addicted teenagers wandering through their neighborhood, stealing cars and breaking into homes. They raised every fear they could possibly conjure up, from tree removal to safety, from traffic to property values. The county decided to initiate a facilitated process with these residents and other stakeholders.

Here is how the three parts of the purpose might affect the convening task:

1. *Issue on the table:* The issue could be defined broadly: Where to locate the new facility? Or it could be defined more narrowly: How can we address the concerns of the residents such that *this* site

might be acceptable? The broader phrasing would necessitate a much broader set of stakeholders, representing all the sites under consideration. The narrower phrasing focuses on the stakeholders in the one neighborhood surrounding the preferred site.

2. *Issue(s) off the table:* In this case, the county had to establish this facility somewhere—so the question of *whether* to establish it was off the table. If they had gone further, they might have made the particular *site* nonnegotiable—in which case the question would have been limited to how, not whether, it would be established at that site.

What is off the table might affect who would be *willing* to participate. For example, if a neighborhood group learns that the county's selection of this neighborhood is nonnegotiable, and that only some details are open to negotiation, they might decide that participation is not worth their time.

3. *Desired outcome:* In this instance, a decision was ultimately needed, and the county clearly had the authority to decide the location. The question was to what extent they would share this authority with stakeholders. If they had wanted only to obtain *input* from the affected community, there might have been no need to identify stakeholder groups—instead, the general public could provide input through a public involvement process (including public meetings and other means of making comments). In fact, the county was seeking a consensus recommendation from affected groups, so a careful identification of stakeholder groups was critical. Where a decision or recommendation is the goal, stakeholder groups need to have representatives present who can enter into agreements (or recommendations) on behalf of the groups they represent.

In contrast, when the goal is not a decision but a deepening of understanding between groups, it's appropriate to have people participate in their individual capacity only, not as representatives of organized groups. For example, some organizations have held dialogues on abortion between pro-choice and pro-life activists, particularly in communities polarized by large-scale demonstrations and violence over abortion, and where neighbors or even family members have stopped talking to each other over differences in abortion views.

The goal in these dialogues is not to try to reach agreement on abortion policy, but to help break down the hatred and prejudice between pro-choice and pro-life advocates and help them see each other as human. One of their ground rules is that the activists speak only for themselves as individuals, so they can reveal the complexity and gray areas in their thinking, rather than sticking to the black-and-white official stances of their activist organizations.

Identifying Stakeholders

It's not always obvious who qualifies as a "stakeholder" in a stakeholder process. There are several criteria:

1. *Who is affected?* Any group that could be directly affected by the outcome of the group process can be considered a stakeholder. In the air-quality negotiation, for example, the businesses that might have to comply with future air-quality regulations were stakeholders. Similarly, drivers who might have to submit to more stringent emission testing were stakeholders (they were represented by an association).

2. *Who has an interest?* In other words, what groups have a stance on the issue at hand as part of their organizational mission or identity? For example, in the air-quality negotiation, an advocacy group dedicated to combating air pollution was an obvious stakeholder.

In some cases, there are interest groups that don't necessarily represent any affected group of people—for example, there might be environmental groups that advocate for threatened or endangered species. If the group members represent a set of interests that bear on the issue at hand, they're stakeholders, unless they fall outside the geographic scope of the effort (see the dilemma of local versus national or international groups, below).

3. *Who has the power to block a decision?* If a group is powerful enough to block a decision, it's wiser to include them in the process

than to have them fight the outcome later. It's tempting to leave out groups who are extremist or confrontational, but this would negate the whole purpose of a collaborative process—it saves time in the long run to allow these groups influence *before* the decision is made. Excluding them also would negate the democratic aims of convening.

4. *Who can help?* Sometimes it is useful to include people who can serve as a bridge between other stakeholders who have opposite viewpoints. For example, in resolving disagreements between the military and state regulators over environmental cleanup of bases, the U.S. Environmental Protection Agency has sometimes served as a helpful bridge—it shares the regulatory role with state regulators but shares the federal-government perspective with the military.

Sometimes there are groups that clearly are stakeholders but do not want to participate fully. In other instances, there are groups that only marginally qualify as stakeholders. Such parties might be considered secondary stakeholders. The process might be structured to allow some lesser form of participation, such as observing the process and perhaps offering comments at designated times.

For example, in the process to select health insurance plans for the municipality, the official who represented city management in negotiations with its unions was invited to observe the sessions but was not at the table. (Management interests were represented at the table by the human resources department.)

Making the Tough Calls

Beware: because a seat at the table means power, the process of deciding who participates can be extremely contentious. Ideally, the convening decisions are negotiated ones, discussed and agreed on among the facilitator, the sponsoring organization, and the potential stakeholders involved. However, there may be groups or individuals who desperately want to participate but who, in your judgment, don't meet the criteria of stakeholders *or* who represent interests already amply represented at the table. For example, at one contaminated former military site, a nearby resident made something of a retirement career of vociferously protesting everything going on at the site—but interviews revealed that he represented no one but himself. As another example, all of the large businesses in a town may want to participate in a planning process, but they would overwhelm, in numbers, the citizens' and government stakeholders.

It's important to declare at the outset of the convening process who is the ultimate gatekeeper. There are several options:

1. *The sponsoring agency decides.* If there is minimal distrust of the sponsoring agency among other stakeholders, that organization might be empowered to make the decision. This follows the logic of "He who pays the piper calls the tune."

2. *The facilitator decides.* If there is appreciable distrust of the sponsoring agency, the process can be made more trustworthy and credible by having an outside, impartial facilitator make convening decisions. This is the one time a facilitator needs to make autocratic decisions. If you're like me, you'll find this uncomfortable—if I liked being autocratic, I would have chosen a different career. Still, identifying and selecting stakeholders is part of a facilitator's expertise and is therefore an appropriate task for the sponsoring agency to outsource. Remember, your decisions, even if autocratic, are intended to serve the process.

Another challenge here is to resist the sponsoring agency's tendency to try to control the facilitator's convening decisions. It's not unusual for sponsors to think they're open-minded about who the facilitator convenes—until they see their enemies or "crazies" on the participant list. If officials in the sponsoring agency aren't willing to give up this control, they shouldn't deceive the public by saying that convening decisions are being entrusted to the facilitator.

3. *The process is open.* If distrust is so high that it's crucial to avoid angering any potential participant, the sponsoring organization and the facilitator might agree that no one will be turned away. In this event, it will be more of a challenge to create a balanced table. Interests with more resources will likely be more heavily represented.

The task, then, will be to recruit enough other participants to result in a balanced (though larger!) table.

My colleagues Chris Moore, Julie McKay, and Jonathan Bartsch convened and facilitated an early phase of the Federal Energy Regulatory Commission (FERC) relicensing process for the Niagara power plant. The area involved in western New York was economically depressed, and the New York Power Authority (NYPA) was the subject of high resentment and distrust. The resentment arose from the considerable profits from operating the power plant; the distrust arose from the region's political culture of backroom bargaining and the suspicion that the public process would be made irrelevant by secret deals.

Given this distrust and resentment, my colleagues and NYPA both felt that no interested parties—whether individual citizens or representatives of organized groups—could be turned away. The result was rooms full of over one hundred people, including business associations, environmental groups, an Indian tribe, government agencies, and individual citizens.

This open process worked for two reasons. First, the level of interest was extraordinarily high—not only because of distrust of NYPA but also because people were hoping that NYPA might be seeking to contribute financially to community groups in order to demonstrate to FERC that it was a good neighbor. Everyone with even a remote connection showed up. Second, this early stage of the relicensing process was limited to "scoping"—identifying issues and assessing what studies needed to be done—so there were no final decisions to be negotiated and thus no need to identify formal representatives.

Note that, when convening decisions are controversial, the options do *not* include that one stakeholder gets to veto the participation of another stakeholder. This is the time to remind people who is the gatekeeper. If someone says, "We won't participate if so-and-so is participating," it's an opportunity for problem solving. You can seek to understand the reasons for the concern, and see if there are ways to deal with it—such as through ground rules.

For example, in a land-use planning facilitation for a state wildlife refuge, one major issue was whether to permit the development of an ecotourism site. The leaders of the town closest to the proposed ecotourism site were strongly in favor of the development, as the town would benefit economically. The mayor strongly objected to the participation of a local activist group that had been formed specifically to oppose the ecotourism site. She threatened not to participate if this group also participated.

In a phone call with the mayor, I acknowledged respectfully that she had every right to decline to participate. I also explained why participation of all stakeholders was important. I asked for her reasons that she found the activists' participation objectionable. Was it simply because they opposed the site, or some other reason? She said that they tended to insult her and others and generally behaved badly. I offered that we could propose a ground rule about treating all with civility and also said I would do my best to address any disrespectful or inappropriate behavior as it arose. The facilitation proceeded with both the mayor and the activist group participating.

Other Dilemmas

Convening is often quite complex. Besides the dilemma of groups who want to participate but shouldn't, it's not always clean or easy to determine how to represent the various interests related to an issue.

Following are some guidelines on handling some common convening dilemmas.

Representing the General Public

One dilemma is how to represent the general public—those not organized into specific interest groups. For example, how can the public concern for clean drinking water be addressed? What about the concern for economic growth, or for containing the economic costs of regulation?

Public-interest groups might fill this need, coupled with opportunities for broader public input outside the stakeholder process. Public-interest groups range from environmental and health advocacy groups to a relatively new movement of taxpayers' groups that advocate for leaner government, lower taxes, and less regulation. As you can imagine, views of taxpayers' groups might be the opposite of the views of health and environmental advocacy groups. This illustrates how, in a sense, the "public interest" is actually quite complex and is best represented by a well-balanced "table" as a whole.

We mustn't forget governments as representatives of the general public, as long as we also remember that they have their own views and ideology and therefore don't represent all of their constituents equally. For example, in public-involvement processes for major transportation projects, the local governments in the project corridor often participate as representatives of their communities. There is then a dilemma of who in a local government serves as the actual representative—elected officials or staff? Elected officials are by definition the chosen representatives of the voters, but staff often have more relevant expertise and need not worry about winning the next election.

Related to representation of the general public is the dilemma of intensity versus breadth of opinion. In other words, there can be a minority with very strong feelings and a much larger majority who hold the opposite opinion but don't feel strongly about it. For example, in the site selection for unpopular facilities (such as jails, landfills, and so on), the people closest to the proposed site are likely to actively oppose it, whereas the broader public might be best served by that location—but few in that broader public are concerned enough to write letters to the city council or put signs in their yards like the opponents do. On the one hand, this is a benefit of a facilitated process over a referendum—a one-person-one-vote system doesn't register intensity of opinion. On the other hand, the danger is that the louder voices—the opponents of the facility—will drown out the larger public interest.

Here, the solutions are similar. Government officials can represent the broader public, in addition to organized groups if such groups exist. In addition, facilitated stakeholder processes can be supplemented by public-involvement processes that feature fast, easy ways for citizens to state their views, so that the relatively apathetic proponents can be heard as easily as the active opponents.

Whether to Include the Ultimate Decision Maker

If the purpose of the process is to make recommendations or provide input into a pending decision, there are pros and cons to involving the ultimate decision maker(s) in the process. Having this authority figure present may dampen the free expression of views—especially in organizational situations, in which people must worry about staying in good favor with their superiors, or, similarly, in contractor-client partnering, in which contractors are straining to impress the client organization. When the decision maker voices her opinion, it may shut down discussion prematurely, even if she was just thinking aloud or playing with ideas.

I once cofacilitated a process among managers in a corporation about reshuffling budget priorities to find funding for a new diversity initiative. Overall, the discussions were careful and thoughtful to the point of being strained—but as soon as the CEO left one meeting for a conference call, the tone turned animated, lively, and more fun and creative. It might have been just as well to have the managers work together on a recommendation and present them to the CEO later.

However, if the eventual solution will have to meet certain goals or fall within certain constraints, the group should know these, rather than discovering only at the end that their recommendation won't fly or their input is irrelevant. If the issues are complex, it may be that the best way to ensure that the solution fits the goals and constraints is to have the decision maker present.

I facilitated a retreat for a nonprofit organization that was strongly concerned with equality and justice, yet whose executive director, who was also the founder and main source of funding, was all powerful. The contradiction between the ideal and the reality there had become unbearable. There was widespread anger among employees about what seemed to be arbitrary use of management power (such as making decisions to stop existing projects and start new ones, causing staff to drop everything and retool), about the lack of women and minorities in leadership positions, and about a failure to adequately involve employees in decision making.

The executive director, sensitive to the contradiction between his overwhelming power and his views on social justice, was so worried about dampening the discussion that he sat almost silently for four-fifths of the entire retreat. While small groups were meeting, I talked with him alone about how the time had come, now that proposed changes were on the table, for him to give his reactions. He wasn't sure how to do this in a nonauthoritarian way, so we agreed that I would conduct a talk-show style interview with him in front of the rest of the employees.

In the interview, he revealed his views on power, his appreciation and high regard for his employees, his thoughts about the future of the organization, and his assessment of the changes that had been proposed during the retreat. He had objections to only one or two of the proposed changes. His participation led to both better decision making and improved morale.

The pros and cons of having the decision maker present should be weighed on a case-by-case basis.

Local Versus National or International Advocacy Groups

This dilemma is a common case of conflict between the "Who is affected" and the "Who has an interest" criteria to determine who is a stakeholder. When the issue in question is local, one can often find local advocacy groups to represent the different views. Such local groups typically meet both these criteria—they have an interest, and they are also affected because they're part of the community.

They usually have a fairly holistic view of the situation, under-standing the competing needs or interests (such as environmental versus economic impacts) and are relatively open to compromise.

In contrast, larger national or international advocacy groups don't need to contend with the multifaceted local impacts of deci-sions and instead are advancing their agendas on a large scale. They may benefit from maintaining ideological purity on their positions and thus may be less open to compromise.

The problem is that local citizens' groups typically don't have the resources to hold their own alongside powerful, well-funded interests such as corporations, industry groups, and government agencies, which may have full-time staff with expertise in the topic at hand. Local groups therefore often desperately need the support (in the form of time and expertise) of larger advocacy groups.[2]

A colleague of mine conducted a project in a developing coun-try to improve relations between a corporation that operated a dam and the nearby citizens. The citizens formed small organizations to represent their interests to the dam operators as well as to the local and national governments. Eager to participate was a large, U.S.-based advocacy group that opposes all dams everywhere. The local citizens' groups had a more nuanced view. They had grievances about community and environmental problems caused by the dam, but they also benefited in some ways from it—through employment as well as through some financial support the dam operator gave the community.

The solution here partly depends on the scope of the process. If the issues are strictly local, it may be necessary to state up front that the goal is to find *local* stakeholders. Then the national or interna-tional advocacy groups might be allowed to participate as secondary stakeholders with a lesser role, or as supporters of the local groups—providing them with technical information, strategy advice, or other assistance. In the case just mentioned, the U.S.-based advo-cacy group observed the meetings between the dam operator and the community and provided information and technical expertise.

Extremists and "Wackos"

As discussed in the previous section, if a group (or individual, for that matter) is powerful enough to block a potential decision, it should probably be included. This is easy to say but hard to implement when the group or its spokesperson is known to be difficult or confrontational, by, for example

- Insulting others, self-righteously implying that others' positions are immoral
- Speaking at excessive length or interjecting irrelevant comments
- Speaking incomprehensibly—through rambling, disorganized statements or overuse of technical terms
- Adhering rigidly to positions and not engaging in problem solving
- Being verbally or emotionally abusive
- Threatening legal action or hostile tactics if they don't get their way

These problems are real: they can turn off other participants, slow the progress of meetings, and possibly discredit the whole process. Yet at the same time, such people should not be excluded if they represent legitimate, relevant interests or have sufficient clout to block a decision.

You can sometimes encourage an organized group to send a different representative, explaining how the individual's approach could backfire. Of course, if the individual is a paid employee of the group, you have to be cautious, as criticism delivered to his employer may threaten his job. Still, your first responsibility is to the integrity of the process you're convening.

In the case of strong, vocal individuals, it may be necessary to assess whether the individual represents anyone but himself, then assess the risks of exclusion against the risks of inclusion.

When No Organized Groups Exist

Notice that the solutions to some of these dilemmas lie in the existence of a multitude of associations, so that you can find an organization to represent every interest. This isn't always the case. For example, in the air-quality negotiation, there were no strong local environmental groups in the metropolitan area in question. Similarly, even some types of businesses were not organized into associations, at least not at the local level.

This problem becomes more acute in developing countries that don't have a well-developed civil-society sector (which includes nongovernmental organizations and, according to some definitions, local governments). In these situations, the powerful industrial interests have unchecked influence over governmental decision making.

There are several possible solutions here. One solution is to recruit individuals (or individual businesses) to represent a broader group informally. This ensures that the point of view is represented, but the drawback is that such individuals can't commit the larger group to implementing a particular outcome. Another option is to organize affected individuals into associations. This takes considerable resources, may require skills that are outside the facilitator's bailiwick, and could raise questions about the facilitator's neutrality. Still, it's not unheard of, and it may ultimately serve all the stakeholders best in the long run.

Another option is to shift from a convened stakeholder process (with select stakeholders represented around a table) to an open public-involvement process (in which there are multiple ways for anyone in the general public to offer input). My colleague Mary Margaret Golten conducted a public involvement process to respond to comments about the likely effects of a planned oil and gas pipeline that would cut through Azerbaijan, the Republic of Georgia, and Turkey. These countries had hundreds of tiny nongovernmental organizations, few of them really compelling as representatives of the vast affected population. There was also widespread fear among citizens of criticizing any of these three national governments openly. Instead of a facilitated stakeholder process, Golten's team conducted confidential surveys in select villages along the pipeline route to obtain input. This involved, in some cases, going door-to-door in small villages and hearing people's hopes for employment as well as their fears about being permanently displaced.

Finally, if there's not a good way to make sure all the voices are heard, you'll have to decide whether to call the whole thing off, as described in the next section.

Power Imbalances

Closely related to the lack of organized groups is when some of the groups are considerably weaker than others—in size, funding, expertise, or overall influence. Although a facilitator can't fundamentally alter these power differences, there are many ways to help create a balanced table representing all relevant interests more equally (some of which have been described previously):

- Ensure that all interests are represented, even if by a few individuals, when no association exists
- Guard against overrepresentation of industry and government interests and underrepresentation of public interests
- Recruit national or international advocacy groups either to participate directly or to support the participation of smaller, local advocacy groups
- Bring in impartial technical experts (funded by the sponsoring agency or by a pool of funds created by the wealthier stakeholders) to provide trustworthy information
- Provide funds (again, from the sponsoring agency or from the wealthier stakeholders) to pay for the time and travel expenses of less-well-funded groups
- Provide funds for less-well-funded groups to obtain supporting staff, consultants, advocates, or other needed resources

- Limit the number of supporting staff, consultants, or advocates per stakeholder
- Encourage groups to select skilled, knowledgeable, articulate representatives
- Provide brief training at the first facilitated meeting on how the process works and how best to participate in it

Ultimately, however, a facilitated process cannot replace the development in society of strong public-interest groups. The facilitator and the participants need to determine whether the table has sufficient integrity to move forward. In other words, are the major interests represented well enough? Will the process be better than the alternatives? These alternatives might include (for the stakeholders)

- Doing nothing, or proceeding with the usual policymaking procedures and the usual means of influencing them
- Engaging in a public-involvement process (which does not require organized stakeholder groups)
- Initiating litigation or other rights-based processes
- Organizing to increase membership and power
- Exercising power by pressuring policymakers through anything from demonstrations to letter-writing campaigns to lobbying

If these alternatives are preferable to participation in facilitation for a substantial number of stakeholders, it might be better to abandon plans for a facilitated process.

Helping Identify Representatives

Once it's clear that a convened stakeholder process will move forward and which stakeholder groups are participating, the next step is to determine who represents them, and how.

Selection Criteria

I strongly believe that every group has the right to determine who represents it. However, the facilitator can encourage stakeholder groups to send representatives who will contribute to a productive process. Following are criteria facilitators can suggest:

• *Credibility with the group being represented.* While it might make your job easier if participants are nice and accommodating with each other, people at the table need to be seen as strong advocates for the interests they are representing. Otherwise, the credibility of the process and the successful implementation of the outcome could be jeopardized. I have come to enjoy tough advocates, as long as they are principled and sincere. Their energetic participation means our process is grappling with the real issues.

• *Negotiation skill and experience.* The participation of skilled, experienced negotiators will make the process more smooth, not less. Ideally they will be skilled in cooperative negotiation in the context of an ongoing relationship, as opposed to adversarial negotiation in the context of once-off business transactions. This does not mean they will be weak; it means they will present their concerns as problems to be solved rather than as demands or ultimatums to which others must yield.

It's the unskilled negotiators who are abrasive and annoying, often attacking or insulting the other participants, the facilitator, and the process. They seem to feel they have no power, and ironically, they act in ways that further undermine their power, such as by demanding something be changed long after the group has already discussed the topic. They often do more harm than good to their cause.

• *Right level in the hierarchy.* When stakeholders are large bureaucracies, the concept of getting people with "full authority to commit to decisions" is a fantasy. The person with full authority is often far too high-level to spend long hours in facilitated dialogues.

Still, you'll need to strike the right balance between people with policymaking roles (who tend to be higher level) and those with technical expertise (who tend to be lower level). My colleagues Louise Smart and Susan Wildau facilitated one of the first public-policy dialogues the U.S. Environmental Protection Agency ever sponsored. A stated qualification was that participants have expertise in the highly technical subject matter. As a result, some of the participating government agencies sent technical staff who had no policy authority. Some of them sat silently looking bored throughout the process. From this early experiment in collaboration, my colleagues learned that it would have been better to involve higher-level policymakers, and perhaps to create a technical-level working group to support them.

• *Ability to devote the necessary time and energy.* Obviously, the ideal representative will have time to prepare for and attend all meetings and to keep constituents informed of progress. In practice, this is often difficult. The solution to this problem may lie in the representation structure.

Representation Structure

There are various ways to structure the representation of groups. Each has advantages and disadvantages.

- *One representative per group.* The simplest approach is for each group to have one representative. This provides the most consistency and continuity. However, there may be problems when the one representative is unable to attend.

- *One representative plus an alternate.* One good way to handle longer processes is to allow each participant to have an alternate. There are two challenges: keeping the alternate up-to-date, and overcoming the disruption of having a new face appear at the table.

- *Two or more representatives per group.* Particularly if there are not many stakeholders, it may make sense for each group to have two or more representatives. For example, in the health-insurance process in the municipal agency, there were five stakeholder groups (three unions, non-union employees, and management), each represented by two to four individuals.

- *Different tiers of representation for each group.* Large, complex processes with highly technical issues often have different tiers of participation, such as a policymaking group of high-level decision makers and a technical working group of their subordinates.

- *One representative plus supporting players.* In some situations it makes sense to have one key representative of each stakeholder group but to allow each representative to bring along needed support. That support may take the form of a staff member, technical expert, consultant, or attorney. The danger here is that well-funded groups may bring an army of supporting players, whereas less well-funded groups may have none.

Convening Questions

In the process of identifying and talking to possible participants, you will need to include some additional questions in your assessment interviews. Following are some typical examples, to be modified, dropped, or added to as the situation requires:

- What is this group and whom does it represent?
- What are your (group's) views on the issue(s) in question?
- Will you gain more by helping resolve the issue or by continuing the battle?
- Who gains from continuing the fight?
- What are your hopes and concerns about participating?

- What would you need to see in order to consider this a legitimate and worthwhile process?
- Who might represent your group? What are his or her style, strengths, and weaknesses as a negotiator?
- Whom else should we be talking to?

This is part of the iterative activity of shaping the process in partnership with likely participants. These questions will likely lead to discussions about representation, the dilemmas mentioned earlier, and getting parties to the table.

Getting Reluctant Parties to the Table

The opposite of the gatekeeping problem is when needed stakeholders are reluctant to participate. You may need them to help balance out the table, or because they are key players with the power to block a decision.

In the air-quality negotiation described earlier, one well-known national environmental group, which had a nearby local chapter, hesitated to participate. This group had sued the state for failure to comply with the Clean Air Act and would have been one of two major environmentalist voices at a table with numerous different business and industry groups.

In another case, CDR Associates was asked to convene and facilitate a group to discuss the future of Rocky Flats, a nuclear weapons facility in Colorado that was being closed. At the time of convening, there was already a stakeholder group called the Rocky Flats Local Impacts Initiative, comprising elected officials and development interests, and formed by the U.S. Department of Energy during a Republican administration. In addition, the Department, now under the Clinton administration, was just forming citizens' advisory groups at all nuclear facilities around the country—composed largely of environmental and community activists.

In CDR's view, it was critical that environmentalists and community activists participate in this dialogue, but these groups were too busy helping start up the citizens' advisory groups. Moreover, they didn't want to join "those damned Republicans" drawn from the Local Impacts Initiative.

In trying to get reluctant stakeholders to the table, the first principle is not to make it a hard sell. It's important to respect the reasons for skepticism. For many activist or advocacy groups and even some business associations, time and resources may be scarce. Moreover, the skills needed for effective participation in a stakeholder process differ considerably from the skills needed for hard-hitting activism, and the resources dedicated to one can detract from success in the other.

There is also a strategic question for stakeholders about how they want to pursue their mission. Participating in a facilitated process with powerful decision makers is a trade-off. On the one hand, it's a rare opportunity to influence decisions directly. Participation may give a small activist group far greater power than it would have through any other action. On the other hand, despite all the talk of "win-win" negotiating, it is rare that any stakeholder will get an outcome that is 100 percent of what they hoped for—they'll probably have to compromise. In the long term, a group may build more power by using a strong, uncompromising stance to draw more members, raise more funds, and influence public opinion. A decision not to participate does not mean the group is obstinate or unwise.

The best approach is to elicit the underlying reasons for the reluctance. Perhaps some of the concerns can easily be allayed with factual information. For example, if one concern is whether the process will be open to the press, and the sponsoring agency has already agreed that it will be, it's obvious that saying so will probably help.

In other instances, you will not be able to allay the concerns fully. For example, the group may worry that

- The sponsoring agency has already made a decision and will manipulate the process to produce this decision

- Secret side deals will be cut between powerful government and corporate interests
- The sponsoring agency will fail to implement the decision or recommendation made by the group
- The public-interest groups will not have access to objective information or will be "snowed" by the more well-funded groups that have their own technical experts
- The public-interest groups will be outnumbered, and thus marginalized, by government and industry stakeholders

These fears are not irrational—all have happened in policy-making and even in facilitated processes. It's impossible for you to reassure potential participants that their worst-case scenarios won't come true. Even if the process is perfect, you can't guarantee that the decision makers will act on the recommendations or input that the process produces.

What you can do is first listen to and express understanding of the concerns. Then, at the culmination of the assessment and convening process, you can recommend to the sponsoring agency whether to proceed or not and describe what conditions will be needed to obtain the relevant groups' willingness to participate.

In the air-quality dialogue, the environmental group declined to participate, but it quietly provided advice and technical support to the other environmental and public-health interests at the table. My colleague and I decided that although the table was somewhat imbalanced in numbers, environmental interests were sufficiently and strongly represented at the table.

In the Rocky Flats case, negotiations with the environmental groups lasted for six months, as they decided whether they could devote their time and energy to the new stakeholder process. CDR insisted on taking that time, because a refusal to do so would have meant an unacceptably skewed process with no environmentalists.

The process in which the facilitator presents results of assessment and convening and enters into discussions with the sponsoring organization about important details of the process will be explored in more depth in the next chapter, on contracting.

Notes

1. The material in this chapter is informed, in part, by Carpenter and Kennedy, *Managing Public Disputes*, pp. 102–105; Cormick, Dale, Emond, Sigurdson, and Stuart, *Building Consensus for a Sustainable Future*, pp. 23–39; Moore, *The Mediation Process*, pp. 147–152; and my colleagues at CDR Associates.
2. U.S. Environmental Protection Agency, *Constructive Engagement Resource Guide*, p. 59.

Chapter Five

Contracting

Setting Yourself Up for Success

A colleague and I once were preparing to facilitate a series of meetings for a management consulting firm, a twenty-member partnership. The firm had begun to decline in revenues and had faced two years of net losses. The partners were seriously conflicted over the firm's future direction and how to turn it around. Some wanted to stick with their historical strength areas of consulting on accounting and financial management. Others wanted to take a risk and venture into the growing market in information technology consulting. The group became polarized, with the first group accusing the second of "crazy opportunism" and trying to "hop on any old bandwagon," and the second calling the first "stodgy," "obstructionist," and "too scared to try something new." The second group, those who wanted to go into information technology, were threatening to break off and start a competing firm.

We met with the board of directors of the firm, which comprised four of the partners and was serving, in effect, as our process advisory group. Because of the degree of internal conflict and distrust, we proposed significant work on relationships and cohesion. We suggested that two out of a series of about ten half-day meetings be devoted to "teambuilding"—a term we thought might be more acceptable to the group's masculine, task-oriented culture than "relationship building." Meanwhile, we also came prepared with a draft list of success criteria, which included, among others, "reduction in conflict" and "improved sense of cohesion."

The board members accepted the list of success criteria as drafted. However, when they looked at the schedule of meetings, they thought it looked too long. One member pointed out that while most of the sessions were devoted to concrete issues, the "team-building" sessions didn't seem to be about anything. He wanted to eliminate them.

In our desire to please the client, we accepted this request without challenge. We silently gambled that we could get at the relationship issues indirectly by fostering cooperation on the substantive problem-solving tasks. This worked to some extent, but in the end, the group's evaluation of the whole process was "good" and not "excellent"—and I believe the difference was largely due to the lack of progress in healing damaged intragroup relationships, despite what felt to them like endless meetings.

This conversation about the teambuilding sessions was a golden contracting moment, and we blew it. In retrospect, we should have said, nonjudgmentally, "We understand that this looks like a lot of meeting time, especially for a group that hates meetings. We'd be happy to drop the sessions on teambuilding, but we would also have to eliminate the objectives of 'reduction in conflict' and 'improved sense of cohesion,' because we can't achieve those without the teambuilding sessions. It's your choice."

Extreme facilitation means taking on challenges when success can't be guaranteed. However, you can be much more in control of your success through good contracting.

What Is Contracting?

In non-extreme facilitation, contracting can be as simple as reaching agreement with the client group about the scope of your services and your budget, along with some agreement with the full group about agenda, outcomes, roles, and ground rules. In extreme facilitation, we define contracting more broadly: it is the process of negotiating agreement with the clients about what they can expect from your services, and what you will need from them to fulfill their expectations. It sets you up for success, because it allows you to participate in defining success, and it helps the client group understand its role in ensuring success.

Contracting covers issues such as the following (presented in roughly chronological order):

- Fees, if you're an outside contractor; or resources and time available for the effort if you're internal
- The scope of your work
- The work plan, including tasks, timelines, and deliverables
- The nature of your role and participants' roles
- Who the client is—specifically: (1) who the paying client or "sponsor" is, (2) who will serve as the point of contact in the client organization, supervising and managing your work, and (3) who the group is that you are responsible to serve
- The time, energy, and commitment the group will give to the process
- The information the client will need to provide
- The purpose of the endeavor
- The definition of success
- The likelihood of achieving success, as jointly defined
- The issues to be discussed, and the issues "off the table"
- The meeting agendas and the schedule of meetings for the entire process
- The ground rules or guidelines

The Contracting Process

Contracting is even less of a distinct stage than assessment or convening. It's an iterative process, with some agreements reached first with a point of contact, later with a subgroup, and later again with the full group. It overlaps with assessment and convening. It begins with the first contact between you and the client, and may continue throughout your entire engagement with the group. This is because the process may unfold in such a way that you may alter your mutual expectations about what outcomes are expected or what it will take to get there. Typically, however, the bulk of the work of contracting is complete by a point early in the first meeting with the full group.

When most people think of a contract, they think of a single document detailing an agreement between two parties. Here I am using the term more broadly. Contracting involves reaching a series of agreements, explicit or implicit, with the participant group, the paying client, and others that may be involved. Not all the points of contracting must be addressed in a formal, written contract. There are three possible levels of explicitness in contracting:

1. *Implicit*. The mutual expectations are never discussed. This is fine when you feel confident that you and the client have a similar understanding on a given point. For example, there may be no need to discuss the nature of the facilitator's role if the client has worked with you before.

Obviously, implicit agreements are easy and convey a certain trust. The disadvantage is equally obvious: you cannot be certain that you are truly in agreement.

2. *Spoken but not written*. You discuss mutual expectations and come to an informal agreement. Many aspects of facilitator contracting are done in this manner. It is explicit, but there could be different recollections or understandings of what was agreed upon.

3. *Written*. The most explicit. Many facilitators use written contracts for fees and financial terms and conditions. Sometimes it's also appropriate to draw up a charter for the group that contains things such as the purpose, ground rules, list of participants, schedule of meetings, and so forth.

Written understandings need not always be formal documents. You might write a quick e-mail summarizing what you agreed on in an earlier phone conversation, for example.

Different aspects of contracting may be handled with different levels of explicitness.

There are different possible groups you might need to reach agreement with on any of the items listed previously:

- Your point of contact—usually, there is only one, but there may be more
- The sponsor (the entity paying for your services)
- The process advisory group (if there is one)
- The group of people whose meetings you will facilitate
- The prime contractor, if you're a subcontractor
- The referring organization, if you are part of a roster

Often, you're reaching agreement with multiple different people at different times. The following example, with a sequence of events from contracting for a large-scale public policy facilitation, will illustrate the complex and iterative nature of contracting:

1. Someone from a government agency puts out a request for proposals outlining a scope of work and asking bidders to submit a summary of qualifications, a cost estimate, and a description of their approach to the project. The scope of work is assessment and convening of a collaborative process to resolve legal challenges to a draft forest plan in an ecologically sensitive area, with the possibility that the same contractor may facilitate the actual dialogue once convened. Your submission and the agency's description of the scope constitute part of the contract with this agency.

2. You are selected, and you and the agency undergo budget negotiations and reach agreement. The agreed-upon budget constitutes part of your contract.

3. The agency sends out a mostly boilerplate contract for signature. This formal contract is only one part of *contracting* as I am defining it.

4. You carry out the assessment and convening, and recommend proceeding with a facilitated dialogue under certain conditions. These conditions may include certain ground rules, certain issues that are on or off the table, and so on. You warn that the willingness of some stakeholders to participate may be tenuous and that the possibility of reaching a hoped-for consensus outcome may be only 50 percent. Any commitments made to stakeholders and the expectations of success you state form part of your contract with the agency and the stakeholders.

5. The agency deliberates internally and decides to go forward with you as facilitator. It extends the scope of your original formal contract. This is a modification to your contract with the agency.

6. You draft a set of operating protocols, including purpose, ground rules, meeting length and frequency, press or publicity provisions, meeting summaries, and what the agency will do with the group's recommendation or input.

7. You hold the initial meeting, during which the operating protocols are revised and adopted. These agreements are now part of your contract with the entire group.

8. You convene a small process advisory group from among the dozens of participants and reach agreement with them on a schedule of meetings and an agenda for the next meeting.

9. You then present these to the full group for modification and approval. You have contracted first with the advisory group and then extended that to the full group.

10. Any of the contracts just discussed may be amended over the course of facilitation.

This is just an illustrative example of a somewhat complex contracting process. It shows how you are contracting with different people at different times.

Contracting for organizational facilitation tends to be simpler, but there may be different complications. For example, I was once brought in by a human resources (HR) director to facilitate in another department. The HR office had been bombarded by both formal grievances and informal letters and calls from employees in a work unit complaining about their manager. The grievances alleged sexual harassment and unfair performance reviews, and the informal complaints said the manager was everything from too loud to dangerously incompetent. The manager, meanwhile, wondered how his previously harmonious workplace had suddenly turned sour, and how he could have gone from effective to incompetent in the six months since this conflict began with the first grievance. He also complained that the employees never talked to him about the concerns or gave him a good-faith opportunity to respond, but just shot letters or grievances to the HR office instead.

The specific grievances were found to be without basis for disciplinary action, but the underlying conflicts remained—and they implicated both the work unit and the HR office. I had to clarify who was the point of contact for what purpose, and what information was to be shared with the HR office once the facilitation was under way. The HR office had to be kept informed to some extent, as they had to fulfill their responsibility of monitoring the performance of both the manager and the employees. Yet a successful process depended on maintaining a considerable degree of confidentiality to ensure candor. We agreed that only a general description of progress (things were going well or weren't) and the final agreement would be shared with the HR office.

Although contracting is a continual process, and not always a tidy one, there are typically a few key milestones. The first is the selection of the facilitator, with agreement on a budget and scope of work. The second is at the culmination of assessment and convening, with a recommendation of whether and under what circumstances to proceed with facilitation, and with what expectations. The third is at an early point in meeting with the full group, when agreement is reached with the entire group on such matters as a purpose, agenda, ground rules, roles, and objectives.

First Milestone: Agreeing on Scope and Budget

Typically, the first milestone in contracting is an agreement that you will be the facilitator for a given scope of work at a given fee or budget. In other words, you are selected to do a particular job. There is also an implicit agreement here that you are qualified to do the job.

Determining the Scope of Work

While it may seem that the clients would know the scope of work before even contacting a potential facilitator, even this aspect may be iterative. The clients may have some sense of what they want, but discussion with you (or a concept paper written by you) may expand or change their thinking and help them formulate a clearer scope. Negotiating the scope of work is an opportunity for you to offer your expertise about how you can best help the group.

Budget and Fees

Budget and fees are part of both early and ongoing contracting. You of course need to reach agreement up front about budget and fees, and what scope of work that budget buys. You also have to manage your budgets, like any contractor. Different fee structures place different contracting demands on you:[1]

1. *Actuals (also called "Time and Materials")*. This means charging per some unit of time (such as hourly or daily), and charging for all the time you work. You will have to make a realistic estimate of the hours you will need—things usually take longer than you expect. Then, if you're going to exceed the amount of time estimated, you must contact the client *before* you exceed it, explain why you

are going over the estimated hours, and give the client a choice of curtailing your work to stay within the original budget estimate.

2. *Actuals not to exceed.* This is just like charging actuals, except that there is an agreed-upon upper limit. This obviously gives the clients some comfort about their maximum total expenditure. The trick is to estimate your hours liberally enough to allow for the work taking longer than you might expect, while not making the budget so high as to turn the clients away.

3. *Fixed price.* This is simply giving one flat price to complete an entire project. Both the contractor and the client are taking a risk: if the work takes less time than estimated, you gain; if it takes longer, the client gains. However, fixed-price budgets will always be to your disadvantage if you chronically underestimate your hours or if you let the scope of work expand without renegotiating the budget. It pays here to be detailed about the scope of work, so that if, for example, you have agreed to conduct ten assessment interviews and the client schedules twelve, you will have grounds to ask for a budget increase.

Second Milestone: Assessment Report

Assessment and convening give you valuable information regarding whether to proceed with a facilitated process, and if so, how. In extreme facilitation, you'll need to give some kind of report at this juncture—whether a written document, a presentation, or both. The conclusions and recommendations in your report serve as part of your contract. (For brevity, I'll refer to this as the assessment report, although it also reflects convening.)

Report Contents

This is your first opportunity to begin to frame a purpose, to craft a schedule of meetings (including what topics will be covered in which meetings), to identify participants, and to offer preliminary recommendations about process design. Importantly, it's also an opportunity to be clear about what you need from the client and the participants to maximize chances of success.

Following is a list with explanations of items you *might* report on at the culmination of assessment and convening. Remember, some of these points may be left unsaid, if you believe that you have an adequate unspoken understanding.

1. *Purpose and issues.* The purpose statement, if you are crafting one, should identify both the subject matter and the hoped-for outcome—decision, recommendation, input, loose "meeting of the minds," or improved relationships or cohesion.

It may also be useful to break down the subject into particular issues or topics. There may be different desired outcomes for different topics. For example, in an annual organizational retreat, it is not unusual to address a variety of issues, reaching consensus on some, coming to a looser meeting-of-the-minds on others, and providing input to a decision maker on others.

Finally, it may be useful to clarify what issues are off the table (as discussed in Chapter Four).

2. *Identification of the client.* Sometimes it is helpful to make clear that you are responsible to the whole group, not to the sponsoring entity, the point of contact, the head of the group, or the management of the organization.

3. *Stakeholders or participants.* In public-policy facilitation, your convening will culminate in a recommended list of stakeholders you hope will participate and a representation structure (one representative per group, one plus an alternate, or other). In organizational facilitation, similarly, you may need to recommend the boundaries of the group or how participants should be chosen. In either setting, you may need to address the question of whether the ultimate decision maker should participate, and if so, how.

4. *Level of enthusiasm to participate.* Your report should reflect the reality of getting people to the table—that there are many more people wanting to participate than would be appropriate, or, conversely, that there are some important stakeholders whose willing-

ness to participate is questionable. In the public-policy arena, participation is usually voluntary, so some stakeholders may choose not to join the process. In the organizational arena, participation is often mandatory. Still, if some employees feel the process is a waste of time, you might point out that they are likely to show up only physically, with their minds elsewhere. Of course, their enthusiasm may depend on how the process is structured, so this item is tied with the other items in your report.

5. *Likelihood of success.* At this point you may or may not have identified specific success criteria. You will likely, however, have a clear picture of the purpose. If the likelihood of accomplishing that purpose is low, it's probably better not to start the process than to waste everyone's time. If success is contingent on other factors, it's important to say what those are (such as, for example, the willingness of participants to commit time and energy to the process).

6. *Schedule of meetings.* At this stage, you may be able to outline a preliminary list of meetings along with general topics or goals for each. This will, of course, be refined in further discussions, but it gives group members a general sense of the amount of time they will need to commit. Even without topics, you may be able to say something about the length and frequency of meetings. For example, in a public-policy facilitation, you may know that some participants can only attend during evenings or weekends—or that some will only attend during business hours. In organizational settings, you may recommend whether to conduct a process in a concentrated block of several days, perhaps off site, or to hold a series of shorter meetings over a longer period of time.

7. *Information needs.* In extreme facilitation involving complex issues, conscious attention needs to be paid to establishing a common knowledge base in the group and meeting participants' concerns about adequate and impartial information.

Public-policy facilitation often includes substantial amounts of time devoted to information dissemination—including technical background, legal and regulatory frameworks, past policy or regulatory action, options, and consequences of options. Some government officials' distaste for public participation is due to frustration from hearing impassioned yet uninformed opinions.

Organizational facilitation also may require information dissemination—such as financial status reports, results from employee surveys, or information on competitors, customers, or trends in the marketplace. Your assessment report is an opportunity to state what information will need to be shared.

Information needs have a lot to do with trust and power. Less-powerful groups may distrust information that comes from particular sources (such as the employer or the government), necessitating a neutral source of information, or perhaps a technical working group that establishes an agreed-upon body of data, or some other creative way to develop information that participants will trust. Your report should state what's necessary to develop and share trustworthy information.

On the flip side, powerful entities may hesitate to disclose vital information—to you, to the public, or to employees. They may fear that the information will be misunderstood, will cast them in a negative light, will be distorted, or will be used against them. If disclosure will be essential for a good process, this is an important chance to emphasize this. A discussion needs to begin about the fears surrounding disclosure and what might be done to minimize risks while maximizing openness and trust.

8. *Impact of the process.* If the process has anything to do with decision making, participants will want to know what will become of the decisions, recommendations, or input coming from the facilitated process. There is no better way to turn willing participants into cynics than by assuring them that their views will be taken seriously, then later ignoring them.

If the group is going to make decisions, what assurance is there that the decisions will be implemented? If they are going to make recommendations, what weight will the decision makers give to the recommendations? If they are providing input, what will the decision makers do with that input? You may have recommendations about what becomes of the product of the facilitated process. Often, participants' willingness to engage depends largely on this item.

9. *Ground rules.* Here again, your assessment may have revealed procedural needs that the prospective participants have. These can vary enormously. Participants might insist, for example, that the process be open to the press and the public, that no one will dominate the discussions, that confidentiality or nonattribution be maintained, or that meeting summaries be distributed by certain deadlines. Even when participants have not indicated any desires for particular procedural provisions, you may have learned about likely procedural or relationship problems and thus can design ground rules to address these. (The next section contains more about ground rules.) This is an opportunity for you to make some preliminary recommendations about ground rules.

10. *Go/no-go recommendation.* Unless it's absolutely obvious that the facilitation will occur (as is sometimes the case with organizational matters), part of your report will be a recommendation to proceed or not to proceed with it—or, just as likely, to proceed only if certain conditions are met. The go/no-go recommendation rests on a number of factors: Is there sufficient agreement about the purpose and desired outcomes? Are enough people willing to participate? Are they committed enough to make the process successful? Is there adequate time for the process? Is there enough deadline pressure to maintain a sense of momentum? Is there a trustworthy source of needed information? Are there adequate funds? Are you qualified to facilitate this process? In summary, is there a sufficient likelihood of success?

You might feel biased in favor of a "yes" response if you are eager for more facilitation experience. If so, one failure will quickly convince you that you're better off being brutally honest about chances for success. It's neither enjoyable nor reputation enhancing to facilitate a process that fails.

Report Audience

Who will be the audience for your report? The general principle is to answer people's request for access to your report while also respecting confidentiality. It seems only respectful to include anyone who has devoted time to participating in your assessment, if they are interested.

A dilemma can emerge if there are confidentiality concerns. For example, I worked with a government entity whose internal conflicts had been the subject of many unflattering news stories. A colleague and I conducted an extensive assessment (including over forty interviews) and reported on our analysis and recommendations in a written document. The interviews had revealed some harsh judgments and accusations among people in the leadership of the organization. Our point of contact at first wanted the report to be only for her. We pointed out that several people we interviewed had requested, quite reasonably, to be privy to the product of these interviews. The problem was that, because there were evidently people among those we interviewed who had been feeding information to the press, we had to make sure our report contained no fodder for further negative publicity.

As a result, we sanitized our analysis to the point that it said almost nothing. In retrospect, we might have been better off not offering any analysis and limiting our report to recommendations on moving forward with facilitation, or perhaps to providing only an oral report rather than a written one. Regardless, it would have been worse to forbid interviewees from seeing (or hearing) the report; this would have only heightened distrust.

Gaining Necessary Commitment

Your recommendation of whether and under what conditions facilitation should proceed is essentially the beginning of a negotiation about what success you can promise and what you need from the client group to fulfill those promises. Now you'll need to hear the group members' response and try to work out an agreement about whether and how to move forward.

The client group and the stakeholders or participants may need to have some internal discussion about their willingness to proceed. This is often a good time for a meeting with a point of contact or a process advisory group, if there is one, to discuss whether they can commit to providing the conditions for a successful process.

Third Milestone: Agreement with the Full Group

Once you've obtained agreement from the point of contact or a process advisory group about how to proceed, the next step is to expand this agreement to include the full group. You will need agreement about such matters as

- Purpose
- Schedule of meetings
- Ground rules
- Agenda
- Roles
- Success criteria

This is often made easier by distributing these items in draft form before the first meeting. Then, at the beginning of the first meeting, you can secure full-group agreement. These understandings can also be made or modified later, if problems or questions arise.

Many common frustrating meeting experiences come from a lack of clarity about these basic procedural matters. For example, I participated in one meeting that was framed by my colleague as how to respond to a particular foundation's newly publicized funding interests—that is, what projects we might undertake that they would fund. I interpreted this as an open brainstorming session in which we would all present ideas, then select the best from all of them.

When the idea-generation got off to a slow start, my colleague who called the meeting asked, "Would it be helpful to have something to react to?" After seeing a few nods of assent, he presented his own idea, and the rest of the meeting became a discussion of how to implement his idea. A couple of times, some participants tried to re-ignite the brainstorming process, while others were immersed in discussing the who, what, when, where, and how of my colleague's proposal. It was like being at two different meetings at the same time.

I felt frustrated and manipulated (though manipulation was not my colleague's intent). I had been lured to what I thought was a brainstorming session and wound up talking about how to act on one person's idea. Yet all that was lacking was clearer agreement on the purpose of the meeting. You can't afford this kind of confusion in extreme facilitation when the stakes are so much higher.

Contracting with the full group may be very easy, if the assessment, convening, and early stages of contracting have been done well. It is not unusual to distribute or post a draft meeting agenda, suggested guidelines, and purpose statement, and to have them accepted by the full group with no revisions.

However, any or all of these items can spark major battles. A colleague and I facilitated a dialogue about how to clean up a severely contaminated industrial facility, in the wake of protests against a federal-government-approved plan to allow some contamination to remain in place coupled with restrictions on future use of the property. The dialogue involved the site manager, the parent company and its attorneys, state and federal government regulators, two mayors, three environmental groups, and five homeowners' associations.

My colleague and I conducted a lengthy assessment and a painstaking convening process. We drafted a set of "operating protocols" that included a purpose statement, a schedule of meetings, ground rules (including provisions for observers and the press), and a description of the many different roles. Despite the thorough preparation that preceded it, this document became the subject of an entire day of negotiation. This was not completely out of proportion to the twelve days' worth of meetings that followed, but it was still arduous.

No doubt, the participants were using the protocols as an opportunity to test the process and their ability to influence it. It was important for us to be patient with what looked like petty wrangling, in order to gain the participants' trust that they truly had influence in the dialogue and decision making.

Following is some elaboration on a few select aspects of contracting with the full group.

Ground Rules

I don't believe in any universal set of ground rules. Even a simple rule like being civil or treating everyone with respect will mean different things to different people, and sometimes will not need to be stated at all.

Ground rules (which can also be called "procedural guidelines," "norms," or even simply "agreements") can serve a slightly different purpose than is commonly assumed. People generally think the main purpose of ground rules is to keep order and decorum and to authorize the facilitator to enforce them. All this is true, and there certainly are times when it works this way. For example, if a group has agreed on a ground rule of speaking only after the facilitator recognizes a raised hand, then if people speak out of turn, I can gently remind them of the ground rule.

Nonetheless, even if there is no such ground rule, I can still do something similar. I can say, "I think this group is large enough that we should go by raised hands. Do you agree?" More simply, I can say, "Hold on, Dave had his hand up." Simpler still, I can just ignore the person who spoke out of turn and focus on the person whose hand I acknowledged. People expect facilitators to maintain order in some way whether there are ground rules to this effect or not.

In my view, ground rules have the potential to serve a more profound purpose. They can set a positive, productive tone for the discussions, they can be used to address relationship difficulties, and they can help a group develop better meeting habits. To serve these ends, ground rules must be generated creatively to address the needs of the specific group. A few quick stories will illustrate how this is done.

- One company had persistent tensions between management and employees. Management felt the employees were always attacking them unfairly. Employees felt management always got defensive after hearing their concerns. I devised the following pair of ground rules: (1) "When raising concerns, identify specific behaviors and their impact on you" and (2) "When on the receiving end of concerns or complaints, ask questions and seek to understand before responding."

- One team within an organization had experienced infighting and distrust. I reassured them that trust was not necessary for productive discussion—indeed, the discussion was intended to solve the very problems that led to distrust. Two ground rules addressed the trust issue: (1) "Work toward specific agreements" (so that trust was not required to ensure their implementation, I explained); and (2) "Before assuming negative intentions, ask yourself if there could be a different explanation."

- In a facilitation to help numerous different local, state, and federal agencies overcome turf battles over developing and monitoring water-development plans, a local regulatory agency requested confidentiality of all the proceedings. The others retorted that sunshine laws probably precluded that, so we explored the local agency's underlying concerns further. They were worried that proposals they made in the course of creative problem-solving might be construed as new policy positions and used against them later—in other words, "You were willing to do X in the meetings about the ABC project, so why aren't you willing to do that now for the DEF project?" I proposed and obtained agreement on the following ground rule: "Proposals made in the course of these discussions should not be construed as new policy positions."

Once ground rules are seen as a targeted way of addressing likely problems in a group, it will become clear that most groups need only a handful of ground rules—typically under ten, and sometimes only two or three.

It may still be helpful to see some sample ground rules here to spark your own creativity. Below is a list of the kinds of topics ground rules might address, along with sample ground rules that help address them:

- *How to keep basic order.* For example, avoid interrupting, avoid sidebar conversations, speak only when acknowledged by the facilitator, turn off cell phones and pagers (or put them on vibrate), let the facilitator know if a break is needed. (Bear in mind these are *possible* rules, not necessary ones. Many meetings work fine with everyone jumping in to speak without raising hands, for example, or with individuals getting up to take their own individual breaks if needed.)

- *How to help the meeting run efficiently.* For example, avoid repeating points already made, limit discussion to items on the agenda, postpone to a future meeting any new topics that emerge, adhere to time limits in the agenda, keep comments brief.

- *How to maintain balanced participation.* For example, monitor your air time, ask to hear the views of people who have not spoken, take a risk to speak if you tend to be quiet, don't wait to find the perfect words.

- *How to keep the discussion cooperative.* For example, refrain from personal attacks, be respectful, be civil, seek to understand others' ideas before responding, explain reasons for your disagreement, criticize ideas but not people, don't take criticism of your ideas personally.

- *How to raise complaints or concerns constructively.* For example, describe specifics rather than generalize, describe behavior rather than attributing motives or intent, state underlying needs or interests rather than making demands, suggest solutions but be open to alternative solutions, be firm about your needs and interests but flexible about how to meet them, limit group discussion to group issues (not interpersonal matters).

- *How to keep momentum toward decision making.* For example, seek to understand the situation before problem solving, explain the reasons for not accepting a proposed solution (rather than simply refusing it), offer alternative solutions, seek solutions that meet the interests of all parties, think beyond the usual solutions, suspend judgment during brainstorming.

- *How to address confidentiality or openness.* For example, agendas will be made public in advance; meetings are open to observers; meetings are for invited participants only; observers may speak at designated times; meetings may not be audio- or videotaped; participants may discuss the meetings generally but may not attribute comments to others; participants may not use anything said during meetings in any future legal, disciplinary, enforcement, or administrative proceeding; meeting summaries may be distributed freely; meeting summaries are to be seen by participants only.

Roles

Sometimes it's unnecessary to make anything explicit about roles, because it's obvious: the facilitator facilitates; the participants participate. However, in extreme facilitation, roles are usually more complicated. Following are some possibilities.

Supporting Staff or Consultants. Role confusion may arise if one or more stakeholder groups are represented by a lead representative plus support people, who may be technical advisers, consultants, attorneys, or staff. Are they full participants, sitting at the table? Or are they more like observers, answering questions only when asked?

In the facilitation about agency turf battles over water planning, two agencies were represented by a staff person as the lead, plus a technical consultant. One of the consultants had been deeply involved in the issues being discussed. She tended to take over the role of representing that agency, and some saw her as more inflexible than the main representative. One participant requested of me, between meetings, that we clarify roles of consultants. We discussed this issue in a full-group meeting and agreed on a loose guideline that the consultants would allow the staff representatives to be the primary spokespersons for their groups.

Role clarification is ideally done at the beginning of the first full-group meeting, but can be done later if needed.

Technical Experts. I just addressed staff or consultants supporting particular participants; separately, there may be people brought in to provide information to the whole group. During the lengthy air-quality facilitation discussed earlier, the sponsoring agency contracted with a technical consulting firm to make presentations and answer questions about sources of air pollution, how pollution forms, what options were available for curbing it, and what the air-quality benefits were of various options. In the health-insurance facilitation described in Chapter Four, the organization's insurance broker was brought in to present information about health insurance options and costs based on proposals he had solicited from a number of insurance companies.

The main thing to make clear is whether the technical experts are also participants in terms of engaging in dialogue and decision making, or whether they are strictly providing information. In the previous examples, they were strictly providing information. In other cases, some participants may double as information providers. The downside of this is that they may be seen as less objective or reliable sources if they also have a stake in the outcome of the discussions. Their role should ideally be made clear up front.

Decision Maker. In convening, you faced the dilemma of whether the ultimate decision maker (if there is one) should participate in the facilitated sessions. If so, he is in a very difficult role. You may need to prompt him about when and how he can offer his views without foreclosing needed discussion—for example, when criteria for good decisions are being set out, or when options are being narrowed and evaluated. In terms of contracting, it may be useful to clarify that the decision maker is there to offer guidance to ensure that the final decisions have his support. Suggesting that the decision maker is there "just like any other participant" is unrealistic except in the most nonhierarchical, nondeferential cultures.

Facilitator. It may be necessary to clarify how you will carry out your role as facilitator. Participants may have certain expectations of what the facilitator should or should not do, often based on experiences with other facilitators. Unfortunately, you may not discover these expectations until you have violated them. You may, however, have discovered them during assessment.

For example, the head of one client organization said during an assessment interview that, having worked with a facilitator before, she didn't want the meeting to be "all about the facilitator." She said she wanted her staff to talk *to each other*; that the facilitator should not be "center stage," as another facilitator had been in the past. I never fully understood what the prior facilitator had done, but I agreed that I would focus on structuring a good process and then letting it roll with minimal intervention.

While this group wanted a facilitator with a lighter touch, sometimes the opposite is true. Particularly if there is conflict, some may want the facilitator to take an active role in moving the group toward resolution. This more active role may entail such things as (1) working to uncover underlying needs or interests when participants are stuck in opposing positions, (2) asking questions that have the effect of challenging negative views of other participants (perhaps in private conversations between meetings), (3) holding a small discussion session between key antagonists to see if they can reach a resolution to propose to the group, or, at the furthest edge of the facilitator's comfort zone, (4) suggesting possible solutions to conflictual issues.

You may need to have a discussion with select group members (ideally the ones who are asking you to do something differently) to try to identify specifically what they are seeking or expecting from you. Then, you will need to reach a realistic agreement about what you can provide.

Objectives or Success Criteria

The purpose statement may be an adequate objective against which to measure success. However, evaluation is one area in which facilitators typically fall short, and good evaluation begins with a definition of the criteria by which success will later be evaluated.[2] This is also part of your contract with the group: How, specifically, can they expect to be better off at the end of the facilitation than at the beginning? It's important to make sure these are reasonable expectations.

You may already have some draft success criteria after conducting the assessment and holding discussions with the point of contact and a process advisory group. In this case you might simply present these for approval. Alternatively, a question about objectives sometimes makes a good opportunity for everyone to speak and make their voice heard early in the first full-group meeting. You might ask something like, "How will you know whether this effort has been successful? What will be the indicators?" or "What one thing do you hope will result from these sessions?" Once you hear the responses, you may briefly negotiate an agreement about what outcomes are reasonable to expect.

I facilitated for one company in which labor-management relations were so distrustful that each side tried to protect itself by sharing a minimum of information, and, in the information vacuum, each side developed conspiracy theories about the other. There was a dormant labor-management council that we revived to serve as the process advisory committee, and it had framed one of the topics as "communication." During assessment, I learned that some people thought that a full-day session would be devoted to improving communication skills. I double checked with the committee about whether they were hiring me as a facilitator or a trainer. They were clear it was the former, and that no training was expected.

Still, when I asked the full group, "What are the most important outcomes you hope this retreat will produce?" a couple of people again said they sought better communication skills. I said that the other objectives were ones I thought we could fulfill (such as achieving greater mutual understanding, increasing trust, and building procedures to improve future communication), and I was able to review and adjust the agenda on the spot, with the group's consent, to ensure it would help meet these objectives. However, I clarified that the meetings would not be devoted to skills training and got the group's approval to proceed with that understanding.

In contracting with the full group, as with the earlier stages of contracting, these questions of ground rules, roles, success criteria, and so on are negotiated. You want to meet the group's hopes as much as possible, but not to the point of promising things you can't deliver. In this way, contracting sets both you and the client group up for success. You're now ready to get into the meat of the discussions.

Notes

1. My knowledge on this aspect of contracting comes entirely from CDR's financial director Paula Taylor.
2. Rothman, "Action Evaluation and Conflict Resolution Training."

Part Three

Conducting the Process

Chapter Six

Process Basics

The Beginner's Guide to Facilitation

We've seen how extreme facilitation requires thorough assessment, convening, and contracting. We now move on to the basics of facilitating group meetings, the actual substantive discussion with the full group.

This chapter will not provide a detailed sequence of specific steps and stages to follow. Such rigid rules can be too inflexible for the customized, creative approach necessary for extreme facilitation. So where do you start? There still has to be some general framework—a "box" that you can think outside of, but one that's flexible enough that you can be creative even when thinking inside the box.

This chapter provides that box. It is intended to give you a solid foundation in the basics of facilitating group processes, so that the later chapters, which help build the extreme facilitator's range of conceptual frameworks and skills, make sense. For experienced facilitators, this chapter may offer a new way of conceptualizing the basics. My approach is less prescriptive and more flexible, allowing room for the customization and creativity that are central to extreme facilitation.

Basic Stages

The stages of a group process will vary greatly depending on the purpose of the process. Still, it's possible to outline some broad, flexible stages:

1. Opening and setting the tone
2. Building understanding
3. Achieving the task
4. Closing

Opening and Setting the Tone

The first words said at the beginning of a process or the beginning of a particular meeting within a process are crucial for establishing the right framework and tone. These may include the following—and not necessarily all of them:

• *Opening remarks by the facilitator or an appropriate leader.* These remarks should help set the tone—whether warm, funny, serious, inspiring, or whatever is needed. In one public-policy process sponsored by a state agency, a top aide to the governor gave opening remarks, impressing upon the stakeholders their important role in making public policy. In a labor-management retreat for a company experiencing significant conflict between management and workers, I gave opening remarks intended to convey both warmth (how happy I was to be working with such wonderful people) and optimism (how I believed that with dedicated effort their problems were surmountable).

• *Personal introductions.* These offer an opportunity for strangers to get to know each other, or for people to learn something new about each other relevant to the topic and purpose. If relationship building is part of the purpose, it may make sense to have people discuss something about themselves they would not learn otherwise (such as hobbies, nonwork interests, or family information).

• *Contracting.* As described in Chapter Five, the first meeting with the full group is an opportunity to obtain agreement on purpose, objectives or success criteria, schedule of meetings, agenda, roles, and ground rules.

• *Start-up question.* People often need to warm up, to get used to hearing their voices in the meeting setting, and to feel assured that their participation is welcome. An opening question to which each participant responds can meet this need.

The start-up question can overlap with other items. For example, it could be an extended introduction that allows for some relationship building. It could relate to contracting—for example, the question might be what each person hopes to achieve through the process (objectives) or what they need from each other for a successful process (ground rules). For a more task-oriented way to begin, the start-up question might delve right into the substance of the discussion (in which case this comes after the other opening items).

Building Understanding

After opening, the next stage is building understanding of the many facets of the issues the group hopes to tackle. It is amazing how often people begin by debating what decision to make or action to take before sharing such knowledge and developing mutual understanding. This impatient rush to solutions is usually a recipe for deadlock and—paradoxically—delay.

Before a group can make decisions, reach agreements, make plans, or achieve any other task, it must develop a shared understanding of the situation. Elements to explore may include relevant information, points of view, the context, and the task.

- *Relevant information.* Exploring relevant information might mean anything from simply sharing tidbits of news with each other to having independent consultants make presentations on complex technical data.
- *Points of view.* To improve relationships, break down misunderstandings or stereotypes, make good decisions, or resolve conflicts, participants need to understand each others' views, interests, perceptions, feelings, experiences, and interpretations.
- *The context.*[1] Problems and conflicts often are a product of their context—the history, external forces, structures, and

cultural factors that may have set people up for inevitable opposition. Coming to a shared understanding of these dynamics helps people take the blame off of each other and view their task as solving a problem rather than winning a battle.

- *The task*. To set the stage for task achievement, the group needs to define its task in light of the understandings developed. This could mean defining the problem to be solved, the issue to be addressed, the dilemma to be resolved, the goal to strive for, or the obstacles to achieving a desired future.

Here's an example of how building understanding can work: in facilitating a dialogue on whether to complete the last segment of a beltway around a metropolitan area, the first meetings were devoted to sharing interests or criteria for a good solution (an example of points of view); hearing presentations of data about traffic forecasts, population and employment growth, and environmental issues (relevant information); and refining the "purpose and need statement" that would drive the screening of alternatives (the task).

As another illustration, recall from the beginning of Chapter Five my work with a management consulting firm that was at civil war over its future direction (whether to stick with its historical strengths of accounting and financial management or venture into information technology). One task we took on was developing a vision statement. In the building understanding phase, we first had a presentation by the CEO on a possible business venture that might or might not be attractive, depending on what business direction the firm wanted to take. This illustrated the need for a vision (which helped define the task). We then asked participants to identify the firm's strengths and weaknesses, and the external factors bearing on them (this combined relevant information, points of view, and the context). Next, we invited everyone to envision the future of the company, by asking questions about both the type of work they wanted to do externally and the type of organization they wanted to be internally in ten years (an example of points of view).

From these activities, some themes and agreements emerged from which I was able to develop a first-draft vision statement, the first step of task achievement.

One last illustration will further illustrate building understanding, specifically of the context. I cofacilitated a process to help resolve issues at a resort community in Colorado that had both year-round residents and seasonal visitors. The resort, a nonprofit organization, was dedicated to having people live harmoniously with nature in environmentally friendly accommodations. The stakeholders included the resort staff, its board of directors, year-round residents, and seasonal visitors. Each group was represented by three to four people.

Conflict among staff, residents, and visitors had reached crisis proportions—the staff felt the seasonal visitors placed unfair demands on them; the residents were resentful that the visitors consumed all the staff time, leaving no time to serve the residents; the regular visitors felt the staff never provided adequate service except in response to complaints; and the board was stuck in the middle and at a loss for funds to increase the staff.

The early stages of the process were largely spent on understanding the factors that tended to make conflict almost inevitable. For instance, one structural factor was that the same staff had to serve the very different needs of residents and visitors—residents simply needed things like trash pickup and grounds maintenance; visitors needed all this plus tourism information, housekeeping services, concierge services, and so on. Another factor was the history: the resort had begun as a reclusive community for year-round residents and had begun receiving seasonal visitors more recently, causing it to shift gears and alter its identity. An additional factor was cultural differences: the residents and staff were of middle-class, mountain culture—individualistic and self-reliant—whereas the visitors largely were wealthy Southerners who expected more deferential, pampering hospitality.

The group began discussing these matters with little prompting from us facilitators. Once they finished, however, there was a palpable reduction in tension and an eagerness, even impatience, to move into problem solving and decision making. In other words, the time spent understanding the context, while on the surface not immediately relevant to the task, in fact laid the groundwork to achieve the task.

Achieving the Task

Once the relevant information, points of view, and context have been understood and the task has been defined, the group can focus its energy on achieving it. This may involve any of a number of activities, which generally fall into five categories:

1. Identifying options for decision or action
   - Identifying known options
   - Brainstorming to generate additional options
   - Researching solutions used by others in similar situations
2. Narrowing and evaluating
   - Developing evaluation criteria
   - Evaluating options against the criteria, which might include participants' needs and interests or standard, objective measures
3. Developing proposals
   - Identifying agreed-upon themes or principles from which to build specific agreements
   - Eliciting group members' proposals aimed at satisfying both their own and others' interests
   - Drafting a "strawman" or "single-text" proposal—a preliminary draft to which all can make changes—as a starting point for negotiation (this is more effective in consensus building than eliciting competing proposals and counter-proposals)

- Assembling small agreements on narrow subissues into a broader, more comprehensive agreement

4. Overcoming deadlocks

- Digging deeper into the needs, concerns, and interests that underlie opposing viewpoints

- Framing disagreements as a task to meet the most important interests of both or all sides

- Inviting key proponents of opposing views to meet separately to negotiate resolution of their differences, and then to bring the resulting proposals back to the full group

5. Refining outcomes

- Negotiating final details of drafts or proposals

- Developing action plans for implementation

- Anticipating obstacles to implementation and planning how to overcome them

In working with the previously mentioned consulting firm on its vision statement, we came to the subsequent meeting with a first-draft vision statement (an example of developing proposals). We then had participants identify language they had concerns with and negotiate modifications (refining outcomes). In the process, one deadlock arose regarding the degree of autonomy staff consultants would have to accept projects that might or might not fit the new vision. This required digging deeper into the interests and needs on that issue, then hammering out agreement and weaving the new agreement into the vision statement (overcoming deadlocks). We completed a consensus vision statement in which the group agreed to stick to focusing on using its existing key skills, such as quantitative analysis, as it carefully explored new fields of application for those skills, such as information technology.

In the transportation dialogue about the possible beltway completion, also mentioned earlier, task achievement included many stages. First the technical consultants identified a "universe of alternatives" to which participants were invited to add (identifying options). The consultants then presented a list of screening criteria based on the participants' earlier discussion of their needs and interests (developing evaluation criteria; narrowing and evaluating). The participants were again allowed to add to this list. The consultants conducted a first screening based on these criteria, yielding a shorter list of alternatives (evaluating options against criteria). A second round of screening was conducted, with further input to develop more detailed criteria, and with more detailed study of the remaining alternatives, complete with planning, design, and engineering. Specific alternatives—such as expansion of one road or light rail along another—were grouped into a few alternative packages (this was, in effect, developing proposals) for final negotiation and consensus building.

Another example will illustrate anticipating obstacles to implementation. I once facilitated negotiations between federal and state entities over the cleanup plan for a closing military base. The state agency had high-level participants who knew they would have no trouble persuading their superiors to approve the agreement. The lead negotiator for the military, however, had many layers of decision makers above him in the hierarchy—and his immediate boss was predicted to be skeptical. Having worked with this boss before, I set up a role play with the lead negotiator in which I did my best impression of the boss challenging the negotiator about why he'd entered into this "stupid" agreement.

The lead negotiator got good practice defending the agreement, which came in handy not only with his boss but also with some of the attorneys in his office. Even though one attorney was at the table during the negotiation, the others back at the office made a sport of poking holes in his work (perhaps a little envious that he got the glory of resolving this long-standing dispute in a mere day and a half). Some last-minute modifications did have to be worked out by phone with the state, but the basic substance of the agreement survived and got approved.

Closing

Closing, like opening, is a fairly quick but important stage. It may involve any of the following:

- Summary of outcomes.
- Next steps identification and planning.
- Evaluation of the process, or of the facilitation. Ongoing groups can help improve their process habits by evaluating meetings as a group. Alternatively, you might distribute written evaluation forms to be completed during the meeting (if time allows) or later.
- Closing ritual. A closing ritual helps people move on from the process, from the problem they've solved, or from the past patterns they've committed to change. This may simply involve an opportunity for last comments about what has happened, what they've learned, or what they've committed to do. Other possible rituals include a champagne toast (or nonalcoholic equivalent) or a closing speech by a respected figure.

Fluidity of This Model

The model just described is fluid and flexible. Not all processes require every stage, much less every piece of each stage. For example, a dialogue process that has the purpose of reducing prejudice and improving understanding across different groups may have no need for any task achievement, except to build understanding. A different kind of case may focus mainly on the task-achievement stage and skip the stage of building understanding. For example, one company had numerous conversations about its organizational values, leading to some general themes. However, this group had trouble reaching closure, so it used a facilitator to achieve the task of coming to consensus on a written values statement—no need in this case for the facilitator to help build understanding first.

Moreover, this sequence of stages either may serve as an overarching structure for an entire process or may occur in miniature in each of numerous agenda items. For example, the stakeholder process about whether to complete the beltway devoted one meeting primarily to opening (stage 1), two to building understanding (stage 2), many to task achievement (stage 3), and the final one to closing (stage 4).

In contrast, organizational retreats commonly have numerous different agenda topics, each of which cycles through the sequence of phases, or pieces of it. One agenda item may focus on building understanding of the financial status of the organization (stage 2 only); another on making a final decision on a topic a committee has been studying for months, such as whether to open a new field office (stage 3 mainly); and another on understanding people's feelings related to another topic and obtaining input that a decision maker will consider (stages 2 and 3). In addition to the opening and closing for the whole retreat, some of these items may have their own openings and closings.

Even the sequence of stages is fluid—the middle two stages, at least, may trade places or overlap. For example, while it usually makes sense to understand a topic fully before embarking on decision making, it sometimes can help first to build a vision of the ideal future state or "optimal model"[2] (part of task achievement) before looping back to better understand the current situation (part of building understanding). Alternatively, it's sometimes useful to tack back and forth between building understanding and task achievement, achieving a piece of the task and then sharing feelings and information about that before working on more of the task.

Basic Interventions

The preceding description of stages may leave you wondering, "How exactly do I conduct these stages?" The basic answers to this are split into two parts in the remainder of this chapter: (1) facilitator interventions—things you can say or do to keep a discussion on course, and (2) formats you can use to structure a process.

During open, unstructured discussions—of which most facilitated processes will involve at least a bit—the facilitator's job is to intervene when needed to keep the discussion moving productively toward a goal. Here are some basic interventions.

Remaining Silent

The most important intervention skill is knowing when *not* to intervene. Before I began my career in facilitation, I had participated in a facilitated meeting only once. The facilitators paraphrased almost every statement we made. This formed my first idea of what facilitation was supposed to be like.

Later, when I started at CDR Associates, I served as a recorder (taking notes on flip charts) for a facilitation conducted by CDR partner Bernie Mayer. The process was intended to find funding for a city's new bus system, and it involved citizens and officials involved in transportation issues. The early discussions went quite smoothly, but Bernie sat mostly silent throughout these early stages. I was alarmed. I thought, "What are they paying him for?" His level of intervention picked up as we moved into achieving the task (which was to make consensus recommendations) and sharp disagreements surfaced. I came to realize that part of what they were paying him for was to use judgment as to when to intervene and when not to.

If we intervene when it isn't necessary, we waste time and turn more attention to ourselves. The group shouldn't be focused on the facilitator; it should be focused on its own goals, relationships, and tasks. If you are selective and intervene only when necessary, your interventions will carry more weight and have more effect.

Asking Questions

Questions can be used to suggest a direction for group discussion. The facilitator poses a question, participants answer, they respond to each other's answers, and the discussion flows from there.

Questions can be used as agenda items. For example, in preparing a leadership retreat for a troubled company, we put the following question as an agenda item: "How can executives balance the need for coordination with the need for autonomy?" This can be more effective than simply proposing a topic (which might have been, in this case, "coordination"), which fails to define the dilemma or tension that the discussion must address.

Questions can also be used to redirect discussion. For example, if participants get too bogged down in the details of an issue that needs to be addressed more broadly, the facilitator might ask, "What's the big picture here?" or "What does this particular scenario illustrate?"

Finally, facilitators can ask follow-up questions to prompt a person who has just spoken to go into more depth or specificity: "How do you mean?" and "Can you explain that a little more?" are examples. Your decision to pose a question will be largely based on your own judgment (informed by your assessment) of what needs to be discussed and understood by others.

Paraphrasing or Summarizing

Paraphrasing and summarizing what a speaker has just said are classic techniques of active listening. They can have several powerful effects in facilitation: first, they prove to the speaker that you heard and understood the comment correctly—which helps to build trust and de-escalate strong emotions. Second, they help other participants understand the point, because you can use different words than the speaker's, and you can perhaps make the point more clearly and simply. (People struggling with difficult issues sometimes "think aloud," resulting in rambling, disorganized statements.) Third, they amplify the speaker's point, since the group hears it twice in different words.

However, paraphrasing and summarizing can be overdone. They may detract from people's confidence in their own ability to express themselves. They may take up unnecessary time. They keep the facilitator at center stage—which may be good in some situations, such as early in a process where there is serious conflict or discomfort among participants in dealing directly with each other. But they can also disempower participants or build their dependence on the facilitator.

I try to paraphrase and summarize sparingly, when it will be the most useful: to help a speaker who has not expressed himself well, to acknowledge strong feelings, or to reinforce important points (including conciliatory ones, as well as compelling explanations for strong positions).

Reframing to Interests

Paraphrasing or summarizing can occasionally be downright destructive. When engaged in a dispute or a contentious negotiation, people often give ultimatums, make threats, hurl insults, or declare inflexible positions or demands. To paraphrase such negative statements can legitimize or reinforce them. I once joked with a training group about paraphrasing the comment "You dumb ass!" as "So you think he's an unintelligent donkey?" More seriously, a well-meaning facilitator might paraphrase a comment such as, "We insist on compensation for the loss of property value of our homes caused by this new prison, and if we don't get it here, we're going to court!" as something like, "I see you're determined not to suffer financially from the building of the jail, and will sue if necessary."

The trouble with this paraphrasing is that it reinforces the position—getting full compensation for loss of property value—as the only acceptable solution. It also reinforces the threat of a lawsuit. Mutually beneficial outcomes are most likely if we focus on the participants' underlying interests[3]—their needs, concerns, or objectives. Therefore, instead of restating the position, you can restate what you believe to be the underlying interests. It may take some additional active listening to know what the interests are.

A reframing of the angry statement about the lost property value might be, "You want to make sure officials appreciate the financial impact of this new prison on you, and you want that to be handled fairly." If you've gotten it right, the participant will say so or show it. If you guess wrong, the participant will let you know and you can ask for more elaboration or try again. You then have something you can work with—a statement of the interests that need to be met, rather than a rigid negotiating position. This simple intervention can transform hostile remarks into useful fodder for further discussion.

Stating Observations

Another simple yet powerful intervention is to state observations of what is going on in the discussion. Your observations, whether spoken or unspoken, need to include not just what is happening overtly in the discussion but also body language, facial expressions, and tone of voice. These give clues as to people's energy levels, their ease or discomfort, their following well or being perplexed, their sense of progress or frustration, and so on. Vocalizing your observations allows the group to confront previously unspoken dynamics and to either self-correct, be receptive to your procedural suggestions, or simply be more cognizant of their dynamics.

Your observations can range from simple procedural notes to profound insights. Procedural observations may include

- That the allotted time for a task or topic is nearly over.
- That the topic or task has shifted—for example, "The discussion has moved from the description of the critical issues into strategies for addressing them."
- That some people have not yet spoken on the topic.

Each of these, obviously, implies a follow-up question or action. For example, noting that some people have not spoken implicitly invites the quieter ones to speak up and the more verbose ones to hold their thoughts.

Deeper observations may include

- Dynamics of the group's culture—for example, "It's interesting that the nurses always address the physicians as 'Dr. so-and-so', whereas the physicians always address the nurses by first name, even the advanced-practice nurses who have Ph.D.s."

- Changes in dynamics over time—for example, "I've noticed that the tone is less tense and more congenial today than in your first meeting" or "You're all much quieter today and seem distant, as if something else is on your minds."

- Cultural differences—for example, "Some of you seem very comfortable confronting each other directly, in an animated way, whereas others of you seem more careful and reserved. Because of this difference, the first group may see the second group as secretive and untrustworthy, and the second group may see the first as volatile and threatening."

- Possible cause-and-effect relationships that the group may not see—for example, "You're all concerned about negative consequences of the tight schedule for this project, but I wonder if the schedule has also helped create the tremendous sense of drive and teamwork that you've displayed."

- The group's success or lack of it—for example, "You may not realize how much you've accomplished in the last several meetings—several key issues have been resolved and you're well on your way to resolving the remaining ones" or "This discussion doesn't seem to be working, and I'm not sure why. We seem to be going around in circles."

After any of these observations, you might either leave a pause, implicitly inviting group members to respond—for instance, with "Yes, we are going around in circles, and I think it's because we don't have enough information to make this decision"—or you might follow the observation with a more explicit question, such as "Do you agree? Why do you think we're not getting anywhere?" Either way, you may end up changing the process as a result.

Making Process Changes

You ordinarily begin a meeting with an agenda and a process design. It is critical to have this plan, but it's just a starting point. You must constantly assess whether things are going well and the process is on course, and if not, make changes.

There are several ways you can go about changing the process. One is to throw the question to the group and discuss and agree on changes collectively. For example, you might say, "I sense that many of you are feeling frustrated by this discussion. What do you think we need to do differently?" Another is to suggest a change yourself—for example, "I sense that many of you are feeling frustrated by this discussion. Why don't we try to capture those points that are agreed on so far and then delegate this issue to a subgroup to come up with a proposal between now and the next meeting?" Finally, you might call a break and ask a small number of people to help you adapt the design: "I sense that many of you are feeling frustrated by this discussion. Let's take a ten-minute break and figure out what to do. If any of you have thoughts about that, come up and let me know."

There are pros and cons to each of these approaches. A "pure" facilitative approach would suggest the first option—letting the group make all decisions, even procedural ones (a process-oriented group might like this approach). As a practical matter, however, this can take a lot of time, and the participants (especially if they're more task oriented) will probably welcome more direction from you, as long as they trust you sufficiently. A more directive approach still leaves the opportunity for group members to object to your suggestion or present alternative ideas—but keep in mind that groups with more deferential or indirect cultures may find it difficult to do this. The last approach, calling a break and soliciting advice, risks making you look incompetent if done too frequently, but otherwise allows group involvement in process decisions in a relatively efficient way.

What if the group is split on what to do about the process? Surprisingly, this is quite unusual in my experience. It did happen to me once during a regular monthly meeting of a local peace activist group—certainly not the kind of facilitation I would have expected to be extreme. I was asked to facilitate the meeting partly because their routine meetings were almost always frustrating and unsatisfying.

In this particular meeting, one newer member, a professor, began pontificating about the then-imminent American invasion of Iraq and how to oppose it, in broad strategic terms. We had many business-type items remaining on the agenda. I suggested that we get through them and then resume this larger topic at the end. The longer-time activists nodded with relief.

Another newer member, however, objected vehemently: "Where else are we going to have such a discussion but here!? This is important and I don't think we should shunt it to the end!"

The longer-term members jumped back in: "We have a lot to do at this meeting, and this wasn't on the agenda!" After some back and forth, the longer-term members resigned themselves to proceeding with the professor's broader topic—and we wound up staying an hour beyond the originally planned end time.

Had I to do this particular meeting again, I would have done more at that moment to test whether people were willing to stay beyond the stated end time, and to seek an explicit agreement either to do that or to drop some agenda items. Regardless, the real problem lay deeper: the longer-time activists viewed these regular meetings as a way to address business items of the group (getting volunteers for particular events, making decisions about financial expenditures) as efficiently as possible. They generally spent a lot of time in meetings and wanted to get on with their tasks—most of which were accomplished in smaller subcommittees. The newer members, by contrast, were excited to have discovered a group of like-minded citizens and wanted to use the meetings to discuss current events and macro-level strategies. After this meeting, I worked with the group to better define the purpose of the regular meetings and to set up some separate meetings for discussion of broad policy issues and strategies.

If a group is sharply split on process, there is probably a deeper issue that needs to be addressed, and the approach is the same: make the observation ("You're clearly split about how we should approach this") and then either throw the question back to the full group ("How do you propose we bridge this gap?"), offer a suggestion, or take a break and invite individuals' suggestions.

Capturing Points of Agreement

One last basic but powerful intervention is to capture points of agreement—orally at first, and in writing later as needed.

There is more art to this than may first appear. Long before a group is aware that it's reached final settlement of a major issue, the astute facilitator will pick up on points people seem to agree on. This requires noticing what's *not* being debated. The group will almost imperceptibly begin to move on to whatever they still disagree about, rarely calling attention to what is now agreed on.

For example, imagine you're facilitating a process involving parents who are organizing a new charter school and residents of a neighborhood where it is going to be located. At first, the residents ask why the school needs so much space. The charter school organizers map out the floor plan, the plans for a playground, the projected number of students, and the capacity of each room. The residents move on to express concerns about noise and the loss of their views of a nearby lake. At that point, the observant facilitator would interject, "Before we move on, I think there's agreement that the school needs about ten thousand square feet of floor space and one-quarter acre for the playground. Is that right?" Stating this kind of interim agreement, even if minor, helps build momentum to larger agreement, builds a sense of progress, and helps the group isolate their remaining disagreements.

A related technique is identifying agreed-on themes from a wide-reaching conversation in which a variety of views have been stated. For example, I asked employees of one troubled organization to come up with their visions of the ideal workplace. Following are some of the key phrases from their visions:

- Ideas from unexpected places
- Rich disagreement
- Support and dialogue
- Light, creative atmosphere
- Accepting and safe
- Good management (creative)
- Celebrate accomplishments
- Time to plan and strategize
- Listen to people
- See each person as an individual (not seen as a "cog")
- Work that doesn't "make me want to punch people"
- Challenge (what you think, do, and so on)
- Be committed
- Work for common good
- Do what is necessary
- Know what it is you want to change
- Believe in your knowledge (but don't impede new learning)
- Change what holds you back
- Help organization become powerful
- Pride of accomplishment is shared
- Mistakes are welcome
- Actions carry meaning
- Creative buzz in the air
- Strive to bring out the best
- Relaxation as the norm
- Creativity toward solutions

- Don't assume, ask what is meant
- A home
- Keep learning
- Cooperate and take care of each other

From these thirty points (there were actually over seventy), I distilled five themes: creative, committed, welcoming, learning, and celebratory. With this forming the basis of a group-wide agreed-on vision, we were able to discuss how to overcome obstacles to achieving it.

As points of agreement are confirmed orally, they are ready to be put in writing. You can do this on the spot (on a flip chart, for instance) or in the form of a more extensive draft consensus or decision document. The stage at which drafting is done varies. The safer stage is after all the agreements that constitute it have been confirmed.

The riskier stage is earlier—in other words, you go out on a limb and draft a document at a point when the group doesn't feel it's in agreement yet. This can be presented as a "strawman" or "single-text" document—something to make changes to. On one hand, such an approach can move groups along fast and may therefore be very welcome. On the other hand, if your draft is too far off base, you may anger the people who strongly disagree. With experience you'll develop a sixth sense of what will likely be acceptable to all sides so that you can put together a good first-draft agreement at an early point.

What's usually a bad idea is to have proponents of one particular point of view draft decision documents—the result will inevitably be biased and objectionable to others. Having an impartial document drafter is one of the key benefits of using a facilitator.

Basic Discussion Formats

The preceding interventions—remaining silent, asking questions, paraphrasing or summarizing, reframing to interests, stating observations, making process changes, and capturing points of agreement—

are ways to guide a fairly unstructured, open discussion. In this section we'll look at some basic discussion formats, starting with open discussion but adding rounds ("going around the room") and small-group breakouts. As with the interventions, these formats may be used during any stage of a group process.

Open Discussion

The simplest format is open, unstructured discussion. The facilitator poses a question or a topic to spark discussion, then lets any group members respond.

Advantages

- Despite all the techniques that are available to structure discussion, groups often need this kind of free-flowing conversation. It allows the discussion to go wherever the group's interests lie.
- Sometimes, creative ideas or insights readily emerge in this environment.
- In many cases, the open forum allows participants to share a variety of viewpoints and perhaps debate divergent positions. This may naturally help move a group toward greater understanding, perhaps greater agreement, or at least a clearer definition of the issue.
- This method allows people who think the issue is important to speak while allowing those who are not so concerned about an issue to defer to others.

Disadvantages

- Full-group discussions may wander aimlessly or lack focus.
- This format is the most likely to produce skewed participation—those more comfortable speaking in front of the group will do so; those less comfortable will tend to hang back.
- Lengthy discussions of this kind may become boring or tiring, especially for task-oriented groups.

Making It Work

- All of the interventions described in the previous section can be used in open discussion. In addition, the recording of key points on a flip chart or other medium visible to all helps keep the discussion from wandering or getting repetitive.

Rounds

A more structured but still simple format is to "go around the room," allowing each person to speak in the order in which they're seated, with every group member speaking once before anyone can speak a second time. A variation is to let people speak in any order, but maintaining the rule that everyone speaks only once until all have spoken.

Advantages

- This format is simple yet orderly, necessitating minimal intervention from the facilitator.
- It can help balance participation, by carving out an opportunity for each individual to speak.
- When a group is deadlocked, it can serve as a straw-polling method, clarifying where each person stands at the moment and suggesting a direction for problem solving.

Disadvantages

- People may start to respond to the previous comments and engage in dialogue before others have had their turn.
- People may not form their thoughts fully before the exercise begins, so they may just echo or respond to others' comments rather than developing their own independent opinion.
- The exercise can be time consuming and tiresome if the group is large or comments are lengthy.
- This method does not reveal differences in the issue's level of importance for different individuals. Therefore, when used as

a straw-polling method, it may make the group sound farther from agreement than it really is. In other words, those who consider the issue less important may be prepared to go along with others' ideas, even if they might have different opinions themselves—but all the exercise elicits is their opinion, not their willingness to accept a different approach.

Making It Work

- Be rigorous in ensuring that everyone gets to speak once before anyone speaks a second time or responds.
- Consider providing a moment of silent reflection before asking anyone to speak, and inviting people to jot a few notes about what they will say.
- Consider inviting people to say how strongly they feel about the issue.
- Try giving a time limit. Surprisingly, time limits often allow people to feel they have more freedom, not less, to express themselves fully while maintaining everyone's attention. A lot can be said in a minute or two.

Examples

- In a fast-growing high-tech company trying to shift out of a constant crisis mode, we used rounds to allow participants to read our proposed purpose statement and say what they wanted the dialogue to accomplish.
- In the public-policy dialogue about whether to complete a beltway, we used rounds early on to elicit each participant's views on his or her interests and criteria for a good solution—for example, a good solution should provide for improved suburb-to-suburb mobility, or should avoid detracting from the habitat of threatened or endangered species.
- In a retreat for an organization seeking to resolve significant management-labor conflict, rounds were used for a closing question, "What do you, individually, commit to do to help

implement the agreements made here and to make this new labor-management relationship work?"

Small-Group Breakouts

All but the smallest groups may benefit from small-group breakout sessions.

Advantages

- Breakouts change the dynamics of the discussion and therefore help maintain energy.
- They allow a more comfortable forum for the more reticent to speak.
- They provide greater intimacy, perhaps allowing deeper honesty or fuller disclosure.
- They allow a certain anonymity, affording greater safety in raising difficult issues. (Views can be reported back as a product of the small-group discussion, without individual attribution.)
- They create efficiencies, particularly when different groups can work on different topics or tasks simultaneously.
- They are a suitable forum for the hard work of problem solving and decision making—small groups can develop proposals for later refinement and approval by the full group.

Disadvantages

- The mechanics of small-group breakouts take time—including dividing up the group, assigning tasks or topics, letting each group settle down and start its discussion, checking on time needed by each group, reconvening the full group, and allowing each small group to report back its results. Report-back time, in particular, often takes longer than expected. The full group then still has to discuss and integrate the small groups' results.

- They may detract from the full-group sense of unity. Group members sometimes resist breaking into smaller groups, especially when they feel they are benefiting from hearing everyone first hand and developing an *esprit de corps*.

Making Them Work

There are two general ways to divide up groups. Many facilitators prefer *mixed groups*—of different levels or departments in an organization, different kinds of stakeholders in a public-policy forum, or people who for whatever reason fall on different sides of an issue. Mixed groups allow for the breaking down of intergroup barriers—it's harder to consider someone an enemy after close-up, face-to-face contact. Mixed groups also make sense when creative ideas are sought—different backgrounds foster different views and therefore different ideas. Finally, mixed groups can be used to help resolve difficult problems or conflicts: if the opposite sides of a controversial issue are represented in a small group, that group is more likely to come up with a solution that will be acceptable to all.

There are multiple ways of dividing up into mixed groups:

- Have people cluster with the people sitting nearest them (if they are not seated within their like groups).
- Set out different topics, and allow people to self-select, based on their interest in each topic.
- Count off, and have each person go to the group number they call out. (The key is to count to the number of *groups* you want to have, not the number of people per group. If you have a group of twenty-eight people and you want seven groups of four people, count off to seven—not four.)
- Get more creative: for example, in large groups, you can divide by month of birth (January through March birthdays are in group one, and so forth), or by first initial.

Equally valuable, however, are *like groups*. These would include members of similar strata in an organization, for example, or other natural allies. Many facilitators shy away from like groups because they may reinforce intergroup divisions. This is a fair concern, but sometimes the divisions are so obvious that it will do no good to pretend they're not there. You will have to weigh the us-versus-them problem against the major benefits of like groups. First, they offer a comfortable means of raising complaints or concerns that individuals are too uneasy to raise directly with members of a more powerful group (the small group can raise the issue collectively). Second, they allow people to strategize with sympathetic peers about how to address issues productively with people in other groups.

Whichever type of groupings you choose, you will need to pay attention to the logistics of starting the small-group activity. It's important to give precise instructions on the task, topic, time frame, and any other specifics, such as guidance on selecting a spokesperson or recording. I've been surprised how many times I've thought I was clear on the instructions on a small-group activity, only to find out later that half the groups misunderstood my instructions.

Examples

- In the large partnering session described in Chapter Two, participants sat at round tables, which formed perfectly sized breakout groups for this purpose (eight tables of about seven people per table). I assigned each table one "critical issue" of the project they were about to commence and asked them to flesh out that issue. Then, if groups had time, they were to identify some strategies for handling the issue.

  Since these were general issues that affected everyone on the project, it was most efficient to randomly assign issues to tables and let people stay wherever they had sat down at the start of the meeting. Each group reported back—the task being only to get a fuller understanding of the issues and some initial ideas about dealing with them. There was little need for further discussion after the reports.

- I facilitated a board-staff retreat for a nonprofit arts organization that was experiencing conflict and role confusion between executive staff and board members, exacerbated by a sense of a loss of clear direction since the founder had resigned as executive director. In the founding days, the board had essentially run the organization, together with the executive director. As the staff grew, it increasingly looked to the board to help with fundraising, and to stay out of the way of making routine decisions, such as what artists to feature each year in its programs. After some relationship-building activities (this was an extremely relationship-oriented group) and an overview of the history of the organization and the context of its current difficulties, I split the full group (board and staff) into five mixed groups, each of which discussed one of the following questions:

1. What is the overall function of the board?
2. Which tasks are handled by the board, and which by staff?
3. What should be the involvement of the board with programming decisions?
4. What are the obligations of a board member?
5. How can board members be recognized and rewarded?

Each group reported a summary of its discussion, and I was able to extract a handful of key themes from across these presentations. These themes—such as "The board provides an overall sense of direction and the staff makes specific programming decisions"—formed the basis of a new, clearer agreement about board and staff roles.

The basic process stages, interventions, and discussion formats described in this chapter will enable you to handle any non-extreme facilitation quite well. These basic skills and structures provide a roadmap for conducting a group process while allowing plenty of room for customization and creativity.

For extreme facilitation, however, you'll need to expand your toolbox. You'll need all these basics plus knowledge of a range of ways to tap into each group's physical, intellectual, emotional, intuitive or creative, and spiritual capacities. The next five chapters will provide you with a range of concepts and tools that will help spark your creativity and enable you to develop customized processes to help groups overcome their most extreme challenges.

Notes

1. This element of building understanding was inspired in part by Moore's Circle of Conflict (Moore, *The Mediation Process*, pp. 64–65), and Mayer's Wheel of Conflict (Mayer, *The Dynamics of Conflict Resolution*, pp. 8–16).
2. Blake and Mouton, *Solving Costly Organizational Conflicts*, pp. 63–66.
3. Fisher and Ury, *Getting to Yes*.

Chapter Seven

The Physical Capacity

The Foundation

Have you ever walked down a hall of hotel meeting rooms and peeked in? In just a few seconds, you can immediately pick up on the mood in the room: it may be jovial and lively, serious and diligent, bored and tired, or tense and hostile. It's easy to read the energy of a group—not just the level of energy, but even the type of energy.

If you and the group you're facilitating are going to take on extreme challenges, you and the participants will need to maintain plenty of positive, productive energy. If participants are fatigued or uncomfortable, that will undermine everything else you do as a facilitator. Imagine for a moment the behavior of a toddler who is hungry, tired, hot, cold, or confined at length in a car seat. She'll get cranky and whine. At the slightest provocation, like being told she can't play with the scissors she's just discovered, she'll throw herself on the floor, screaming and banging her fists, getting only louder or more violent at any attempts to control her.

It's important to remember that adults aren't all that different. We have essentially the same reactions, but we've learned to restrain ourselves—somewhat. Instead of screaming and throwing ourselves on the floor, we make fist-pounding angry pronouncements or conduct hostile cross-examinations. Instead of grabbing each other's toys, we interrupt and dominate each other. Instead of falling asleep in the car seat, we tune out and daydream. Instead of biting the person next to us, we shoot down his ideas. Instead of whining . . . well, we still whine. Does this sound like any meetings you've been to?

Conventional wisdom says you should limit all meetings to no more than three hours. This is nonsense—I have successfully facilitated meetings as long as two consecutive eight-hour days, and participated with enthusiasm in ones that were considerably longer. The three-hour limit holds true only if everyone sits around a conference table in the same motionless format the entire time, with only a break or two to ease the monotony. There is much you can do to maintain participants' energy besides keeping the meetings short.

This chapter is about drawing on people's physical capacity—their ability to stay physically energized, productively engaged, and, at the same time, reasonably civilized. You might not notice when you've tapped this ability well, but you will definitely notice when you haven't. There are four keys to drawing on the physical capacity of groups: comfort, movement, variety, and progress.

Comfort

Any physical discomfort can distract attention, deplete energy, and sour attitudes. How cheerful and productive can you be when your back is aching? Unfortunately, we are often at the mercy of our clients or employers—and their budgets—when selecting and setting up meeting rooms. Still, we often can influence them. For that reason, it's worthwhile to consider all the factors that lead to an ideally comfortable meeting setting.

• *Water.* I live in Colorado, where the high altitude and dry climate can easily dehydrate people. I've been astounded at how listless and irritable I can become before I realize dehydration is to blame. When facilitating, I try to make sure water pitchers and glasses are within easy reach of every chair.

• *Food.* Tasty and visually appealing food helps promote happy attitudes and a sense of abundance (the opposite of a scarcity mentality, which promotes defensiveness and turf protection). The standard meeting fare of sugar and caffeine yields only short-lived energy spikes. Healthy food with some protein content helps energy last.

So does the ability to snack between meals. When possible, I request snacks such as nuts, fresh or dried fruit, cheese and whole-grain crackers, and vegetables and dip. Breakfast should at least include some bran muffins, and ideally some eggs, yogurt, and fruit.

• *Light*. Some people work in places with no sunlight, so they're used to 100 percent fluorescent lighting. I'm not. Hotel conference rooms with four windowless walls are a pet peeve of mine. Even if only a few members of your group are used to sunlight, windows should be a high priority. I once worked with a group of airline employees who were in the midst of a four-week training program, all held in the same basement-level hotel conference room. Even though many of them were used to working without any natural light, I had to use every trick I knew to keep them energized.

With or without sunlight, it's also important to make sure the overall amount of light is adequate. If people are straining to read documents, they'll tire fast.

• *Fresh air*. If any group members are used to being outside a lot, the ideal spaces will have either windows that open or quick access to the outdoors. (This is also helpful for smokers.)

On nice days, participants may be eager to move the meeting outside. This sounds delightful until you remember all the possible discomforts: bright sun glaring in people's eyes or burning their skin, wind blowing papers around, insects buzzing, itchy grass, uncomfortable seating, ambient noise. In some warm countries, lovely outdoor restaurants and meeting spaces that avoid many of these problems are common; in the United States these remain rare. One meeting site I used had a porch with shade and good seating (and a nice view too!), but it wasn't big enough for the whole group. Small-group breakouts are an excellent opportunity for people to enjoy the outdoors for a while, as we did successfully in that case. Otherwise, however, until there are more good outdoor meeting sites, I'll generally (if reluctantly) keep my meetings indoors.

• *Temperature*. Another bit of conventional wisdom is that if people are just a little too cool they'll stay energized. Perhaps this explains why hotel conference rooms are often over-air-conditioned—another of my pet peeves. In my experience, being either too hot or too cold is distracting and irritating.

One more pet peeve here is people who think the room will cool down faster if they set the thermostat to 50 degrees Fahrenheit. It doesn't. When facilitating, I sometimes conduct a "temperature survey," asking participants to raise their hand first if they're too hot, then if they're too cold, then if they're just right. This beats having enterprising group members adjusting the thermostat themselves to their own liking. I sometimes also suggest to group members that they dress in layers so they can adapt to the indoor climate.

• *Chairs.* The best chairs are ergonomic office chairs with lumbar support and seat-height adjustment. The ones that automatically rock back to a slightly reclined posture are awful. Standard hotel chairs are usually serviceable, though some people get uncomfortable in them after a couple of hours. Couches are an alternative that offers an informal, social atmosphere, which may or may not be desired. As for going without seating altogether, I don't think most adults can sit on the floor for more than a very short time—I've occasionally done small-group breakouts on the floor, but not long ones.

• *Tables.* I once facilitated a retreat for a thirty-person group. Since this was out of town for me, I didn't see the meeting room until the morning the retreat started. The hotel staff had set up a large U-shaped arrangement of tables and chairs. It looked elegant, but the seats seemed terribly far apart, making the setting much too stiff and formal for this hard-working but young and casual group. I consulted with a few members of my client group, and we agreed that, since there were few documents involved, we would get rid of the tables (except a few along the walls for personal belongings). The hotel staff said they would charge $200 to change the arrangement on the spot—enough for the client to decline the help. So, shortly after opening the meeting, I quipped that we had a "teambuilding exercise" and enlisted the group's help in removing the tables and setting up the chairs in an oval (the room was a long rectangle). They cheerfully obliged, and many thanked me for the change.

If many documents will be passed around or if people want to take notes, tables are important, but if the group is large, the effect will be formal, which may or may not be intended. A series of round tables might be better. If round tables are unavailable, a "starburst" design can be substituted (Figure 7.1).

There may also be other creative solutions. For example, college classroom chairs that each have a little one-person table top attached might be appropriate in some cases (though they might make people feel like they're in school). You could also experiment with clipboards or lap-top writing surfaces.

• *Sound.* Sound becomes an issue in groups over about thirty to fifty people, depending on the acoustics of the space. I don't love microphones—they can be intimidating, and they make conversation more stilted and unnatural—so I generally try to see if we can make do without them first. Still, straining to hear is at least as irritating as straining to see. We have to be aware of this, particularly as baby boomers approach the age of possible hearing loss.

Some high-tech meeting rooms have individual microphones at each person's seat. Cordless microphones are another helpful meeting-room innovation, as are small lapel microphones. Each arrangement has different advantages and disadvantages.

Yet another of my pet peeves is starting a meeting only to begin hearing construction going on down the hall or a loud meeting just on the other side of a paper-thin wall. I haven't managed to prevent such situations, but I've sometimes managed to move the group to a quieter room.

• *Space.* There are large cultural variations in what is considered an adequate amount of space. Comparatively, Americans like a lot of it. Regardless, I try to ensure that the group won't feel lost in a huge meeting room, and conversely that people won't have to suck in their abdomens to walk past each other.

If there's any chance you'll use breakout groups, you'll need a place for them. Too many small groups in the same room can make it hard to hear, especially for those with hearing impairments.

Figure 7.1. Starburst Seating Arrangement.

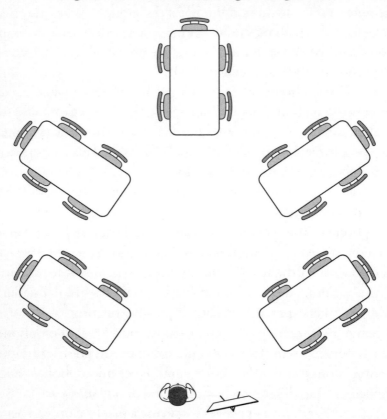

• *Accommodation of disabilities.* It's a good idea to invite groups in advance to tell you of any disabilities or physical needs that will require accommodations, such as wheelchair accessibility or large-print handouts. Many disabilities are invisible, so be careful of assuming that you know.

Again, we often can't control the selection of meeting space, and even if we can, the perfect space often doesn't exist or isn't affordable. Keep in mind that seemingly cheaper spaces such as schools become much more expensive if you have to pay for catering, rent furniture and audiovisual equipment, and expend costly staff time on setup and tear down. This makes hotels and conference facilities a better value than they first appear.

Movement

You've achieved a lot if you've set up a space where people won't be burdened by physical strain or discomfort. Yet even with the perfect space and seating, most of us tend to wilt if we're sitting still for too long. How long is too long varies, depending largely on what people are accustomed to. On one hand, those who work at desks all day will have much higher tolerance for sitting and may actually groan and roll their eyes at your attempts to get them moving. On the other hand, people who are constantly on the move, such as hospital or airport workers, will get either fatigued or agitated after even an hour or so in their chairs.

Extreme facilitators need an arsenal of ways to get people up on their feet. The more participants are used to moving, the more we have to use these techniques. Following are some ideas; you may come up with others.

• *Breaks*, obviously. The ideal is typically about once every ninety minutes, although people's needs vary. I always invite people to let me know if they need a break, but I can often tell by their body language.

• *Small-group breakouts*. These require people to get out of their chairs at least twice—once to go to the small group, once to return.

• *Gallery walks*. When small groups have generated flip charts or other displays with a summary of the product of their discussion, the standard is to have them report from the front of the room. For more movement, have each group set up its display at a different place along the perimeter of the room, have everyone cluster around that spot for the report, then walk to the second group's display for its report, and so on.

• *Write-and-post methods*. People tend to assume that all meetings involve sitting and talking to each other. Sometimes a good alternative is to have participants write points down, post them, then read each other's points.

You can be creative in applying this idea. For example, you can conduct a brainstorming session by posing the question and having people write their ideas on sticky notes, one idea per note. Then, if needed, you could invite group members to help you categorize or cluster the notes. As another example, you could post alternative proposals on flip chart paper with plenty of extra space, then allow people to write their comments, concerns, or pros and cons of each proposal on the flip chart paper.

Write-and-post methods have advantages and disadvantages. They afford all participants an equal chance to contribute, but they cut out the give-and-take of spoken communication (which could still happen before and after). Regardless, they're another way to get people out of their chairs.

• *Cocktail-party format.* Another alternative to the standard plenary-discussion format is to pose a question or topic for discussion, then have people mill about as if at a cocktail party (minus the cocktails), talking informally one-on-one or in small groups about the topic. This can be a good relationship-building exercise, if the questions posed have to do with getting to know one another better. It can also serve as a way to begin the process of building understanding of perspectives about a particular topic.

I once used this method during a partnering session at the beginning of a large construction project. I called an extended break to allow me to draft the key elements of a partnering charter based on the previous discussion, and I asked participants to talk to people they didn't know already. As a result, we achieved the stated objective of improving relationships while I made progress on another objective, completing a partnering charter.

• *Straw-polling methods.* It's often helpful to straw-poll a group—for example, to test for consensus, to conduct multivoting to narrow a list of options (more on this in Chapter Nine), or even to conduct exercises such as the "temperature survey" mentioned in the previous section. The standard method is to have people vote by raising their hands. For more movement, have them stand up in place instead, or invite them to vote by getting up and placing sticky dots on a flip chart.

• *Floor diagrams.* Sometimes people's opinions, values, or tendencies can be expressed in terms of where they stand on a continuum or in some kind of diagram. You can draw the continuum or diagram on the floor with masking tape, then have people stand at the spot representing "where they stand."

For example, I was working with a consulting firm to overcome conflict about its future direction. In a phone call between meetings, the president of the firm identified several key questions on which there were conflicting opinions. One question was whether to "run lean" or "run fat"—that is, whether to have minimal staff, work long hours, and reap high profits, or staff up, leave the office promptly at 5:00 P.M., and accept a narrower profit margin.

We set up an imaginary line on the floor with "fat" on one end and "lean" on the other, and had members of the firm stand on the spot according to their preferences. We looked for where people clustered and invited discussion about why people were on different parts of the continuum. In this particular example, the younger partners were on the "leaner" end and older ones on the "fatter" end (referring to staffing preferences, not physiques). This reflected the different values they placed on ambition and profit versus a balanced, less-stressful lifestyle. The discussion eventually led to creation of a policy on part-time work that enabled those nearing retirement, those more interested in lifestyle, and those with significant family responsibilities to work less and be paid less if they chose.

Floor diagrams are also excellent ways to discuss personality inventories. Results of many such inventories can be plotted on some kind of diagram. For instance, the Strength Deployment Inventory (from Personal Strengths Publishing), which focuses on interpersonal communication styles and relationship values both when things are going well and in conflict situations, yields results in the form of two points on some part of a triangle model.

When administering this inventory, we sometimes draw a huge triangle on the floor with masking tape and have people stand at the spot corresponding to their inventory results. Particularly if participants are in the same organization, this can lead to interesting conversations about the organizational culture or about whether differences correspond to different work functions or other variables.

It is also interesting to see patterns when participants move to the spot that represents their conflict results.

Again, you may find additional ways to get participants out of their chairs. The key is to get the right amount of movement based on the group's needs—how much sitting they're accustomed to—and to use techniques that best fit the group's goals and culture. Senior corporate or government officials may scoff at placing sticky dots on a flip chart but may welcome a small-group breakout; young workers in creative fields may welcome all manner of games and activities and may feel quite out of place sitting around a conference table.

Variety

When people get fatigued, they often are simply tired of one particular activity but still have reserves of energy available for doing something different. For example, when I was in college and studying for long stretches toward exam time, I would find it refreshing and energizing to clean my room or wash dishes. Conversely, when I was home on maternity leave, doing the manual labor of child care around the clock, I was relieved when I could sit and read for a while—the more intellectually engaging the book, the better.

This principle can be applied in numerous different ways with groups. Following are some ways to provide variety.

• *Vary the physical setting.* You might find a way to change the setting: have people switch seats, move the flip charts or visual displays to a different part of the room, change the arrangement of chairs and tables, or go on a site visit. These changes will seem less hokey and arbitrary if they support the group's goals in some way—for example, changing seats promotes more relationship building; site visits may promote greater understanding of the issues.

As for offsite retreats, I'm not sure I subscribe to the theory that luxurious settings promote productivity. (I favor such settings but for different reasons—such as showing appreciation for employees or volunteers.) However, I do suspect that if people are away from their usual physical surroundings they might have something beyond their usual thoughts. The simple fact of a change of environment can be energizing.

However, too much change of setting can be draining—as occurs with frequent business travel. Frequent travelers might be pleased to spend a day or two in the office conference room.

• *Vary the format.* Think about what mix of formats will be most energizing—open discussion, rounds, breakout groups, or the many formats listed in the previous section on movement.

• *Vary the topic.* Changes in subject matter can help revitalize. Weigh the pros and cons of switching topics versus getting the sense of accomplishment of achieving closure on one topic before moving to the next. When a deadlock arises, sometimes the group needs to go deeper and understand more richly the underlying needs, concerns, and interests that people feel are threatened. Yet sometimes the group may need just to take a break from the issue and return to it later with a fresh perspective.

• *Vary the task.* Sharing perspectives requires a kind of mental engagement different from creative brainstorming, which in turn requires engagement different from evaluating and decision making. The goals of the process will probably dictate which tasks you need to do when, but beware of too much of one kind of task, such as multiple back-to-back presentations.

Progress

In all kinds of human activity, a sense of progress and accomplishment helps energize people to keep pushing to the final goal. Conversely, continued effort with little results tends to depress and deplete energy. I call this phenomenon the progress principle.

The Progress Principle

There are two parts to the progress principle. First, people are energized by frequent successes. Experts in political activism recommend setting modest goals that allow near-term victory. Computer games that provide some sense of a win every few minutes are addictive. So are slot machines at which you win a little money after every few minutes of constant play, even if you run a net loss.

Second, people are energized by knowing how far they have come and how much farther they have to go to reach the final goal. Long highways have frequent signs showing the mileage to the next major city. High-tech exercise machines display the minutes that remain to reach your target time.

Here are some ways to apply the progress principle to process design—that is, to structure the process not only to make progress but also to ensure that participants are aware of their progress.

• *Separate the process of identifying issues or questions from the process of solving or answering them.* For instance, in extended question-and-answer sessions after a presentation, it may help to elicit all the questions first and list them before the presenters answer the questions. Then everyone can see, at any given moment, how many questions remain. (This also reduces the firing-squad dynamic of the questions, and it gives the presenter a chance to come up with more thoughtful, less defensive responses.)

• *Use the classic brainstorming process of generating a long list of ideas before evaluating any of them.* This also helps promote creativity, which is dampened by having ideas shot down as soon as they're uttered.

• *Simply have a written agenda.* This helps provide a sense of progress, as people can see at a glance what they've covered and how many items remain.

• *Allow more than ample time for each agenda item, despite the temptation to squeeze more into the meeting.* Beside the usual fact that most things take longer than forecast, it's energizing to be ahead of schedule and discouraging to know you've fallen behind. No one will complain if the meeting ends early.

• *Address easier issues first.* This is most suitable for processes in which the issues in contention can be boiled down to (or a single issue broken out into) a small handful of issues.

Examples

One application of the progress principle illustrates separating the issue identification from issue resolution. I cofacilitated, with my colleague Mike Hughes, a negotiated rulemaking process to help a state agency develop a regulation limiting the environmental damage of numerous chemical products used in households and small businesses. After a considerable amount of discussion and hammering out agreement on some broad issues, the agency staff drafted a regulation. We came to the next meeting ready to fine-tune the wording and iron out the narrower issues.

We had two possible ways to do this. One would have been simply to go through each section, asking people what concerns they had, and resolving them on the spot. This isn't bad as far as applying the progress principle—most sections were short, so we could have demonstrated progress every time we successfully completed one section and moved on to the next. Better yet, however, was to survey people's concerns about the whole draft at the start and display them in some visual manner, so that the participants had a sense of the entirety of the task ahead and how close they were to finishing.

We had participants write one concern per sticky note and post the notes on the wall by section (each page of flip-chart paper represented one section of the document). We further had people use one color of sticky note for items that truly required discussion (potential "deal breakers"), and another color for items that were more minor, such as edits, which they could live without if necessary. We allowed anyone to strike out any of the minor changes that they objected to. We then focused on the sticky notes with concerns that required discussion. As each item was resolved, we removed it from the wall. As for the minor items, we could simply hand those to the drafters for incorporation without the need for further discussion.

Another scenario illustrates addressing easier issues first. I once facilitated resolution of a team conflict in an organization. Employees felt the supervisor used a divide-and-conquer strategy. They alleged that he unfairly delegated plum assignments to certain favorite employees, more rigidly enforced policies and rules with others, and failed to communicate important information to everyone. The supervisor, meanwhile, felt the employees were ganging up on him, were not respecting his supervisory duty to manage performance individually and to maintain confidentiality of personnel issues, and were acting on their concerns in passive-aggressive ways (such as gossip) rather than raising them constructively.

The first two issues we started with were information dissemination (primarily of interest to employees) and how employees raised concerns (primarily of interest to the supervisor). Even though these issues were not necessarily the most central, they were easier to resolve. We obtained agreement fairly readily that the supervisor would hold weekly meetings to share information with all his staff. We then achieved agreement that employees would raise concerns directly with their boss, possibly talking to just one coworker first for guidance. These early agreements helped provide a sense of progress and momentum before we got to the core issues of favoritism and polarization.

Reading Physical Energy

Tapping a group's physical capacity begins during process design but continues throughout the entire facilitated process. We must constantly read a group's energy and make adjustments as needed, whether that means addressing discomfort, getting people out of their chairs, changing something for variety, or switching to a task that will provide a near-term sense of progress.

There are many ways to read a group's energy. One is through obvious, visible clues: people's eyelids droop, they slump in their chairs, they get up individually to go to the bathroom or to stand rather than sitting (if the culture and the tone you set give people a sense of permission to do this). There can also be obvious, audible clues: a lower, slower tone of voice; longer pauses between comments.

Often, however, the clues are more subtle. One clue is an increase in the kind of misbehavior discussed earlier—the adult versions of the toddler's tantrums, such as cutting people off, dominating, and other negative interactions. Then there's an even subtler clue. Once I worked with a municipal government agency that was trying to plan in the face of severe budget cuts—on the order of 25 to 30 percent. The group was trying to come up with some overarching priorities to guide the line-by-line budget cutting. We developed a draft statement of priorities, then came to the stage of revising it. A disagreement was raised about the wording of one particular point in the priority list. The group went round and round on it, debating the minor changes as if they had tremendous significance.

Early on in a process, when a new group has been convened for the first time, this kind of nitpicking can be a way of testing the trustworthiness of a process. That didn't explain this situation, in which participants had good relationships and were closer to the end than to the beginning of their discussion. It finally dawned on me: they were worn out. Their minds had reached the point where they couldn't discriminate between important issues and trivial ones. I called a break, after which we tackled a different subject for a while (for variety), then came back to this minor issue and re-solved it in minutes.

Your Physical Capacity

Thus far we've been discussing the physical capacity of groups we facilitate, but as is true of all the five capacities, the facilitator's own physical capacity is important too. The energy you bring into the room will set the tone for the whole group—as long as it's not so far different from the group's energy that you seem like you come from a different planet, in which case you'll fail to establish rapport. (I once lost a bid to work with a library system because I was too "bubbly" and "high energy" during the interview—which was conducted by four librarians.) You will also be best able to think on your feet and respond with clarity to unexpected challenges if you're physically in top form.

It would be easy for me to recommend a familiar checklist of self-care advice to help you stay at peak physical energy: eat properly, get plenty of sleep, exercise regularly, keep your stress level manageable. I don't know anyone who can consistently conform to this ideal.

Instead, I recommend cultivating self-awareness about what affects your energy most. For example, I can cope pretty well with short-term sleep deprivation—if I've slept poorly for a couple of nights, I can still get through an important meeting without a problem (though I'll collapse afterward). What diminishes my spirit noticeably is chronic sleep deprivation month after month. I've found the conventional wisdom about sugar consumption to be mildly true for me—I do feel better when eating healthy, but only marginally. I've also found that exercise is key to maintaining my energy, and that emotional agitation wears me out as much as sleep deprivation does.

Emotions, in fact, are closely related to physical states. Drawing on your own and your groups' emotional capacities is the subject of the next chapter.

Chapter Eight

The Emotional Capacity

Welcoming and Working with Feelings

Once I was facilitating a process involving a business and a contractor. They had worked together at length on a project to renovate a building. The business representatives felt the contractor had failed to do the work properly, requiring the undoing and redoing of several steps in the construction. The contractor, in contrast, felt the business people had failed to express their specifications clearly and were expecting the contractor to read their minds. The project was so far along that neither side wanted to break the contract and let a different contractor complete the job.

On the first day of meetings, the tension mounted as each side blamed the other. At one point, an exasperated supervisor from the contractor's staff looked straight at the business's project manager and burst out, with sweeping hand gestures, "I don't know whether you're *trying* to make my life hell or if it's just incompetence, but you people need to get your act together. Stop blaming my people for your lack of planning!" He went on, in the same angry tone, to detail incidents that supported his point.

The client business's project manager, motionless except for the clenching of his jaw, waited until the contractor representative took a breath, and said to me coldly, "If you allow this kind of behavior to continue, I'm walking out of here."

The extreme facilitator needs to be at home with strong emotions. If emotional outbursts like the one described above are your greatest fear, you're not alone. Anger, shouting, crying—or the prospect of these—make many of us anxious and uncomfortable.

There are some good reasons for this: when people are over-whelmed with emotion, their capacity to think rationally is dimin-ished.[1] If they are filled with rage, they may lose control and become violent. If people are angry at *each other*, we may feel we've failed as facilitators. Worse, if someone is angry at *us*, deep down we may fear that they're right—that they have correctly identified some error or weakness that we'd rather not admit.

Despite these good reasons for trepidation, emotions are also a capacity, a force to be welcomed and channeled to productive ends. Emotions can be a kind of knowledge—we can know things with our heart before our brains have fully comprehended them. In the example, even without understanding the details of the construc-tion contract or the sequence of events prior to the meeting, we can understand that the contractor representative felt frustrated, unfairly blamed, and stuck in a dreadful situation. We can also understand that the business's contract manager felt deeply threat-ened by the outburst, and also unfairly blamed. This is as much part of the reality of the situation as the facts and figures. As the facili-tator, my own emotions after this exchange—alarm, regret—also told me that I needed to change course.

At the highest level of a group's emotional capacity, group mem-bers can overcome their self-protective anger and blame and actu-ally empathize with each other. Tapping this capacity is the greatest challenge of a facilitator in an extreme, conflictual facilitation.

The extreme facilitator must be not only comfortable with and receptive to emotions but also able to manage the level of emotional expression in the room to fit the group's culture. In the preceding example, I was so pleased with my own progress in becoming com-fortable with emotional outpourings that I forgot that some partic-ipants were not—hence the project manager's anger that I had allowed the outburst. To tap a group's emotional capacity, the emo-tions must be expressed at a level of intensity that will not leave anyone feeling threatened or overwhelmed. At the same time, if the emotions are not expressed intensely enough, people who need to become aware of a problem may remain oblivious to it.

Welcoming Emotions

Emotions are universal, though how people express them varies widely with culture. People from cultures that don't express emotions very much are likely to fear overt emotional expressions the most. Conversely, people from very expressive cultures will tend to view the more emotionally restrained as stiff and boring at best, devious at worst ("they must be hiding something"). All of us need to become comfortable with not only other peoples' emotions but also their way of expressing them—whether more overt or more restrained than our own.

Let's take a deeper look at a few of the emotions or emotional expressions we may fear, since greater understanding is the first step toward greater comfort.

Anger

Anger usually involves a combination of some kind of pain, frustration, anxiety, or loss with a calculation (which may occur instantly or emerge slowly over time) that this shouldn't have happened—it wasn't deserved.[2] This means that to understand someone's anger, we must understand the underlying pain.

Interestingly, this also means that it takes a certain measure of self-respect for people to reach the conclusion that they don't deserve the pain. In this regard, anger can be healthy. If someone has been mistreated for a long time, especially if she is in a lower societal status, she may tend to accept her mistreatment, perhaps unconsciously, as part of the natural order of things. Then one day she realizes that she deserves to be treated as well as anyone else, and she gets angry. The anger is liberating, the first step in a struggle for equality.

I knew someone who underwent this kind of transformation with a tyrannical older sister. He'd been teased and mentally tortured by her throughout his childhood, all the while not questioning his assumption that his big sister must be right. Then, at age fifteen, he had a sort of epiphany, realizing that this kind of treatment was just wrong. He began to stand up to the teasing and insulting. Meanwhile, he became so full of anger that he hated his older sister—it was the only way he could feel good about himself. Over time, as he grew more self-assured, the anger subsided and the relationship improved.

Of course, anger does not always work in such a positive way. An angry outburst can represent a loss of self-control, and it can have a variety of negative effects on the people it's directed toward: they may feel hurt, unfairly blamed, or unjustly attacked. They may respond by withdrawing, getting defensive, or going on the offensive—responding in kind or even more vehemently. In this way the expression of anger may escalate conflict. In the extreme, it can lead to physical aggression and violence.

As facilitators, ideally we promote the productive aspects of anger and limit the destructive aspects. There are several ways to do this. First, we can appreciate the positive potential of anger to provide the impetus to change an unjust or unhappy situation. Second, we can judge when we need to protect participants from each other's anger (by meeting with angry individuals one-on-one) versus when people can have a constructive dialogue about what's making them angry in a way that won't escalate the conflict. Third, we can recognize that the anger is coming from genuine pain or frustration, and we can seek to understand what that is.

Another negative function of anger is to protect our own egos by displacing blame onto others. This is a common dynamic of conflict. For instance, a colleague once took me to task, twice in one week, for failing to give him credit for work to which he had contributed. I started to wonder if I was in fact hogging the credit or otherwise behaving badly. I didn't want to believe this, so my initial reaction was to blame him—he's oversensitive and overreacting, I thought, and he's blaming me for his own career problems. If I had maintained this blaming posture, he would have become more resentful and angry at me, which would have in turn increased my anger at him, and the conflict would have escalated.

Instead, over time and with support from my husband, I was able to admit my mistake. I had a good dialogue with my colleague in which I learned from him about how I'd been behaving and coming across to others. I not only mended my relationship with him but I learned and grew. Many people never get past the defensiveness to the point where they are prepared to examine and learn from their mistakes.

A facilitator who is empathic and understanding (as my husband was with me), while also being able to gently point out mistakes, can help participants get beyond their self-protective blaming and into a mode of admitting mistakes, learning, and growing.

An extreme facilitator will need to become well acquainted with anger, as well as with distrust.

Distrust

Distrust is a common dynamic in extreme facilitation. For instance, activists don't trust that a government agency is really going to take their input seriously. Agency officials, in turn, fear the community members are trying to score political points by making the agency look bad. Employees don't believe their management is being honest when they say they want workers to express their concerns directly—they fear being labeled troublemakers. Managers, meanwhile, fear their employees are conspiring against them.

Distrust is a variant of fear. Like anger, it comes from some kind of pain or distress. Distrust is a fear that future pain will occur, and it often is spurred by past pain. The fear of the pain recurring may or may not be related to the situation at hand in facilitation. For example, the community group may have past negative experience with *this* government agency—that's relevant. Alternatively, the distrust may be based on past negative experience with a different agency, or with other authority figures—police, teachers, or even parents.

Again, it's not the facilitator's job to discern where misplaced distrust is coming from (that's a job for the therapist or the best friend). It is the facilitator's job to remember and respect that there is or was some actual pain that the distrustful person is reacting to. This lays the foundation for negotiating the conditions in which trust can be gradually rebuilt.

Meanwhile, we can help cultivate trust by making sure we, as facilitators, always act in trustworthy ways: say what we mean, do what we promise we'll do, be willing to admit our own mistakes, always be truthful. If participants feel they have to fear sneaky behavior on the part of the facilitator, they will have a hard time getting out of a watchful, distrustful mode with each other.

Crying

Crying, of course, is not an emotion, but rather a symptom of several possible emotions. If you're one of those who fears strong emotions, you probably don't relish the prospect of a participant breaking down in tears.

We tend to associate tears with sadness, loss, or despair, and it certainly can signify those. However, it can also signify a number of different feelings. Tears can express joy or relief after an extraordinarily stressful situation has come to an end—imagine, for example, the soldier's wife welcoming her husband home from war, or the parent who learns that his child's mysterious growth is *not* cancerous. Crying does not necessarily mean sadness.

An interesting thing about crying is that it discharges emotional tension. While we're struggling through a trying situation, we're often in survival mode—on guard, ready to handle whatever attack or challenge comes at us next. It's when we get out of survival mode that we release the struggle through tears.

For instance, I was once home with my four-month-old baby while my husband traveled, and I came down with an illness that sapped my strength. For two days I struggled along trying to care for both myself and my baby, hoping the infection would cure itself, before I finally called my doctor—a woman with a particularly empathic manner. At the sound of her soothing voice, I broke down in tears on the phone, relieved to feel that someone was taking care of me.

This aspect of tears means that we can welcome them—they are a sign of relief, of letting down one's guard a little bit and allowing oneself to truly feel the underlying emotion, to accept it, and finally to progress through it. Most likely, the deepest pain occurred before the bout of crying, not during it, so our pity may be misplaced.

When someone cries, we should not assume we know the reason. We can use the active listening skills described further on in this chapter to get at the underlying emotion and the reason for it. We must also offer the person the choice of having privacy or of continuing to engage in the conversation. Depending on culture and personality, crying can be extremely embarrassing or shameful.

Joy

Let's not forget positive emotions. In cultures that eschew emotional outbursts, joy may be downplayed as much as sadness or anger. It's important for people to notice and celebrate their achievements and triumphs, their feelings of connectedness and belonging, their excitement and anticipation, their moments of silliness and fun. In expressive cultures, this may mean yelping, dancing, and jumping for joy. In less expressive cultures, it may mean, depending on the situation, a subdued round of applause, a toast of congratulations, a little laughter, or a simple statement like "I really enjoyed this." The point is not to get so hung up on fixing negative feelings that we forget to facilitate the celebration of positive feelings.

Responding to Emotions

We've explored some of the emotions and emotional expressions people tend to fear, and identified some reasons to welcome them and some ways to do so. We now turn to skills for responding to strong emotions.

Empathic Listening

Empathic listening (a variant of active listening, mentioned in Chapter Three) is a skill widely taught in courses on psychology, therapy, communication, mediation, and facilitation. It's not new, but I've found that it is, in fact, incredibly powerful in welcoming emotions and channeling them positively.

For starters, empathic listening encourages the simple act of talking about a situation and the feelings it produced, which is immensely cathartic. When done well, empathic listening yields a visible, palpable release of tension in the speaker—you may notice a relaxing of physical posture and a calming in the voice. Moreover, freed of the grip of the emotion itself, the speaker can now focus on accepting or changing the underlying problem (or in the case of joy, replicating the happy events). It uncovers the speaker's own capacity for constructive problem solving, which was previously drowned in a sea of emotion.

In essence, empathic listening involves seeking to understand the emotions occurring and the reasons for them, then conveying this understanding back to the speaker in some way. It is typically taught through a formulaic sequence: first listen and ask open-ended questions as needed, then feed back "You feel _____" (fill in an emotion word) because _____" (fill in the reasons). This can be one good way to do it, if it fits with your culture and personality, but there are other ways.

I believe that if you welcome the emotions and truly work to identify and understand their source, the right responses will come naturally.[3] Sometimes the best response is to honor the disclosure with attentive, respectful silence. Sometimes you might reflect understanding in the way you phrase the next question (such as, "Have there been other times when you've gotten more support than you're getting now?"). Sometimes your natural facial expressions—the furrowing of your brow or the turn of your lip—will demonstrate you got the point. Sometimes you may indeed want to articulate your understanding—through a metaphor ("Sounds like you're up a creek with-out a paddle"), through paraphrasing ("You really have no one to turn to"), through some piece of the formula just cited ("Must feel lonely"), or even through a little exclamation ("Hmm!"). There's no need to calculate which of these is appropriate—again, if you turn your focus away from your own reaction and onto the speaker's experience and feelings, the right reactions will follow.

With anger, it's helpful to understand not only the anger itself, but the underlying pain or distress. This is because reinforcing anger could reinforce blame. For example, if a resident is angry at a nearby factory because of a toxic spill, it's more productive to say something like, "You were worried about the effects on your and your family's health" than "You were angry that they let this hap-pen." The latter statement could sound as though you accept the assumption that the managers of the factory are to blame. If the fac-tory managers are part of the group you're facilitating, you'll lose their trust just when you've gained it with the others.

It's not always easy for people to identify the pain that under-lies their anger. In one group I facilitated, a supervisor was highly aware of her anger at an employee who dealt with her own anger at her boss by talking about her gripes with everyone else on staff. The supervisor had a harder time articulating what was the underlying pain. I tried to guess at it and feed back my hypothesis: "You're wor-ried she's harming your reputation." She shot back: "I think she hurts her own reputation more by doing this."

In that moment, I didn't succeed in putting my finger on the underlying pain in a way that resonated with the supervisor, and she couldn't articulate it herself. It became clear over time, however, that she had become something of a pariah among her peers, her staff, and her own boss. She felt unappreciated for holding her employees to high standards of performance (part of the issue in dispute), worried about her job security, and isolated. My inability, in this case, to cap-ture her feelings made it more of an uphill battle to earn her trust. I eventually succeeded, but not before she reached the conclusion that

I was biased in favor of the employee. Most of the time, my ability to discern each participant's feelings allows me to establish trusting relationships with people of sharply divergent views.

Using Empathy in Facilitation

So when in facilitation do you use this listening skill? The short answer is almost anytime.

One advantage of conducting one-on-one or small-group interviews during assessment and convening is that they are an excellent opportunity to draw out emotions and help work through them. For this reason, the higher the level of conflict, the more important it is to talk to participants in advance, either one-on-one or in small, like-minded groups, and use empathic listening. This one simple step helps participants come to the full-group meeting ready to be constructive instead of ready to burst with emotions. This can also be done between meetings if fresh events have generated more strong feelings.

Empathic listening is also helpful in full-group settings. Expressing your own understanding of someone's feelings helps others understand too. I've often gone through long stretches of facilitation doing little but calling on raised hands and listening empathically, to positive effect.

Calling a Break

Besides empathic listening, another helpful response to an emotional outburst is calling a break. This can be particularly helpful if someone is so physically agitated that they are becoming violent, can't function, or have horrified the rest of the group. Sometimes the passage of time and the opportunity to cool off work wonders. (For this, a typical ten- to fifteen-minute break may not be enough; the cooling-off effect may not show up until the following day.)

Still, unless you're in physical danger, it pays to combine the break in some way with empathic listening—either one-on-one during the break; right after the break; or perhaps, if it feels right, in the full group just before the break.

Be sure, too, that you're taking the break for the right reasons: for the sake of the agitated person or for the sake of the group—not for the sake of managing your own comfort level.

What Not to Do

All of this may sound obvious. In practice, however, I've found that many novice facilitators have quite different responses to emotions. Following are some steps that you might be inclined to take, but that probably won't help.

Enforce the Ground Rules. Let's go back to the business and the contractor. The contractor representative had an outburst, in which he accused the business project manager of incompetence and making his life hell. Perhaps you had a ground rule about being civil or respectful or not making accusations. He clearly broke it. You have the authority to enforce ground rules, right? Certainly. However, this approach is likely to alienate him and unlikely to get at the underlying issues.

Instead, you can use empathic listening with *both* of the individuals involved. To the contractor, you might say, "You're feeling exasperated, and unfairly blamed" and allow any further elaboration (which will probably come out more calmly). Then you might turn to the business project manager and say, "That couldn't have been easy for you to listen to" and invite more explanation.

Focus on the Facts. Wouldn't everyone be better off if they could put aside their emotions and focus on the facts? Can't you just ask them to do that? Maybe if it's an extremely reserved, unexpressive culture. Even then, though, the emotions are part of the story, part of what the group needs to work through to get to their goal. It certainly helps if participants focus on the facts of others' behavior rather than name calling. However, when it comes to participants' own emotions, prohibiting them may only intensify them.

Tell People to Calm Down.   If you've ever tried this, you know it can backfire. How do you feel when someone tells you to "calm down"?

Explain One Person's View to Another.   If you are more naturally attuned to emotions, you may be tempted to explain one person's viewpoint to another: "Well, Mr. Business, I think what Mr. Contractor is trying to say is that he's been receiving confusing and contradictory instructions from your company." Despite your good intentions, this will make it sound like you are an advocate for (in this case) the contractor. You might instead paraphrase the contractor back to himself, "So what you're trying to say is . . ." The other party (the business person, in this case) will hear you.

Managing the Level of Emotional Expression

As a facilitator, you need to manage the level of emotional expression to match the group's overall culture in terms of comfort with overt emotional displays. If some people are more expressive than most in the group, the others will feel uncomfortable or even threatened by emotional displays. If some are more reserved than most, the more expressive others will miss the point when the reserved ones express themselves in an understated manner.

Following are some ways you can adjust the emotional "volume" to fit the culture.

Using Ground Rules

If a group that's not highly expressive has emotional issues to discuss, group members probably have some idea of what they want *not* to happen during the full-group meetings. You may see fit to codify these in the form of ground rules. These may include any-thing from "Take a break if you need to cool off" to "Express your views calmly." If a group is more emotionally expressive, you may simply want to remind people to articulate the reasons for their feelings rather than just letting loose the emotions themselves, or perhaps to focus on describing the impact of specific behaviors on themselves rather than attacking others.

Remember, while ground rules do imply enforcement author-ity for the facilitator, there are dangers to enforcing ground rules overtly. Instead, their greatest power is to set the tone for the process at the outset.

Determining When to Intervene

If the group culture is more expressive, you may need to restrain your own tendency to cut off an emotional exchange. Conversely, if the culture is more reserved, you may need to insert yourself more often (through empathic listening, calling a break, or paraphrasing to less emotion-laden language) to keep the emotional volume down.

Adjusting How You Empathize

While the skill of empathic listening can be used universally, *how* it's done may need to be adjusted. With expressive groups, it may make sense to use feeling words: *disappointed, frightened, lonely, ecstatic*, whatever. Reserved groups may find this too "touchy-feely," making other, more subtle expressions of understanding—metaphors, for example—more appropriate.

Encouraging Disclosure

A more expressive group may welcome your probing to draw out feelings. A more reserved group may find this inappropriate and in-trusive. For example, asking someone who has been under verbal attack, "How did it feel when you heard that comment?" may be appropriate for a more emotionally expressive group, but uncomfortable for others. In an emotionally reserved group, you might substitute, "Does it seem like you're on the firing line?"—and it might even be better to say this privately, during a break (in which case, you might encourage the speaker to repeat the answer to the full group in a way that he sees as appropriate).

Naming the Differences

Of course, the hardest situation is when there are sharply different levels of emotional expressiveness in a group. In this situation, as with any cultural differences, it is helpful to name the difference, and enlist the group in helping to bridge the gap. For example, you might say, "I've noticed that some of you are more open than others about expressing emotions. That may be a cultural difference." Then, you might offer a suggestion, such as, "Maybe we should try to meet in the middle—those of you who are more expressive may want to try to keep your tone even keeled; those of you who are more reserved may need to push yourselves a little to articulate what you're feeling." Alternatively, instead of offering a suggestion, you might ask the group, "How can we bridge this difference?" There is more on bridging cultural differences in Chapter Twelve.

Enabling Empathy in Others

If you can welcome emotions, respond to them empathically, and calibrate the level of emotional expressiveness in a group to fit the culture, you have come a long way toward helping emotions serve the group. By welcoming emotions, you create an atmosphere in which participants can express them. Through empathy you help relieve the emotions and allow participants to work through them to the underlying issues. By adjusting the emotional "volume," you facilitate participants' ability to hear each others' emotions—they'll neither be so overpowering people will shut them out nor so understated people will miss them altogether.

There is, however, a way to use the emotional capacity of a group even further. With a combination of skill and luck, you can help people in conflict examine their own responsibility for creating conflict, transcend blame, and empathize with their enemies.

I say this requires some luck because some people are fundamentally unable to let down their defenses, let in others' perspectives, and overcome blame. They remain closed to the possibility that they, too, may be partly responsible for the conflict. Good facilitation is no substitute for strength of character.

However, we can sometimes enhance people's capacity to acknowledge responsibility and empathize. The following approach sometimes works.

Empathize and Earn Trust

First it's essential to create a trusting relationship with the angry person or group. This requires a full-fledged effort to do all the things already discussed in this chapter—welcome emotions, respond with empathy, strike the right level of emotional expressiveness. The angry person will need to be convinced that you completely understand her views. This may take time and patience. Some or all of it may need to be done outside the full-group sessions.

Encourage Story Telling

If each side in a conflict can recount his or her experience of the conflict as a story, others' empathy more likely will be aroused. Stories are much more powerful than factual arguments in evoking empathy.

It's crucial, however, that the story relate only the speaker's direct experiences, not inferences about others' motives or intentions. For example, "I discovered that my coworkers were trying to exclude me" relates inferences about the coworkers' intent. Instead, "I was told that my coworkers invited the boss out to lunch when I was away on vacation" relates direct experience. You might explain this distinction up front (perhaps in the form of ground rules); or, when you hear attributions of intent, you can probe for specifics of the experience: "What led you to the conclusion that they were trying to exclude you?"

Suggest an Alternative View

Once you have earned trust, and once stories have been exchanged, you might ask a question or state an observation about the speaker's contribution to the problem or about explanations that make another person's offensive behavior understandable. For example, you might ask gently, "Is it possible your coworkers didn't mean to exclude you—that they just arranged the lunch by coincidence when you were on vacation?" or "You've mentioned you've been feeling cranky and cynical lately—do you think that could make your coworkers less inclined to include you?"

This must be done in the supportive tone of an ally, not the adversarial tone of a lawyer conducting a cross-examination or a police officer conducting an interrogation. It takes a sense of security to admit responsibility, transcend blame, and empathize with others. Warm support will enhance this security; accusations will undermine it.

You may not get a positive response. Even still, the idea may "percolate" in the person's mind, and he or she may come around later to understanding others' actions and accepting his or her own piece of responsibility.[4]

Some might say that this level of engagement with people in conflict is beyond facilitation, that it's really mediation. My response is that while these skills do indeed overlap with the skills of mediation, they are an essential part of the extreme facilitator's toolkit. Extreme facilitation means stepping into war zones and creating conditions in which participants feel comfortable laying down their arms.

Putting It All Together

A story may illustrate how welcoming emotions, responding with empathy, managing the level of emotional expression, and enabling empathy in others can all work together.

I was facilitating a consensus process about whether (and if so, how) to build a new convention center in a mid-size city. The city government had handed us a template for convening stakeholders: the group was to contain representatives of each of the neighborhoods bordering the convention site along with two local environmental groups and two local economic-development associations.

During convening, my colleagues identified a national advocacy group dedicated to preserving local neighborhoods. The city government ruled out their participation on the grounds that they were neither a local group nor an environmental one. The group leaders were angry at being excluded. They did, however, manage to participate in the process in other ways—one member served as the alternate for an environmental representative, the other as the technical committee representative for that same environmental group.

Still angry at their exclusion, they used the "public comment" portion of each of the meetings to make mini-speeches about their views. This angered other participants, who felt these activists were "taking two bites of the apple" (speaking both as meeting participants and as members of the general public). My colleague tried in vain to talk the activists out of this approach just after the meeting.

I then had the idea to hold a special meeting with this group—an example of welcoming emotion rather than running the other way. We facilitators met with the group members with the stated goal of discussing their role in the process and helping them maximize their influence. They first talked at length about why they were angry, while we listened as empathically as we could. They were animated and fiery. In this setting, we left the emotional "volume" button untouched and stayed engaged with the conversation even when they were yelling.

Over the course of the meeting, we seemed to earn their trust and respect gradually. As we were suggesting to them ways to be more effective in influencing the process, one of our suggestions was to be a little less abrasive with other participants and the city government. This seemed to help them accept a certain amount of responsibility for others' tendency to shut them out. We also pointed out that the city was actually being more inclusive than in the past, when such committees included only the neighborhood representatives and no public-interest organizations of any kind. This seemed to notch up their empathy a bit, and from then on, they were considerably more constructive participants.

Meanwhile, one of their key complaints was that the city had established too tight a timeline to study the potential impacts of the convention center development. We had already begun to share the same concern. Our meeting with this group helped spur us to have some frank conversations with our paying client—the city—and to persuade them to slow down the schedule in order to maintain the integrity of the study and decision-making process. If we had run away from this group's emotional agitation, we might not have taken this crucial step.

Your Own Emotional Capacity

Your ability to embrace and be comfortable with others' emotions is related to your own emotional capacity.

Welcoming Your Own Emotions

How much do you welcome your own emotions? Can you name the emotions you're feeling at any given moment, or are you inclined to deny or ignore them? Do you let yourself feel your own pain, or do you tell yourself you don't care? Can you relate to your feelings, or are they strange and foreign to you? The more you can welcome your own emotions, the more you'll be able to welcome the emotions of others.

It's a commonplace belief that women are more emotionally attuned than men. This may be true, but many women have been socialized to be attuned to others' emotions more than to their own. The danger of this is that their own emotions, if they're unaware of them, can sneak up on them and pounce unexpectedly.

For example, I am sometimes unaware that I've been pushing myself too hard and becoming increasingly frazzled and frustrated—until I suddenly snap and lose my temper with someone undeserving. In other words, my lack of emotional self-awareness temporarily obliterates my sensitivity to others' feelings.

I have found there is a great deal of individual variation in emotional self-awareness among both sexes. Many of us, men and women alike, could stand to increase our own emotional self-understanding.

Welcoming Others' Emotions

Beyond emotional self-awareness, we can also cultivate our ability to embrace others' strong emotions. In mainstream American culture at least, it is common to want to distance ourselves from someone who's overcome with feeling. If instead we can approach that person and openly receive his or her emotions, our power to heal is multiplied.

Once during a family visit, my niece, seven years old at the time, was playing with her slightly older, male cousin, who was more physical and adventuresome. She was struggling to keep up with him as he played ball and roughhoused with the other children. She seemed to be feeling competitive with him and probably envious. At one point, the two got into a tug of war over who got to ride the swing, and he won. She screamed at him in rage, and then collapsed onto a lawn chair in tears of fury and defeat. At that moment, her little brother, then only three years old, crawled up onto the lawn chair, hugged her, and remained snuggled next to her until their mother arrived.

That little boy remains my role model for embracing others' emotions. I hold this scene in my mind when I approach a participant who's erupting. It helps me to be present and receptive until the emotions are discharged. Then I can focus my own and the group's attention on discussing the issues to which the emotions are attached.

Part of that dialogue involves engaging the intellect to understand and analyze the informational content of the issues. If you're ready to be done with emotions for a while, the next chapter, on intellectual capacity, should give you some relief.

Notes

1. Goleman, *Emotional Intelligence*, pp. 13–14.
2. My views on anger have been influenced by Rosenberg, *Non-violent Communication*, and Tavris, *Anger: The Misunderstood Emotion*.
3. Mayer, *The Dynamics of Conflict Resolution*, pp. 120–122.
4. Bush and Folger, *The Promise of Meditation*, pp. 159–161.

Chapter Nine

The Intellectual Capacity

Facilitating Complex Issues

If you're not the type who fears intense emotions, perhaps you fear a different extreme challenge: complex technical issues. The extreme facilitator often must take on issues that are complex scientifically, technically, legally, or bureaucratically. For example, I once helped resolve issues about soil and groundwater cleanup at closing military bases in one state. The issues were complex in all these ways:

Scientific. There were detailed and shifting calculations of the effects of various contaminants on human health and environmental quality.

Technical. There were various methods of cleaning up the contaminants and various estimates of the amount of time these methods would take to clean them up successfully.

Legal. There was a complex legal test as to whether the state's more stringent cleanup standards should trump the federal standards, and no clarity (or agreement) about whether they did so.

Bureaucratic. The issue involved people at four different government agencies (two federal, one state, and one local) and at five or more levels of the hierarchy in each agency. How all these people communicated with each other, both within and across agencies, was complex. Moreover, the people with the technical expertise were not those with the legal expertise, and neither of these were the people with the policymaking authority needed to resolve the issues.

This is an extreme example. But even in a case as simple (on the surface) as helping an organization select a slate of health insurance plans, the technical complexity of comparing different health plans on at least half a dozen different variables requires the help of a technical expert.

Sometimes it's tempting to gloss over technical information. For example, suppose an organization is deciding on a new marketing strategy. If everyone intuitively likes the same approach, it's tempting to feel self-congratulatory about the consensus and not to dig up the data that answer questions such as the following: What is our market? Who are our customers? How do they see us compared to our competitors? Who are our competitors? What are they doing better, worse, or differently? How do our prices compare? How do our products compare? How does our image compare? What trends do we see in the marketplace? This kind of information is essential for good decision making.

Sometimes the facts tell us things we don't want to know, but we must confront them.[1] The company in our example might not want to acknowledge, for instance, that they're being surpassed by competitors on the quality of a product line they've always identified with most. The executives might be in consensus about continuing that product line unchanged. They'd all feel good, but they'd all be wrong. The extreme facilitator will be astute enough to point this out, even if it dissolves the consensus, and to offer to design a process that incorporates solid information.

This chapter will help you deal with technically complex issues, break them down into manageable pieces, and draw on the intellectual capacity of the group to generate, assimilate, and analyze this information in order to incorporate it into good decision making. It also will help you put technical information in its place, to see it in a context of values, personalities, politics, and other factors that may be equally important.

Managing Complex Issues

Working through complex issues requires a structured, deliberate process to allow the group to identify, digest, and analyze information. Designing this aspect of the process can be as creative as any other aspect. There are no set formulas. As usual, it must be tailored to fit the group (including its level of technical expertise), its goals, and its culture.

Getting a handle on complex information might involve any combination of the following steps, depending on the situation:

- Laying out the background information, educating participants as needed, and developing a picture of the context.
- Defining the issue—crystallizing the real question(s) the participants are trying to answer, the problem(s) they're trying to solve, or the issue(s) they're trying to resolve. There may be one or many key issues.
- Generating options—identifying possible solutions, decisions, actions, or outcomes.
- Developing evaluation criteria by which to compare these options. These criteria are rarely just technical. They will usually reflect individual or group interests as well as external constraints. This is one of the points at which to integrate technical data with other factors.
- Evaluating and narrowing the options. This can include an analytical process of applying the criteria to the options, but final decision making tends to go back to values, interests, and politics—again, technical analysis is not the end of the story.

You may notice that this list roughly follows the classic problem-solving sequence: identify the problem, identify criteria for a solution, generate a list of options, apply the criteria to the options, select and refine. This doesn't make it a rigid formula. You may use only one or some combination of these steps, you may do them in a different order, and the way you implement any of them can be highly creative.

Below we take a closer look at each of these steps.

Laying Out Background Information

In the example of the company developing a marketing plan, all the information mentioned earlier (who the competitors are, how their products compare, and so on) would need to be presented and considered. In the negotiations to determine how to reduce the level of ground-level ozone in a metropolitan area, participants had to understand how ozone forms, what contributes to it, and what the history was that led to this issue being so contentious.

This step overlaps with two of the components of the building understanding stage described in Chapter Six: sharing information and understanding the context. If some or all of the participants need to gain a better understanding of the technical issues, this step can include education. Here are some specific possible techniques and how to make best use of them.

Handouts. It may be useful to distribute information in advance of a meeting, if the following conditions are met:

- You have some confidence participants will actually read it. If some read it and others don't, those who do might become resentful of the others for holding up progress.

- You can get it to them far enough in advance that they will have time to absorb it. If you set unrealistic expectations about this, it can damage trust and increase tension.

Discussion. If different participants have different pieces of relevant information, an open discussion may be a good way to let the information flow out and begin to form a complete picture.

Presentations. Sometimes a technical expert may need to educate the group about background information. For example, an outside technical expert was hired separately from the facilitators in the air-quality negotiations. In selecting a slate of health insurance plans for an organization, the insurance broker served as the technical expert. In the base cleanup example, the staff scientists and engineers across the four agencies presented background information to their policymaking superiors. In the company devising a marketing plan, the staff marketing specialist who had done the market research would most likely present it.

The trouble with presentations is that the people with the technical expertise to make them are often not the best at communicating with a nonexpert audience. They often need some coaching on how to do it well. We can encourage them to

- *Use plain English.* Presenters may need to be reminded to avoid technical jargon and acronyms that are unknown to some participants.

- *Use visual aids.* By presenting information both verbally and in some graphic form (charts, graphs, diagrams, flow-charts, pictures, and so on), the presenter can increase comprehension.

- *Keep it short.* Technical experts are often enamored of their subject matter and enjoy talking about it at length. You and the presenter will need to be clear what the group needs to know and why. Then you may need to encourage the presenter to stick to that. The presenter should err on the side of brevity, then allow questions to fill in gaps.

- *Plan how to handle questions.* You and the presenter will need agreement on which of you will facilitate the question-and-answer period. If the question-and-answer period is likely to become contentious, you might want to insist on facilitating it yourself.

There are many possible variations on how to handle questions. You can allow any questions during the presentation, hold all questions until afterward, or allow only clarifying questions during, and the rest afterward. You might allow both questions and comments at any time, or, if the comments and ensuing discussion could become lengthy, you might invite only questions first, then comments later. If people are using the question-and-answer period to make speeches, you might propose that questions be submitted on index cards (this imposes some formality, however). If the questions could become a series of attacks against the presenter, you might also elicit all the questions first and post them before having the expert answer any of them.

Defining the Issue

Once the background has been laid out (or sometimes beforehand), there needs to be clarity on the issue the group is charged with addressing.

In the military base cleanup scenario, the technical staff, who were at relatively low levels in their respective hierarchies, had elevated the contentious issues more than once before. However, the issues were so complex that their superiors tended to throw their hands up, not knowing what they were being asked to resolve. Disputed issues fell into a bureaucratic limbo, being bounced up and down the chain of command.

My colleague Louise Smart and I developed a concept called the Joint Issue Statement, which would document the background information that the technical staff across the agencies agreed on and which would clearly spell out what the issues were. The issues were stated in the form of questions to which they needed to work out answers. This simple innovation allowed the higher-level officials to be clear what problems they were being asked to solve, and therefore to more easily solve them.

Defining the issue is not always such an elaborate process. However, as part of defining the task, it is an essential one. You may be able to define the issue in advance of any full-group sessions, as is sometimes the case in public-policy facilitation when a group is formed to address a specific issue. Alternatively, mapping out the range of concerns and boiling them down into a manageable handful of issues may be a large part of the group process, especially in organizational issues, partnering, or other situations in which there are long-term relationships.

Defining an issue well is an incredibly powerful step in helping a group resolve it. It also helps lay the foundation for determining what information is needed, what options need to be explored and analyzed, and what criteria need to be considered.

Here are some guidelines for defining the issue.[2]

Select a Neutral Word or Phrase. In the first iteration of defining the issue—which may occur during assessment, in writing the agenda, or during full-group discussions, it often helps to find a key word or phrase that captures the topic.

The phrase should not favor a particular solution. Let's take the well-known issue of abortion. The word "abortion" does not imply that abortions either should or should not occur. That's why the news media tend to use the phrase "abortion issue" rather than, say, the "reproductive choice issue" or the issue of "unborn children," each of which implies a stance.

It's also important that the word or phrase not take an accusation at face value. In the military base cleanup dispute, the issue was not "the military's violation of state regulations" or "the state's disregard for federal taxpayers," but simply "cleanup levels."

Use an Open-Ended Question. As the issue is defined further, that key word or phrase can be incorporated into a question, the task being to answer it.

People often phrase issues initially in terms of a yes-no or either-or question: "Should the beltway be completed?" "Whose cleanup standards apply—the state's or the federal government's?" The problem with such phrasing is that it suggests only two options. It forecloses the possibility of a wider range of options that will meet the needs of all participants.

A simple improvement is to turn such closed-ended questions into open-ended ones. The question, "Should the beltway be completed?" becomes "How can we improve mobility in the study area?" The question, "Whose cleanup standards apply?" becomes "What should be the cleanup level?" or, since that question still presupposes that the solution is simply a number, "How should we clean up the contaminants at the site?" is even better.

Incorporate Key Interests. If the issue is contentious, you can go one step further in phrasing the issue so that it orients participants to solving it in a way that meets competing interests. When an issue is controversial, there is usually a tension between two or more competing needs. Once you know what these are, you can craft a question that incorporates them, in the form of "how can we both _____ and _____?"—that is, How can we meet both or all of these competing needs?

For example, in the military base cleanup, the state's main interests were to have their regulatory authority respected and their regulations "substantively" followed. The military wanted to maintain nationwide consistency and avoid a costly precedent. The issue of cleanup levels now becomes, "How can we clean up the site such that the state's authority and regulations are respected while the military maintains national consistency?" Notice how this question leaves far more room for creative thinking than "Whose cleanup level should we apply?"

Following are some other issues phrased as questions that capture competing interests:

- How can we achieve a more family-friendly workplace while also promoting profitability and growth? (instead of "Should we introduce flex-time?")
- How can decisions be made in a way that is inclusive without becoming cumbersome? (instead of "Should we

continue to include first-level supervisors in weekly management meetings?" or "How do we deal with huge, unproduc-
tive meetings?")

- How can we reduce the budget while maintaining key
  services to the public? (instead of, "Do we need to lay off any
  staff?" or "What programs should we eliminate?")

Depending on the situation, you can work on phrasing issues
on your own, with the help of a process advisory committee, or
with the help of the whole group. Keep in mind, however, that all
but the most process-oriented group will get frustrated if this careful crafting takes up lots of full-group meeting time. I learned this
the hard way when one participant barked at me, "When are we
gonna stop talking about what we're *gonna* talk about, and just start
talking about it?"

Phrasing issues is more of an art than a science; more driven by
interests and values than by information. However, it is a key tool
for imposing order on the field of information when the subject
matter is technically complex.

Generating Options

Once the issue has been defined, a logical next step is to generate
options for solution. The topic of brainstorming, which is intended
to stimulate creative thinking, is addressed in the next chapter.

Before creative thinking begins, there is often a first step of
identifying and researching known options. In the air-quality negotiations, the technical consultant researched air-quality regulations
in other states and districts around the country to come up with an
initial list of possible ways to reduce ozone. Then my cofacilitator
and I invited participants to add to the list. In the dialogue on possible completion of a beltway, the client agency and the consultants
generated a list of different alignments for construction of new free-
ways, improvements of existing roads, and transit lines. Again, participants were invited to add to this list. In the process of selecting

health insurance plans for an organization, the insurance broker developed a request for proposals to health insurance companies and obtained over a dozen proposals.

Not all issues require this extensive process of identifying and expanding the list of options. This is for issues that are complex in terms of the range of options that exist. In other situations, the tangible solutions become obvious after the more important work of building understanding among participants and encouraging empathy for each other's viewpoints (as discussed in Chapter Eight).

Developing Evaluation Criteria

In a complex situation, you may have not only a long list of options but also a range of sharply divided opinions on which of them is the right answer. Instead of having participants pick their favorites and debate with each other which is best, it will reduce contentiousness if they state their interests and you reformulate these as evaluation criteria. You might ask, "What would characterize a good solution?" or "What would the ideal solution accomplish?"

For example, in the transportation project, we elicited participants' interests, then reformulated them as a list of over twenty-five criteria (some with sub-points), ranging from "improve suburb-to-suburb mobility" and "promote business development" to "protect open space," "avoid excessive noise," and "reduce contribution to sprawl."

Some criteria may be based not on participants' interests but on objective factors or external constraints. Examples include funding or affordability, compliance with laws and regulations, achievability within time constraints, and acceptability to decision makers or powerful interests not at the table.

Criteria may be generated either before or after the identification of options. There are pros and cons to each approach. If done before, the criteria discussion can be a good transition from building understanding to task achievement (identifying, narrowing, and evaluating options). If done after, participants can look at the list and ask themselves, "Why do I like this option and not that one?" and the answer is a criterion: "I like this option because it doesn't disrupt residential neighborhoods."

Evaluating and Narrowing the Options[3]

For those processes in which a long list of options is generated, narrowing those down can seem daunting. There are many techniques that can make this process easier and more orderly. You might use one or a combination of these—or some variation you invent yourself—to fit the particular situation.

Fatal Flaw Elimination. Sometimes a good way to shorten a long list of options is to invite the group to eliminate those with "fatal flaws." The ground rule here is that if one participant nominates an option as fatally flawed but another participant wants it to stay on the list, it stays. In the air-quality negotiations, we used this method to eliminate about fifteen of some one hundred options.

Straw Polling. There are many methods of polling the group to shorten the list of options. This is not a scientific approach—it does not involve any rigorous evaluation based on criteria. Instead, it ensures that the least-popular items are eliminated, yielding a list that's more manageable for an in-depth evaluation or discussion. I often use this approach in strategic planning retreats when participants have listed dozens of possible goals for the organization.

One well-know technique is called "N/3."[4] This involves taking the total number of items in the list—"N"—and dividing it by three. Each participant may then vote for that many items. For example, if an organization has identified thirty potential different goals for the year, each participant votes for ten favorite goals.

Before you do a straw poll, the option list should be clean—in other words, similar or overlapping items should be grouped together. Otherwise, votes could be split among multiple similar items, resulting in their undesired elimination.

Of course, the N/3 method is somewhat arbitrary. It doesn't take into account how many people are in the group, for instance, or how many items you'd like to have remaining. With larger groups you could do fewer votes per person (N/4 or N/5, for instance).

Moreover, this method does not register strength of preference. To do that, you might allow participants to distribute their votes with more than one vote per item. Be careful, however, in a situation in which two polarized groups are each wedded to a favorite solution—each will put all the votes allowed onto that favorite, and you'll be stuck with just the two options they've been fighting about already.

You might get creative in other ways. For example, you might allow people to give away their votes, so that those who care more about the issue have more votes.

There are innumerable voting methods—ask for a show of hands, give each person sticky dots (the kind used as price labels at garage sales) to place on a list of options written on a flip chart, allow each person to write check marks on the flip chart, allow each person to write his or her votes on index cards and have someone tabulate them, and so on. Each method has obvious pros and cons—for example, the check marks require trust that participants will not vote for more than their allotted number of items; the index card method requires trust in the tabulator.

Assessing Pros and Cons. This is a more methodical evaluation method than straw polling but a simpler one than applying criteria. You ask the group, or an appropriate expert, to identify pros and cons of each option. This may be done with or without a list of criteria.

Applying the Criteria. This is the most rigorous evaluation method—assessing each option according to the criteria generated by the group. Because this is usually time consuming, you may want to have this done by an expert or a small group outside the meeting, then let the group review and comment on the analysis and ranking.

There are many variations on how this can be done. For example, you might assign different weights to the different criteria. (However, this could get contentious if the criteria spring from strong value differences—how do you weight "promoting business development" versus "protecting the environment" for example?). You might give each option a score based on how it meets the criteria overall or even each specific criterion. The trick with this, as for all the narrowing methods, is to balance the necessary level of rigor with the need for efficiency.

This rigorous analysis will not automatically yield the right answer. Participants will still need to digest, discuss, and struggle with the top options that result from the analysis. The techniques listed in Chapter Six under Achieving the Task (developing proposals, overcoming deadlocks, and refining outcomes) will still need to be used.

The Limits of Analysis

One danger in group processes dealing with technically complex issues is "paralysis by analysis." Yes, information is important. Sometimes it's powerfully eye opening. Issues must be understood before they can be resolved; decisions must be grounded in facts and reality.

However, participants sometimes get into an endless loop of receiving information, challenging it, then requesting more information, challenging that, requesting more, and so on, trying to eliminate their ongoing uncertainty. People keep looking to the data to resolve values differences, to yield an unassailable answer, to settle conflicting perceptions once and for all. Occasionally, data can do this. In complex issues, it usually can't.

One example comes from the transportation arena. There is a values continuum when it comes to transportation development. At one end of the continuum are those who fully accept that our society is automobile dependent and who want to make driving as congestion-free and convenient as possible. They see mobility (via automobile) as an enabler of economic growth. On the other end of the spectrum are those who envision a world that is far less automobile-dependent, where people can live, shop, and work in the same pedestrian- and bicycle-friendly neighborhoods, and where they take longer trips by bus, subway, light rail, or other mass transit. This values difference is an offshoot of the broader growth-versus-environment values conflict.

The difference is over values, yet people who hold these different perspectives often fight it out through data analysis. When traffic forecasters and modelers predict the need for or benefits of a new road, for instance, the pro-growth people say the data prove additional roads or lanes are needed, that there clearly is an unfulfilled demand. The environmentalists argue that the demand is "induced"—that building new roads lures people to drive more than they would otherwise, induces development to occur farther and farther away from the urban core, and makes driving more attractive than the environmentally friendly alternatives.

The pro-growth people point out that denser development will produce only continued (or worsened) traffic congestion, which produces more air pollution (from idling cars). The pro-environment people point out that if roads are less congested, people will tolerate longer commutes, move farther from their jobs, and so total miles driven increases and sprawl worsens.

Who is right? I'm not sure anyone knows. The war is fought over data, analysis, and projections: What will be the effect of building versus not building this road? Yet the answers are no more certain than weather forecasts. The models incorporate assumptions about human behavior, which are in turn influenced by culture. Do the participants accept that culture (for instance, the American tendency to drive everywhere if we can), or do they work to change it? This is not a matter of data analysis. It's a matter of values.

As an extreme facilitator, you need to help your group strike a sensitive balance between obtaining necessary information and coming to terms with inevitable uncertainty, conflicting perceptions, and values differences. You might need to do any or all of the following:

- *Agree on informational needs up front.* Before beginning lengthy technical study and presentations with handouts and charts and graphs, you can work with the technical experts and the participants to agree on what information will be needed and why. Then, you can refer back to this agreement when people ask for more and more data.

- *Call it.* Note when the group has hit this endless loop (information-challenge-requests for more information), gently point it out, and suggest they move on. If you're unsure whether additional data will be helpful, you can ask, "Before we send the technical experts off to do this research, are we confident it will bring us closer to a solution? Or are we just delaying the inevitable task of grappling with your underlying differences?"

- *Ask what hinges on it.* When participants request further data or analysis, you can ask them to consider how the resulting information will affect the group's decision making: "What hinges on the answer to the question you're asking?" or "How will your conclusions be different if the data say x rather than y?"

    There may be a persuasive response—a clear indication that more data are indeed necessary. This response will help the technical experts be clearer about what question they're being asked to answer. Alternatively, participants may realize that they're going to hold the same view regardless of what the data say—in which case, gathering further data or conducting further analysis is pointless.

Your Own Intellectual Capacity

When I tell people I am a facilitator, they imagine me standing in front of a group and interacting with people. They imagine my work is all about interpersonal skills, emotions, and relationships.

Indeed, my work does involve these—but my informational skills are just as important. I need to be able to

- Absorb lots of subject-matter information (to delve into technically complex issues)
- Analyze information—break it down into manageable chunks
- Detect patterns in a mass of information (to identify themes or points of agreement)
- Find the right words (to reflect understanding of people's concerns, and often to find the right language to bridge differences and obtain agreement)

This is one part of extreme facilitation that is greatly enhanced by formal education.

Academic Education

There are certainly limits to the usefulness of academic education. It rarely does a good job of building your emotional capacity (the subject of Chapter Eight), and it does a mediocre job at best of developing your intuition (the subject of Chapter Ten).

However, academic study is an excellent way to hone your intellectual capacity. A quality education involves constant exercise in reading (absorbing lots of information), analyzing, synthesizing (detecting patterns), and writing (finding the right words). You can do all this on your own, and there are some remarkable examples of self-taught intellectuals. For most of us, however, the structure of the classroom and the feedback of an instructor are unparalleled accelerators of progress.

What subject you should study is another question.

Subject-Matter Expertise

As facilitators, we advertise ourselves as experts in designing and managing group processes. Therefore, the best preparation for extreme facilitation focuses on processes of human interaction, such as conflict resolution, social psychology, organizational de-velopment, business management, or public administration. Our expertise need not necessarily lie in the subject matter of the group discussion.

This raises an important question, though, especially when the subject matter is highly complex: How much subject-matter exper-tise does a facilitator need?

My experience indicates that if I am to be a lead facilitator in a situation with technically challenging subject matter, I need to be *familiar* with the subject. This means having sufficient understand-ing to know the jargon and follow the conversation. The goal is to avoid having to slow the group down to ask for explanations, or having to divert one's energy to a struggle to comprehend the discussion.

There are several ways to acquire this level of knowledge:

- Serving as a cofacilitator with a lead who is more versed in the subject matter.
- Doing background reading.
- Getting a tutorial from a knowledgeable colleague—either a fellow facilitator who has worked with similar issues or a technical expert who is not part of this facilitation.
- Asking participants for minitutorials during assessment interviews. This is a bit dicey; remember, you are supposed to be serving them, not vice versa. Learning about the specific issues to be addressed through facilitation is part of serving them; gaining a general subject familiarity is a different matter. However, some technical experts are happy to give a quick education—at least a definition of some key terms. (I often try to interview lower-level personnel first— they often have more technical expertise and less time pressure.) It's important to be honest about your technical qualifications prior to accepting a facilitation assignment and clear about how much time you'll have to spend getting educated.

In determining how much expertise you need, an important variable is the extent to which all group members share subject-matter expertise. When some of the participants are lay people, part of our jobs as facilitators is to build in a process of technical education for them—which conveniently allows us to get educated as well. We also have to ensure that the more expert participants speak in terms that the nonexpert participants can understand. In doing this, it actually helps somewhat to be novices ourselves. Even in such situations, however, I have worked only as a cofacilitator alongside a lead who was more technically conversant.

In contrast, I facilitated one process involving six participants who were all engineers or scientists specializing in the same technical area. I was facilitating solo, and I was in way over my head. I did raise a concern in advance about my level of technical knowledge, but my point of contact assured me that the problems in the group were personality problems, not technical disagreements. She was correct on that point, but she probably took for granted her own ability to follow the technical discussion, which I found myself struggling to do.

One group member took it upon himself (out of pity, I guess) to be my quasi-assistant, pointing out when someone had made a key point and sometimes translating that point into lay terms. This was helpful, but I was still putting so much energy into trying to follow the conversation that my attention was diverted from what I was hired to do—manage the process and mitigate the personality clashes.

I also was unable, due to my technical deficiency, to write the first draft of a consensus document, which meant that a group member composed the first draft. Predictably, it came out slanted toward his organization's viewpoint. The group stumbled its way to a minimal consensus (which was the substantive goal), but relationships emerged even more strained than when I entered the picture. In retrospect, I should have turned down the job or recruited a lead facilitator who was more versed in the technical subject.

Still, this is not to argue that the only person who could facilitate in that situation would be another engineer or scientist. Indeed, my colleague J. Michael Harty later facilitated in a situation with almost identical subject matter. He had no problem. The difference was that he had built up years of experience facilitating and mediating when similar subject matter was involved.

Understanding the technical subject matter, absorbing and analyzing information, and managing the process by which the group members engage their intellectual capacity are important components of extreme facilitation. This type of intellectual work relies heavily on the linear, logical left hemisphere of the brain. The other half of the brain is important too. It is largely responsible for creativity and intuition, the subject of the next chapter.

Notes

1. Collins, *Good to Great*, pp. 65–73.
2. This section reflects the teachings of my colleagues at CDR Associates.
3. This section reflects common techniques taught at CDR Associates and written about widely. See, for example, Rees, *The Facilitator Excellence Handbook*, pp. 145–171.
4. Interaction Associates, *Essential Facilitation*, section 2, p. 12.

Chapter Ten

The Intuitive Capacity

Sparking Insights and Ideas

Analysis and logical reasoning are as important in facilitation as they are in other endeavors, but they're not the end of the story. The right hemisphere of the brain possesses a complementary and almost magical ability: it puts together, albeit unconsciously, innumerable bits of information into a whole picture. This is the holistic side of the mind, the nonverbal, intuitive part. It generates creativity, flashes of insight, and gut-level understanding.[1]

When ideas pop into our heads, that's the right brain at work. When we dream in images that symbolically illustrate the goings-on of our lives and our unconscious thoughts, that's the right brain at work. When we tell or listen to a story, forming vivid images in our minds, the imagery is a product of the right brain (though the words themselves are processed by the left brain). When we can size up a person or a situation, intuiting far more about them than we have explicitly been told, that's the right brain at work. When we make music or art, dance or theater, we employ our right brains. To some extent, when we have empathy for someone, imagining what it would be like to walk in his or her shoes, our right brain is at work.

The right hemisphere of the brain can be an indispensable tool in

- Understanding others fully, even across sharp differences
- Gaining clarity on the dynamics of organizations or complex relationships
- Gaining insights into issues or problems

- Generating ideas that will innovate, bridge differences, or solve problems
- Envisioning better futures toward which to strive

Far too often, meetings and group processes (much like our educational institutions) rely too heavily on left-hemisphere activity: talking, reasoning, and analyzing. They fail to capitalize on the remarkable power of the right brain. What a shame it is to neglect this awesome capacity in our group processes, especially in extreme facilitation, when we need every resource we can muster.

Creating Conditions for Intuition

Typical meetings lack the conditions for unleashing the power of our intuition and creativity. In many meetings, people are tense, concerned about how others are judging them, and somewhat formal. Much of the conventional format is verbal—talking, presenting data, and so forth.

Our intuitive, creative powers flourish in conditions that are relaxed, playful, nonjudgmental, and receptive. We must feel we have permission to break with convention, to be off-the-wall. We mustn't be too worried about offending.

We can help create these conditions in a number of ways: by instigating games or fun activities, by not taking ourselves too seriously (perhaps using a little self-deprecating humor), by being nonjudgmental of group members, and by being receptive to unconventional ideas. However, creating these conditions can be challenging when the culture of the client group is formal, judgmental, fear-oriented, or hypersensitive. I can think of many organizations that meet this description.

To a large extent, we have to work within the cultural norms of our client groups. We can't push people too far beyond their comfort zone, or we will be ridiculed and rejected. We have to establish rapport with our groups, and this requires, in part, doing in Rome as the Romans do. Once we have established this rapport, however, we can sometimes push the boundaries a little, if we explain the benefits and obtain explicit permission.

I once facilitated a planning retreat for a government agency that was facing drastic budget cuts for the upcoming year. The culture of this group was deliberative, process oriented, and conservative (in terms of what constitutes normal office behavior). Many of the participants were scientific or technical specialists. While planning the agenda, I concluded that before we went into the detailed, methodical work of setting goals and priorities for each program, the group members needed first to develop a guiding vision of what they most wanted to accomplish with their limited resources.

The ideal process of developing a vision involves first helping participants settle into a deep state of relaxation before asking them to visualize a future scenario. For this group, the whole concept of a visualization exercise, let alone deep relaxation, was already far outside the participants' normal mode of conducting meetings. I talked to my two contacts, neither of whom was the director of the group, about conducting a visualization session, and they consented. However, I didn't even broach the subject of deep relaxation. I knew it would seem far too new-age or touchy-feely for them.

When I explained the visualization process to all the group members and obtained their permission to begin, the director got a smirk on his face that reminded me of the look my older brother would give me when teasing me as a child. The director seemed to think the exercise was silly, but he also seemed to suspend judgment (perhaps to avoid undercutting his two staffers who had worked with me to plan the meeting), and he didn't openly object.

I proceeded to explain the exercise. I asked participants to close their eyes and imagine that they were at a party at the end of the next year, toasting the accomplishments they had managed in the "past" year despite the unprecedented budget cuts. I then had them jot down a few notes to indicate key points they would make in their toasts. We then went around the table asking each participant to report what he or she envisioned.

Several common themes emerged from their various visions. I captured these in a brief bulleted list which I projected from my laptop computer with an LCD projector. As the group members went on to the detailed tasks of goal setting, prioritizing, and cutting, they frequently referred back to this list. In an end-of-day evaluation, the director acknowledged that he had been skeptical of the exercise, but that he was now persuaded of its value.

I succeeded, in other words, in pushing the group a little beyond its comfort zone. I remain convinced, however, that if I had asked the participants to lie on the floor while I did a deep-relaxation exercise, I would have been laughed out of the room. You have to start where the group is and connect with its culture and norms. Then, when you can give a reason for it, you can ask group members to go a bit outside their norms to help access their capacity for creativity and intuition.

Some Activities for Tapping Intuition

There are many ways to tap a group's creative and intuitive capacity, and innumerable more waiting to be invented. Let these techniques spark your own creativity, and see if you can devise custom activities that will help the group achieve its goals in a way that's not too far outside its culture.

Brainstorming

Brainstorming is a well-known technique for coming up with creative ideas.[2] However, I've often seen groups fail to tap the potential of a true brainstorming exercise. Too often someone just asks for ideas on a particular topic and writes them down.

At its best, brainstorming can maximize the creativity needed to come up with solutions to seemingly insoluble problems. There are several keys to truly unleashing this creativity:

- *Promote a playful atmosphere.* Ideally, brainstorming is preceded by a game or activity that gets participants out of their serious-discussion mode and into a more playful frame of mind. Perhaps you have them play some simple ball game with beanbags, conduct a contest to come up with a new name for the office cafeteria, or play musical chairs.

- *Pose the dilemma.* Articulate the dilemma that needs to be solved—for example, how can we reduce the budget while maintaining essential services? Or, how can we develop this parcel of land while promoting environmental quality and species habitat? (See the section "Defining the Issue" in Chapter Nine.)

- *Aim for quantity, not quality.* Be clear with the group that its job is to come up with the *most* ideas, not the *best* ones. Of course, everyone is hoping that brilliant ideas will emerge— that's the whole point. Paradoxically, though, they're more likely to emerge if people are not worried about being judged on quality. If people are wondering, "Gee, will my idea be shot down?", they'll be inhibited and creativity will be squelched. The stupidest idea may spark someone else's idea that may be a perfect solution. I've occasionally split groups into teams and had them compete to come up with the longest list of ideas. This adds another bit of fun and silliness, and therefore creativity.

- *Capture all ideas.* Whoever is recording the ideas generated must write down every one—no matter how ridiculous, impractical, illegal, or immoral. The facilitator and recorder must model nonjudgmental receptivity.

- *Curb any judgment.* This is one time to be rigid in enforcing a ground rule: there is no judgment of any idea until after the brainstorming is completely finished. In almost every brainstorming session, there's someone who can't help themselves from interjecting, "Oh, that could never work, because . . ." You must then respond with something like, "We're not evaluating ideas now. Do you have a different idea for the list?"

I once used brainstorming with a group of frontline supervisors from an airline to come up with ways to deal with a fictitious irate customer who missed a connecting flight because his first flight came in late due to weather. The dilemma was how to satisfy the customer while respecting the standard policy that the airline is not responsible for weather-related delays. Before the exercise, all agreed there was little they could do but express sympathy. By the end of the brainstorming exercise, they'd come up with over thirty options, including several that were viable, such as letting the customer wait in the elite-customer lounge.

Visualization

Visualization, as illustrated in the previous section, can be a powerful tool for planning, problem solving, improving relationships, and probably other purposes as well. Sports psychologists and others tell us that if we can visualize success, we can achieve it. The vision makes the possible seem much more real and tangible, and it motivates us to achieve it.

Visualization can be an excellent method for improving complex group relationships, such as inside an organization or in a long-term contractor-client relationship.[3] When such relationships are troubled, people often have different diagnoses as to what the central problem is. For instance, in a troubled organization, you might see low morale, poor communication, low productivity, distrust, and uncertain leadership. These are interwoven issues. There isn't just one key problem—it's a complex system. The classic problem-solving method is therefore not the best approach—if you can't agree what the problem is, how can you solve it?

Instead, visualization can be used to form a picture of an ideal future relationship. This often works like a charm, in part because people tend to want similar things from their working relationships—respect, inclusion, communication, and trust (though the specifics of these vary from person to person and culture to culture).

Once the vision has been established, you might take the next step of identifying (1) forces that help promote this ideal future, and (2) obstacles to it. The group can then discuss how to strengthen the favorable forces and conduct problem solving to overcome the obstacles.[4]

Several steps maximize the power of a visualization exercise:

• *Invite relaxation.* Relaxation is a powerful aid to the creative and intuitive capacity. If the group members are open to it, consider walking them through a relaxation process. First, they find a physically relaxing posture (in chairs, on couches, or even on the floor). Then use any of a range of relaxation techniques: slow, deliberate breathing ("breathe in for four . . . now out for eight . . ."); conscious relaxation of muscle groups in sequence ("first relax your neck, then your arms . . .); or visualization of a beach or other relaxing place.

• *Warm up the imagination.* To help warm up the right-hemisphere powers, you might give a non-task-related visualization exercise first. I once participated in an exercise adapted from Elise Boulding's workshops on envisioning a world without weapons.[5] After we were deeply relaxed, the facilitator asked us to imagine we were standing on the roof of a tall building. We were to imagine what we felt like, how the air smelled, and what we saw and heard, and report this to the group.

One of my fellow participants had had a past career as a construction worker, and he had experienced this very scenario in his work. He said that it was common to "feel the pull"—to experience an urge to jump off the building and fly into the vast landscape. He reported "feeling the pull" during this exercise. Some other participants reported vertigo. I remember feeling the vastness of the sky, the horizon, and the cityscape below. Our imaginations transported us far beyond the meeting room where we were sitting in a circle in chairs. It prepared us for the more task-related portion of the exercise.

• *Pose the task.* You might ask people to envision themselves as individuals acting or performing in some improved way: an ideal future working relationship; a successful event, process, year, or decade; or an ideal future state for an organization—what the organization will be doing, how it will be organized, what its niche will be in the field (this latter kind of vision development is a major component of strategic planning).

In an individual example, I once worked with a woman who was having conflict with her teammates. I discerned that part of the problem was that she felt powerless, perhaps more powerless than she really was. With her permission, I helped her relax, then asked her to imagine herself at a meeting with her colleagues, being calm, confident, and powerful. Once she had this image in her mind, I asked how it felt, what she might say, and how they might respond to her. The next meeting of the team went a great deal more smoothly, and the team members resolved their specific issues fairly readily.

At a broader level, I helped a firm establish a vision for where it wanted to be in ten years—what kind of work it would be doing, what kind of ventures it would be taking on, how it would be organized internally. There was a complex set of steps involved in building this groupwide vision (described in Chapter Six under "Building Understanding"), but one of the steps was simply asking the group members to imagine themselves feeling highly successful ten years on, then asking them what had led to that success and what its components were.

• *Call on multiple senses.* The term "vision" implies visual imagination. Yet some people are more adept at imagining things in terms of sounds or tangible feelings or actions. So you might invoke a vision by asking participants to "imagine" rather than "envision" a scenario, and suggesting they imagine not just visual observations but auditory, tactile, and maybe even olfactory ones.

When I worked with an organization that wanted to change its workplace culture, I asked the participants to imagine an ideal workplace culture and environment—and to think about what they would see walking around the office, how they would interact with each other, what they would be saying and hearing, and how they would feel. An image will be more powerful if it draws on multiple senses.

• *Plan what to do next.* Once you've asked individuals to create visions, you may end up with as many visions as you have participants. You may just want to leave it at that, perhaps pulling a few common themes from the various visions, as I did with the government agency facing budget cuts. In developing a vision statement as part of organizational strategic planning, you may need to identify key differences in individuals' visions and treat them as a series of issues to work through using problem solving. Visions may serve simply as individual motivators, or they may serve as the raw material for developing an agreed-on vision for the group.

Pictures and Visual Images

When we forget about words and create or look at pictures, we access the powers of the brain's right hemisphere. In this way, we often can come up with new ideas, insights, or resolutions.

I once participated in a teambuilding exercise at CDR in which my colleagues and I were each given a sheet of flip-chart paper and asked to draw a house. The basement was to represent the values we brought to our jobs, the first floor the skills we brought, the second floor what we wanted to get out of our jobs, and the attic our hopes and aspirations. We were to draw pictures or symbols that somehow captured each of these, then to present them to the group.

I was skeptical at first, but I found that even though most of us had worked together for years, the images helped us connect to each other in whole new ways. Moreover, in many cases one image had multiple meanings. For example, one colleague who was then new to the organization drew mountains in the "what we want to get out of our jobs" floor of her house. She explained that they represented not only where she now lived but also the difficulty and exhilaration of her steep learning curve in her new job—much like climbing a mountain. That simple image conveyed her experience more immediately and profoundly than words alone could.

In another example, my colleague Louise Smart participated in a workshop led by Geoff Ball in which the introductions were done via pictures. When participants first entered the room, they were asked to draw pictures representing who they were on half-sheets of flip chart paper. Then they introduced themselves, referring to their pictures. What people said during these introductions was "amazing," according to Louise, and "nothing like we would get through the typical introductions."

In yet a different example, I learned from a training participant in a seminar I taught, who was herself a trainer for a county human service agency in Colorado, a story that shows how visual imagery can make a concept real in a way that words can't. The whole state was shifting to a new computer system to manage the administration of food stamps, welfare, and so on. It was my training participant's job to train employees in the new system. The problem was that the state had been talking about the change for so long, and with so many delays, that it seemed to employees as if it would never really happen. Employees seemed to think that if they ignored it, the whole thing would go away.

My trainee and her colleagues needed a way to make the change real to the employees so that they would be motivated to learn the new system. They thought about holding a "funeral" for the old system and sending it to "heaven," but they quickly changed their minds and realized the old system deserved to go to hell instead (people had always found it frustrating). The trainers decorated a trash barrel with paper flames. They rounded up the employees and symbolically sent the old system to hell. The old system had components with acronyms that could be represented by objects: the CACTIS component was represented by a cactus, the COIN component with coins, and the CARS component with toy cars. The trainers threw these objects into "hell," and employees were invited to throw the most hated forms there as well.

Finally, the fact of the change became real, and employees got engaged in learning the new system.

Stories

Stories, as discussed in Chapter Eight, are much more effective than factual arguments in bridging differences and building understanding. This is, in part, because they evoke potent imagery, tapping the intuitive capacity. We can imagine ourselves in the storyteller's shoes and mentally re-create the experience.

I once worked with an organizational conflict in a call center for a large company. The supervisor of the customer service team—the people who actually handled the calls—complained of being excluded from the meetings in which policies were developed about how to respond to particular requests and complaints. She tried to explain that this was to make sure that the policies would reflect her team's expertise and would be practical to implement. However, the policymakers thought her complaint stemmed mainly from her need to feel included personally and to have her status respected, and they didn't take her concern seriously.

During assessment, the supervisor had told me stories not only of explicitly asking to attend meetings and being refused, but also of being stuck asking her staff to implement changes that did not make sense. For example, they were given language to use in response to a particular question that was too lengthy and difficult for callers to comprehend. I suggested that she share a couple of these stories with the others, and I indicated where in the agenda this would be appropriate.

As she told the stories, her colleagues listened with unusual attentiveness. (I have often found in conducting training, too, that participants are riveted by a story, whereas they might yawn while I explain theory or methodology.) They seemed for the first time to understand her complaints. They proceeded to work out a protocol for keeping her updated, getting her input, and including her in meetings.

Stories can be used in a number of ways:

- To help people in conflict understand each other's perspectives and humanize their stances
- To aid in teambuilding—stories can help people get to know one another better
- To energize or inspire people—for example, in a board-staff retreat I had the founder tell the story of the start-up days of the organization, which helped build commitment to the organization's cause
- To provide an example of recurring types of dilemmas so that a group can work on handling them

You might listen for stories during assessment and when you hear one that's particularly powerful, you might encourage the storyteller to tell the story to the full group. You might explicitly invite stories during meetings. You might even put them on agendas.

Metaphors

If we listen carefully as people tell stories or discuss issues, we find that they often use metaphors that potently indicate how they view the world.[6] As facilitators, we can bring these to people's conscious awareness (they often use them unconsciously), help the group derive insights and ideas from them, and perhaps even suggest an alternative metaphor.

Here are some examples:

- One firm had a chronic problem with its partners overcommitting to clients, so that staff would have to work late into the night to meet clients' expectations. Staff called this phenomenon "crashing" and "fire drills," resulting in a commonly used metaphor, "burnout." I highlighted these metaphors and initiated a brief discussion about what they connoted. I later captured the participants' desired model of working in the phrase "well-oiled machine"—that is, they would become more methodical about managing client expectations and planning their work processes. This had some gradual but positive effect.

• A growing company had previously thought of itself as "one big family," but as it grew, some were lamenting the loss of this intimate connection. While I showed appreciation for their grief over this loss, I also discussed with them some of the downsides of the family metaphor. For instance, family members are accepted regardless of the quality of their performance, and families often favor people of the same race and ethnicity. I suggested an alternative metaphor of "community."

• I was helping a government agency overcome conflict between its acquisitions and operations staffs. The acquisitions staff felt they were being treated like "lackeys" and subordinates—that they were not being consulted or included in the process of determining what contractors were needed, what the scope of work should be, and so on. Instead, the operations staff (themselves under a lot of pressure) would often request acquisitions' help at the last minute, not allowing time to do it right.

Both sides acknowledged that the acquisitions staff had valuable expertise that could help the front end of the contracting process. I asked if it would make sense to think of the acquisitions staff as "consultants" to the operations staff on acquisitions matters. A consultant, I explained, is accountable to the client but is not a subordinate.

Meanwhile, the operations staff explained a reason for their resistance: the acquisitions staff, whenever presented with an idea from operations, would only "throw up roadblocks"—what the errors and dangers were in their thoughts or actions so far. What operations needed were positive suggestions and guidance. I rephrased this as being "shown the right path" for doing acquisitions properly.

Metaphors, like pictures, quickly access our intuitive capabilities. A simple phrase like "road blocks" speaks volumes about an experience. The extreme facilitator can "pounce" on metaphors and (to mix my metaphors) "milk" them for meaning and implications.

Drama

Once during an annual staff retreat I participated in, we came back from a break to find the front of the room transformed into a makeshift stage and members of the retreat-planning committee transformed into actors. The "set" included a conference table and chairs. The cast then performed a rendition of how we typically started our internal meetings. The scheduled meeting time had arrived. One staff member came along, peeked in the conference room, saw it empty, and said, "Oh, I guess I have time to make that phone call," and walked away. Then another colleague looked in the conference room, also saw no one there, and said, "Hmm, guess I can finish writing that e-mail." Another and another came by and did the same thing.

We all laughed hysterically, recognizing in this scene our own behavior, which we'd been only semiconscious of previously. For years, our meetings typically started fifteen to twenty minutes later than the scheduled start time because of this chronic pattern. If someone had simply said, "Can we do something about starting our meetings more punctually?" it would have had little impact. In fact, we might have dismissed it as uptight whining. In contrast, this little bit of drama brought about an immediate and surprisingly permanent change in our habits.

In another situation, we were holding an offsite retreat for part of our staff. To help in teambuilding, one of my colleagues led us through an exercise in which we silently formed a "human sculpture" representing the organization and how we all worked together. One colleague knelt on the floor, representing the foundation, the center of gravity. Another touched someone in the middle of the sculpture but reached with the other hand away from the group, representing being part of the organization but working outside it and in some way being apart from it. The sculpture helped us better understand how we each saw our roles—not just our formal job descriptions but the informal roles we played in the group.

The interesting thing is that we first moved *intuitively* to where and in what formation we felt we belonged, and only afterward found the words to make sense of it. With the help of a ground rule of total silence, the exercise primarily used our intuition. It allowed us to gain insights about how we all fit together and worked together that were previously outside our conscious awareness.

A final example occurred in a group of advanced-practice nurses I was consulting to. My colleague Susan Wildau and I designed a simulation of a meeting of these nurses and the physicians they worked with, based on the real-life meetings they had described to us. Even though all the roles were played by nurses, those playing the doctors took control of the agenda and dominated the meeting, and those playing the nurses passively let this happen. I pointed out the dynamics as soon as they occurred, and their eyes seemed to pop out of their heads. They immediately learned how they might change these destructive dynamics, such as by stating that the meeting was not following the agenda and suggesting that the two groups discuss and agree on all agenda changes.

Theater and creative movement require a willingness on the part of the group to go considerably beyond the usual sitting-around-the-conference-table format. I once asked members of a group if they might like to use a skit to act out some of the conflictual dynamics in their organization. They wisely declined—the sensitive people in that particular case might have been offended by the sight of other people role-playing their inappropriate behavior. Still, in the right circumstances, the potential for using theater and creative movement to productive ends is enormous.

Music

If drama is unusual in facilitation, music is more so. Music goes straight to the heart and has the power to help people see beyond their differences.

An example of this involved Turkish and Greek Cypriots who participated jointly in a peacebuilding training conducted by the Institute for Multi-Track Diplomacy at a time when Cypriots from both sides of the "Green Line" dividing the island were forbidden to cross to the other side. These participants were proponents of peace, yet there were still conflicting perspectives and considerable distrust among them.

One evening after dinner (and long after the formal meeting time was over), participants were sitting together, drinking wine and talking. One participant had brought a guitar, and participants were passing it around and playing songs. At one point, when the Greek-Cypriot participants were singing a folk song, the Turkish-Cypriot participants found, to their astonishment, that they knew the same song (but in their own language). They all continued singing the song, alternating between the Turkish-language and Greek-language versions. The poignancy and the sense of unity were palpable.[7]

Music can help groups understand each other and transcend differences in ways that are otherwise nearly impossible.

Your Own Intuitive Capacity

Your own intuitive capacity can be a tremendous tool, not only in tapping a group's intuition and creativity but in many other ways. The ability to "read" a group, for instance, is primarily intuitive— you pick up a few specific clues almost unconsciously and conclude that the group is excited, bored, skeptical, disappointed, relieved, or whatever. Understanding the dynamics of conflict is also sometimes intuitive. What's really going on for this person? What's the real reason she's so angry? Getting a handle on a group's culture is intuitive—Chapter Three gave you clues to look for, but you won't have time to spend months doing an ethnographic study. You'll have to be observant for clues and quickly form a picture of the culture in your mind. Finally, process design brings together intuition and creativity. You intuit what this particular group needs, imagine it playing out to see if it would work, and weave your ideas creatively into an agenda and a set of techniques or activities to support it.

In contrast to your intellectual capacity, your intuitive capacity will probably not be helped much by formal education (with the possible exception of artistic fields of study). In fact, it might be hindered. Formal education tends to favor the scientific method, treat hunches as suspect, and submit all ideas to logical rigor. Science is a marvel, but an exclusive focus on it leaves our intuitive abilities immature and undeveloped.

Incidentally, the danger of intuition is that it is hard sometimes to separate true intuition from prejudice. If you have a hunch, for example, that someone is not very smart, is it because you've genuinely picked up clues as to his intelligence? Or is it because he's ugly, of a different ethnicity, disabled in some respect, or a second-language speaker? For this reason, it pays to try to get some other confirmation of your hunches when important and feasible. It also pays to sharpen your intuitive ability over time to the point where you know when you can trust it.

Fortunately, building your intuition is fun. (Creativity was addressed in Chapter Two; we'll focus on intuition here.) I am lucky to have a highly intuitive husband, who has been an inspiration for me to develop my own intuition. The main thing it takes is practice—ideally with some way to test the accuracy of your intuitive insights. Here are some ways to strengthen your intuitive capacity:

- Be open to intuition. Listen to your gut. Remain open-minded that prejudice might be at work, but don't dismiss your instincts as illogical or baseless.

- When you meet someone new, try sizing them up on sight, or after an initial, brief conversation. As you get to know them, you can find out where you were right and where you were wrong.

- With people you know well, see if you can detect from the moment you see them what's going on in their lives: What emotions are they experiencing? What might be happening that has led to these feelings? Then ask how they're doing, explore as appropriate, and see if you were right.

- Practice predicting the future. Who will win the next election? What will become of your organization's new initiative? Which team will win the big game? Remember your predictions and see if you can improve your rate of accuracy.

- When you have a difficult decision to make, ask yourself what your gut is telling you, and compare that to what logical analysis is telling you. See which ends up leading you in the right direction. Try also integrating them—what did you pick up by intuition that your pros and cons list (or other analytical approach) failed to account for?

- Try to remember your dreams, and interpret them. The dreams themselves are an intuitive experience that's mostly outside of our control (some people claim they can manipulate their dreams—I can't), but the process of assessing what the images represent is also intuitive.

Early in my career I worked on a large project led by a difficult, capricious manager I'll call Ed. He frequently made arbitrary changes in his instructions to the team, delegated authority and then seized it back, and generally made the work extremely stressful. I was an entry-level employee, and he was three levels above me in the hierarchy. My immediate supervisor shared my feelings and was doing everything she could to handle the situation (to little avail).

While this was going on, I had a dream about large, cockroach-like insects burrowing under the skin of my arm. I woke up feeling creepy, and I had no idea what this image symbolized. I told my husband about the dream, and, using his well-honed intuition, he said the dream was obviously about Ed. Then it all fell into place in my mind: I was letting Ed get under my skin—figuratively in real life, literally in the dream. This image helped me learn to distance myself emotionally from the situation, accept what I could not change, and just get through the project.

I have since improved my own ability, through practice, to determine what the feelings and imagery in a dream relate to in my own life. This requires less logical analysis and more whole-picture, right-brain intuition.

As your intuition improves, begin using it in facilitation. Use your intuition to offer hypothetical insights that may help the group or help you understand an individual's perspective. You might offer an observation such as, "Sometimes in situations like this, employees feel they're being intentionally slighted, when in fact the manager's mind is just occupied with something else" or "Sometimes in intergovernmental relations, people can feel defensive about their agency's turf and what authority they have over what. In those situations, it's often helpful to focus on the underlying goal you're trying to achieve." You can check whether the "sometimes" scenario is indeed happening here. If it is, the group will benefit, and you'll get credit for having a lot of insight and wisdom.

The intuitive capacity is a remarkable human ability that's waiting to be tapped in helping groups deal with extreme challenges. We can learn to cultivate this innate ability in ourselves as well as in our groups. For even more unconventional approaches, we turn next to the role of spirituality in facilitation.

Notes

1. Edwards, *The New Drawing on the Right Side of the Brain*, pp. 27–47.
2. See, for instance, Fisher and Ury, *Getting to Yes*, pp. 62–67.

3. Blake and Mouton, in *Solving Costly Organizational Conflicts*, call this "developing the optimal model," pp. 63–66.
4. Blake and Mouton, *Solving Costly Organizational Conflicts*, pp. 67–68.
5. Boulding, *Building a Global Civic Culture*, pp. 172–176.
6. Lederach, *Preparing for Peace*, pp. 73–78.
7. James Notter, private communication to author, 2004.

Chapter Eleven

The Spiritual Capacity

Helping Groups Transcend Their Limitations

What could spirituality possibly have to do with facilitation? Physical, emotional, intellectual, and intuitive abilities all seem relevant, but what point is there in calling on a group's spiritual capacity?

If you look at the essence of spirituality, separating it from particular religious institutions or traditions, much of it concerns helping people rise above our base, selfish, animal natures—to transcend them. By tapping people's spiritual capacity, we help them to be their best, to rise to the toughest of challenges, and possibly even to make peace with their enemies.

Any extreme challenge, especially severe conflict, can bring out people's worst. We can all think of terrible things we've said or done to others when we were angry or felt under siege—things we may not be proud of but that we felt we had to do to protect ourselves or to even the score. This can range from yelling at our spouses or children in anger to things much more severe. To give a particularly extreme example, the genocide committed by Rwandan Hutus against Tutsis and moderate Hutus occurred after a systematic propaganda campaign led Hutus to believe that if they did not kill Tutsis, the Tutsis would kill them. They felt their only choices were to kill or be killed.[1]

Where do some people get the strength to rise above this tendency to commit evil in order to protect oneself from evil?

At the Abu Ghraib prison in Iraq, where Americans detained and interrogated Iraqi prisoners, there were abuses involving humiliation and psychological torture as well as some actual physical torture in 2003 and 2004. The psychological torture included such things as making male prisoners pose nude with each other as if performing homosexual acts and putting dog collars around prisoners' necks while they lay on the floor—this in a culture in which homosexuality is frowned upon and dogs are considered filthy pests. The physical torture included a gamut from letting dogs maul the prisoners to suffocating and beating them.

During investigation of these abuses, it became clear that such behavior had become common at the prison and was on some level condoned. The army reservist who was photographed holding a dog leash around the neck of a naked Iraqi prisoner (she was charged with physical assault as well) explained that she was acting under orders from superiors. More interestingly, she saw the point of the orders: she said the acts of humiliation were "psy ops" (psychological operations) and were succeeding in their aim of rendering prisoners more forthcoming during interrogation.[2]

When I read this, I suddenly understood the point of view that could make these repulsive acts seem reasonable. It was a simple case of the ends justifying the means, in the eyes of the perpetrators. They were willing to commit acts of evil they saw as relatively minor in order to win a war and, in a misperception fed by the U.S. government, to prevent another terrorist act on the scale of the September 11, 2001, attacks.

Yet while some saw a logic in performing acts of humiliation, others protested. Military police officer Spc. Matthew Wisdom said that witnessing these acts made him physically ill, and he demanded reassignment away from the cellblock where the abuse happened. Platoon leader Sgt. 1st Class Shannon Snider "once barked so loudly at soldiers stomping on prisoners' toes that one witness later told investigators, 'I never thought that that voice could come out of somebody so little.'" Both of these and several others complained to their superiors repeatedly.[3] Why did these soldiers resist these injustices when others got caught up in their "logic"? Why do some people act out of ongoing fear or need to lash out against enemies while some have the courage to stop the cycle of cruelty?

While this question probably can't be answered definitively, I believe part of the answer lies in our spiritual core—not necessarily organized religion or conscious spirituality, but inner, spiritual strength. In my view, therefore, spirituality is an important element of extreme facilitation, particularly when severe conflict is involved.

So what does spirituality in facilitation look like—prayers, rituals, sermons? New-age crystals, pyramids, chanting? None of the above, necessarily. Calling forth our participants' spirituality need not be visible, audible, or detectable in any way. Instead, our own spirituality, magnified by the power we have at the front of the room, can help invoke it in others.

If we succeed in doing this, what is the result? In my experience, there are rare and seemingly inexplicable moments that groups experience as magic. These might include moments when

- Erstwhile enemies recognize each other's humanity
- People feel hope or faith in the face of pessimistic circumstances
- People let go of resistance, hidden agendas, or selfish aims in favor of serving the greater good

Spirituality and Facilitation

What is spirituality? Analyzing spirituality is worse than explaining a joke—it drains all the magic from it. Still, to look at spirituality independent of any particular religion, we need to examine the common themes across spiritual traditions.[4] Some of these include love, faith and its close relative hope, gratitude, truthfulness, and community.

Love

Most religious traditions enjoin followers to show compassion, caring, and love for other people or perhaps all living things. The ability to feel compassion or brotherly love even toward people we disagree with or dislike is a profound spiritual capacity.

What's more, everyone needs love, even the most aloof, intim-idating people. In fact, they're often the ones who are most in need of love. This provides a ready entrée for facilitators: if we can help people feel loved, not only can we win them over and establish a relationship with them, which on its own is valuable, but we can help free them from the sense of siege and of living in a dangerous world that renders them suspicious and hostile out of self-protection.

Offering love need not be overt. You needn't go up to the grumpy bully and hug him, kiss him, or tell him you love him. Instead, you just naturally exude it. Have you ever met someone who seemed to exude love? In some cases it's overt, but for other people, it just seems to radiate from them. It's something in their eyes, or something you feel when you're around them.

The only way to cultivate this kind of aura of love is to feel it. Genuinely. Depending on your beliefs, you may regard love as orig-inating with God, and so the worship of God expands the love you can offer others. Alternatively, you may regard love as originating within your innate spiritual self. Regardless, any time I have not been able to cultivate a heartfelt sense of brotherly love toward people I've worked with as a facilitator, I have failed to form a trust-ing relationship with them, and I've also failed to break through their intransigence.

Early in my career, for example, I was working with the owner of a motel. He was part of a planning process for redeveloping the tourist area of a small town that served as a stop-off point for many travelers on the way to mountain resorts. The town wanted to use the power of eminent domain to condemn and raze the existing old hotels and restaurants. In return, it was offering significant com-pensation, tax breaks for property owners to rebuild, and the prospect of more and better-heeled travelers staying in the town and increasing profits for all. The owner of this particular motel was dead-set against the whole redevelopment plan.

He also struck me as rude, selfish, and self-aggrandizing. I didn't like him, and I couldn't get past it. While I could certainly appreciate the merits of some of his arguments, I couldn't manage to feel any love for him as a human being. Perhaps as a result, he never yielded an inch from his intransigent opposition to the city's plans.

In contrast, I once cofacilitated an organizational meeting for the faculty of a university department. My cofacilitator was CDR partner Mary Margaret Golten, a person who naturally exudes love. One of the issues we were addressing was the professors' tendency to burrow in their own individual worlds and avoid any engagement in the collective life of the department, despite severe conflict that needed to be resolved.

One participant was known to be particularly averse to meetings and departmentwide functions. At one meeting, we had unusually low attendance. As Mary Margaret and I opened the meeting with questions about what we could accomplish with the smaller group, this professor began rising from his chair to leave, muttering, "Well, this isn't going anywhere."

Immediately, Mary Margaret replied, "No, why don't you stay, until we decide what we're doing." How did she get away with being so directive? She was decisive and firm, but her characteristic warmth was still there. The professor slunk back in his chair like a schoolboy and stayed—and participated!—for the rest of the meeting. We found, moreover, that underneath his grumpiness lay some valid concerns that merited discussion.

Going back to the motel owner, there are several things I could do differently today to overcome my blockage to feeling brotherly love toward him. These are things anyone can do when they can't find love for someone difficult.

- *Look for the pain.* In general, I believe that everyone has a good inner core, and that their negative ways, from the distasteful to the downright evil, arise from pain or deprivation they have suffered sometime in their life. Most people who commit cruelty were victims of cruelty at some point in their past. If we can understand the pain that underlies the negativity, we can invoke our compassion.

The motel owner was an earnest businessman trying to eke out some modest success in a small tourist town. His customers, he explained, were often on vacation flings, partying and leaving wrecks behind them and often lying about such matters as bringing in dogs. He also felt that the city government took too lightly his dread of seeing the cherished establishment he'd worked so long to build knocked to the ground. He constantly felt trampled, and now more than ever. These were some of the sources of his obstinacy.

• *Approach rather than avoid.* There are many people who at first seem unlikable to me until I understand them better. Unfortunately, we all tend to avoid people we can't relate to—birds of a feather really do flock together. As facilitators, we need to do the exact opposite: work harder to understand the people we can't relate to. We need to have one-on-one conversations with them and try to understand their background and how they formed the views or tendencies we at first can't understand.

I once had to interview people from a point of view opposite of mine as part of an assignment in graduate school. I have always supported a right to abortion. I used to think antiabortion activists supported the subjugation of women and were moralistically judgmental regarding women's sexual behavior.

I went to an abortion clinic and interviewed antiabortion activists demonstrating outside. I consciously put my own views aside and pried my mind open to understanding theirs. I came to realize that these activists truly saw a fetus's life as equal in status and value to that of a person who has been born. It follows from this belief that killing a fetus is no more a valid "choice" than it is for me to kill an adult.

I still don't agree—I don't see a tiny, new embryo as a full-blown person. However, I recognize that my views on this are as arbitrary as theirs, and I've come to see the abortion issue as one on which reasonable minds may differ. I came honestly to be able to love those pro-life activists, and I believe I could work with them effectively as a facilitator.

• *Understand our own prejudices.* We need to acknowledge our prejudices and stereotypes and to understand their genesis. Understanding why we hold a prejudice drains it of its potency. Some stereotypes are culturally pervasive and we unconsciously absorb them—racism is an obvious example. Some biases come from past pain we've experienced—if we had an abusive parent, for example, we'll have a hard time with anyone who reminds us of that parent. Finally, some prejudices come from seeing in others things we don't like about ourselves—for example, it's often said that the person who hates gays or lesbians may be in denial of some tiny homosexual desire they harbor themselves.

This latter type of prejudice was at work with me in the case of the motel owner. Looking back on it now, I realize that he fit into a stereotype I had that might best be described as the "ugly American."

In the years I lived overseas, I saw many American tourists who made me want to hide my nationality. In England, they were loud and abrupt where the cultural norm was to speak quietly and delicately. In France, they could only complain about the lack of the right kind of toilets and toilet paper instead of appreciating the fabulous art, architecture, and cuisine. In Egypt, they could only condemn the country's dust and dirt or the corruption-ridden bureaucracy instead of understanding the wonderful spirit and warmth of this people who had seen foreign rulers come and go for two millennia. The motel owner reminded me of these kinds of Americans.

Yet I'm American and am proud to be one. While being American means many positive things, I too can sometimes be ignorant or contemptuous of others' cultures or overly attached to my material comforts. The tourists I dreaded encountering were living examples of those tendencies in myself I'd rather not admit to having, and on some level in my mind the motel owner was one of them.

Since the case with the motel owner, I've had many occasions to work with people who initially repelled me but whom I eventually came to understand, respect, and love in the brotherly sense.

From working with such a broad variety of people, I've overcome many of my prejudices and continue to work through those that remain.

I am reminded of the work of international mediator Adam Curle, who writes of the importance of feeling genuine caring, respect, and friendship in his conflict resolution work, even with leaders who have committed acts of barbaric violence.[5] If he can feel love for such evildoers, I can find it in my soul to love a cantankerous motel owner.

Faith and Hope

One of the most profound interventions facilitators can make is to lend hope to a situation that otherwise looks hopeless. This hope may spring from our faith in God, our faith in human potential, or our faith that good will ultimately prevail.

We have probably all experienced how we reach new heights of human accomplishment when someone has faith in us. Maybe it was the coach who knew you could beat your own best scores or fastest times if you just kept practicing and practicing; the parent who trusted that your classmates would eventually stop teasing you if you held your head high and ignored them; the professor who expressed confidence that you could ace that difficult assignment if you put your mind to it. When someone places such faith in us, somehow we find new strength to achieve the impossible.

Hope has something of a placebo effect. There is something about going to a doctor for an illness and having that doctor seem to know what to do that starts making us feel better even before any treatment has begun. A similar thing can happen with a facilitator. There may be bitter conflicts, dire circumstances, bewildering complexities, or overwhelming emotions. Participants may feel exhausted, defeated, or helpless. If a facilitator enters who can calmly examine the group just as a doctor examines a patient, there is an injection of hope. If the facilitator approaches the situation with faith in the group members and hope that something positive can come of their effort, somehow group members feel their own commitment and hope refreshed.

Hope and faith do not substitute for a sober assessment of the chances for success, as addressed in Chapter Five (Contracting). Rather, the two complement each other. You might give a conservative estimate of the prospects of achieving a goal, while maintaining hope that participants will rise beyond what is realistically predictable and having faith that participants have the capacity to exceed their limitations.

Once a colleague and I worked with division directors in a government agency who had been treating each other horribly. They had taken their complaints about each other to the media and were fighting it out in the press. With our help, the directors reached consensus about the underlying issues and restored a considerable amount of harmony.

We later reconvened the group to collectively present the results of the facilitated discussions to the agency administrator. The administrator's executive assistant, after listening to the presentation, walked over to us facilitators and said, "If you ever need a reference, I'd be happy to provide it, because I think I've just witnessed a miracle." We never promised this degree of success, but we also had faith that the participants could transcend their vicious behavior, and they did.

Sometimes I have given brief words of inspiration indicating the faith or hope I have. This may be as simple as saying that I've dealt with groups in much tougher circumstances and they pulled through it. In one case, I made a longer statement to a group of leaders locked in combat that they all had the capacity to be visionaries and to see a way out of this deadlock. I notice that when I make these kinds of minispeeches, everyone's attention is riveted. I think people often hunger for a little encouragement, faith, and hope.

I recently met the executive director of the Rio Grande Council of Governments, Jake Brisbin, while he was attending a training I conducted. Even though he'd never had any formal training in facilitation, he found himself frequently convening leaders of member local governments to help them negotiate the resolution of fierce battles, often involving water distribution. Jake said he began every such effort with the simple declaration, "We *will* get through this." It seemed to work. In his six years at the helm of the Council of Governments, there has not been one lawsuit filed by one member municipality against another.

Gratitude

There seemed to be another reason for Jake's success. He was grateful—for his job, his wife, his children—and he exuded positive energy and warmth. He had suffered an injury while fighting in Vietnam that forced him into a wheelchair for about a month per year, but he was even grateful for the injury. Why? "Because for the rest of the year, every time I get up out of a chair, I'm thankful." How could this spirit of gratitude not rub off on the local leaders he worked with, helping them be less selfish and more magnanimous?

Most religious traditions emphasize gratitude toward God or other spiritual figures for all the goodness we enjoy. Life is hard, and we can always find things to complain about. It's easy to direct all our attention and energy to things that need to change—problems and deprivations and losses. It takes a conscious effort to appreciate what is right in our lives—hence the various prayers and rituals that exist to affirm and celebrate our bounty (think of saying grace before a meal, for instance).

All of us, no matter how rich or poor, can probably find examples of both abundance and scarcity in our own surroundings. People commonly refer to a "scarcity mentality" as a source of hostile, turf-protecting behavior. I believe there is considerable truth in this. If people feel there are adequate good things to go around—whether money, recognition, power, or love—they are less likely to feel the need to fight over it. Encouraging people to count their blessings, literally, is one way to help foster this attitude.

Of course, this best starts by counting our own blessings. The resulting positive attitude will be contagious. Do I go into a group meeting cursing how early I had to get up or how overworked I am or how difficult this client has been, or do I gratefully accept the opportunity to connect with new people, to learn, to help, and to be creative? Whichever attitude I bring, I know it shows. I have seen other facilitators expose their attitudes to groups inadvertently.

With our own gratitude as a foundation, we can then ask questions that invite others to look at the bright side: What's the best thing that has happened in this meeting today? What do you appreciate about the other participants in this group? In what ways will things be okay even if you don't get the specific outcome you are seeking? How can you make the best of it?

I recently worked with a small firm in which employees felt chronically overworked and underappreciated. When I scratched the surface a bit, I found that the partners of the firm felt almost the same way. On the second afternoon of a two-day meeting, we worked through a great deal of decision making and problem solving. I had put on the agenda a closing item in which participants were invited to say what they appreciated about each other—either their superiors, subordinates, or peers; either something specific or something general. In the time pressure of finishing the more substantive tasks, I almost sacrificed this agenda item. The exercise seemed a little silly, and I wasn't exactly sure to what extent it would suit this group's culture.

As we finished up the other tasks, the "appreciation" agenda item got squeezed from fifteen minutes down to about three. On the spot, I decided to go ahead with it anyway, in part because I had no better idea for a closing activity. I posed the question to the full group, gave them fifteen seconds to think, and then said anyone could just shout out their responses.

I was moved by what resulted. People thanked individual staff members who had worked hard to make difficult but important changes; they thanked the whole organization for the career opportunities it offered; they recognized various departments or units for their contributions. Some people's eyes welled up as they were thanked. Despite the hard work of the preceding two-day meeting and the general fatigue of all involved, there was an air of energy and enthusiasm as we closed the meeting.

Of course, I followed this by thanking all of them sincerely for the opportunity to serve their remarkable group.

Truthfulness

Morality is a theme that spans many religions, and what it means differs considerably across different faiths and cultures. One piece of morality that is fairly universal and that I've found crucial to facilitation is truthfulness. To facilitators, this means not only being honest ourselves but also promoting honesty in our clients and participants. Lest we get too self-righteous, however, we also need to be understanding and compassionate of those who might be inclined to be less than truthful. We need to promote honesty in a humble, loving way.

I once facilitated the development of a land-use plan for a state wildlife refuge. A developer was interested in building an eco-tourism site near a town within the refuge, and several groups opposed this. The town stood to benefit from the tax revenue that would be generated by the ecotourism site. The facilitation participants included the state agency that was charged with developing the plan, as well as the town, the developer, and various public interest groups. While there were several points of disagreement in developing the plan, the tourism site was the most controversial. The public interest groups suspected that the state agency was not only beholden to the developer but also under the undue influence of the town. Their distrust of both the state and the town was extremely high.

Midway through the facilitation, I learned that the state agency and the town had been discussing a cost-sharing plan by which the town would pay about a third of the costs of the land-use planning process, including the costs of technical studies and facilitation. A representative of the state agency mentioned this information to me in passing and requested I keep it in confidence, explaining that the cost-sharing plan might not "look right" to the public and the participating stakeholders.

At first I agreed, eager both to please my paying client and to demonstrate my trustworthiness. Immediately after this conversation, though, I could only think of how dishonest this would be to the public and to the participants. I put in a call to the state employee who had told me this news, but I had to wait hours for a return call. In those hours, I grew increasingly agitated and indignant. How could they be so dishonest? How could they think that it was ethically acceptable for a partisan interest to help fund the process, especially when they intended not to disclose this to the public? I also made assumptions about the town's intentions in cofunding the study: clearly, in my mind, they were purchasing influence.

By the time the state representative called me back, I was ready to explode. I unleashed my accusations. He calmed me down (what a role reversal!), and he clarified several points on which I had made false assumptions. First, it already looked like this cost-sharing arrangement was not going to go forward (thank God—I no longer had a dilemma to face), not because of ethical concerns exactly, but because of "strings" that might be attached to the town's offer of funds. Second, the state had approached the town about the arrangement, not the reverse, because the state was facing a severe budget crunch. The town had already planned to spend money on a study of this ecotourism proposal, and it turned out that the land-use plan would be incorporating the same questions, so it seemed to make sense to economize and conserve public funds. In other words, there was no nefarious intent.

This example illustrates two points. First, we need to promote our clients' and participants' truthfulness (as well as our own, of course). Had the state and the developer carried on with a secret cost-sharing plan, I would have continued to oppose it, ultimately stepping down from the project if necessary. Even if the town's funds had no substantive influence on the plan, the arrangement would have been a breach of public trust.

Second, when we promote truthfulness, we need to do so in a humble and compassionate rather than self-righteous way. I fell into the trap of assuming the worst of the state agency and the town and of reading in evil intent where there was none. I attacked the state representative with my accusations. Instead, I should have approached the matter with questions that first sought to understand the motivations and then raised my ethical concerns in a caring, understanding manner. This would not have lessened my resolve to promote truthfulness; it's just a different, and probably more effective, means of doing so.

Community

We move further from individual experiences and attitudes to a group level of spirituality. Why is it that so many spiritual traditions involve either congregations or strong values about service? What is it about a group or collective that is necessary to spirituality?

The answer, I believe, lies in the concept of community. Human beings need to draw strength and support from others, to identify with a group, and to feel a sense of belonging. We also probably need to see ourselves as contributing to a community. While people seem to need this to different degrees depending on personality and stage in life, it's clear that people generally do need to give and not just to take.

We are not purely selfish beings. There is too much evidence to the contrary.[6] Why do people give to charity, leave tips for people they'll never see again, or do good Samaritan deeds that few will ever see or know about? Some of this has to do with serving our own individual identities as good, decent people, but some of it also has to do with serving the community to which we belong.

It seems to me we are at our best as human beings when we're both enriched by belonging to a community and can see ourselves as productive contributors to that community. There is always a balance to strike between our individual freedom and autonomy and our need for belonging, and that tension often produces conflict. When we do strike this balance—when we can feel a sufficient degree of personal freedom within the role we play in a community—both the individual and the community flourish. This seems to make the most of our God-given gifts of independence and interconnection.

What if we could draw on this community strength, this desire both to belong and to contribute, when we're facilitating groups in severe conflict? What would it take for belligerent participants to give up some of their own selfish aims for the benefit of the larger group, or better yet, to see them as compatible? What if we could help participants draw strength from the others in the group rather than seeing themselves only in competition with them?

We can't force it, but I believe we can facilitate the occurrence of these things. One way is to care about the group genuinely, which helps group members feel cared for and enhance their sense of belonging. This is another application of love as described above. Here are some additional ways:

• *Seek ways to affirm the group identity, the relationships within the group, and the* esprit de corps. All the myriad teambuilding activities that focus attention explicitly on relationships help do this, but even in the most task-oriented groups that want nothing to do with teambuilding, there are innumerable ways to affirm group identity. We can commend the group's achievements, remind them that they have far more potential as a group than as separate individuals, have someone overview the group's history, or establish tasks for the group to achieve together. Identification with and relationships within the group are powerful motivators for people to serve the needs of the group.

On three different occasions, I have had someone overview the history of an organization I facilitated for. One was a nonprofit arts organization, one was a medical practice, and one was a political consulting firm. While this was done for a different purpose in each case, in all cases it helped participants build a sense of pride, of belonging, and of being part of a project larger than themselves.

• *Affirm people's identities as good, decent, contributing members of the community.* This can be done directly through praise or indirectly through implication. We might ask participants what they do in their personal lives and show interest in their activities that contribute to the community. We might acknowledge that the "difficult" participant is trying to do right by the people she represents. We might ask outright what she thinks would be the good and right thing to do in this situation.

I once had a difficult participant in a contentious public-policy facilitation dealing with land-use planning. He was an advocate of alternative transportation. He rode his bicycle almost everywhere, showing up to meetings with his pants tucked into his socks and his bicycle helmet on. He complained loudly if meetings were scheduled in places accessible only by car. He frequently jumped into discussions at inappropriate moments to make his pitch for mass transit and bike paths. People tended to roll their eyes whenever he opened his mouth.

Whenever I spoke to him, though, I kept in mind his admirable sense of cause and his vision of a more livable and sustainable world. I asked him questions about his tiny, cash-strapped organization with appreciation and encouragement. I eventually earned his trust and was able to coach him to be a more constructive participant. I believe that his trust and his openness to my feedback depended on my recognition of his positive contributions.

• *Encourage an atmosphere of welcoming and accepting all group members, even if specific negative behaviors must be confronted.* A sense of acceptance and belonging helps prevent the need for a self-protective, kill-or-be-killed mentality. When confronting negative behaviors, we can avoid making individuals feel attacked or ostracized. This may mean confronting the person privately rather than embarrassing him publicly. It also means approaching him as an ally with helpful advice about how he can persuade others more effectively by being more constructive, cooperative, or polite. This doesn't mean you can't be firm. You often must be firm, but you might also add how much you value the person and his contributions.

I once worked with a children's advocacy organization that had a dual strategy of trying to elect candidates friendly to its perspective and trying to influence public opinion. During one election year, one manager in the organization became convinced that the only strategy the group should focus on was getting pro-child candidates elected. She herself worked extremely hard to do this. Her colleagues appreciated her work but felt that it was important to keep up the longer-term work of influencing public opinion so that any candidate elected would have public support to make child-friendly policies.

When we were discussing the agenda at the beginning of their planning retreat, this manager repeatedly interrupted others by saying, "All I want to talk about is how we elect pro-child candidates" and "How will that agenda item help us elect pro-child candidates?" She was hijacking the meeting. On the third instance of her interrupting like this (after my more subtle interventions failed), I interrupted her interruption, and said "Just a minute, just a minute" firmly until she stopped.

I then said calmly, "You have been a leader in helping this group focus its attention on pro-child candidates, and you've done a great deal to find the most effective ways of doing this. What I'm hearing from others, though, is that the public opinion work remains equally important and can complement the electoral work." Then I asked the group, "Is that correct?" and others piped in expressing their frustration with her behavior but also their appreciation of her important efforts.

Prior to this meeting, I had been concerned that this manager was going to resign from her job and pursue the pro-child agenda by working full-time for a political campaign. Instead, she remained with the group, and she became a much more cooperative participant.

• *Encourage the group to work to understand what underlies others' intransigence.* When people seem stuck in a seemingly unreasonable position, there is often fear, an unmet need, or an unachieved goal behind it. We can try to enlist all group members as allies of the intransigent party in finding a solution that meets his or her needs while also meeting the needs of the rest of the group (the coveted "win-win" solution).

• *Encourage group members to consider the greater good, particularly when win-win solutions cannot be found.* We might simply ask what is the greater good to be served, or ask participants to imagine themselves in each other's shoes. We might ask them to consider the general public interest, if the issue is a public-policy one. In organizational facilitation, we might ask what's in the best interests of the organization or the people it is intended to serve (customers, clients, or service recipients).

If people feel that the end justifies their questionable means, we can ask what kind of precedent they might be setting. The new CEO in a company I worked for had succeeded in dislodging the prior CEO by waging a behind-the-scenes campaign to discredit him. The prior CEO, in the eyes of the new one, was a destructive, short-sighted tyrant. The new CEO felt he'd done the right thing by unseating him and taking his position. Not surprisingly, however, he had a hard time gaining the trust of the rest of the executive team after this power maneuver.

The new CEO felt somewhat remorseful over his tactics but also felt it was for the good of the company. Over the course of several months, while my colleague and I facilitated a process to unite the executive team and address a range of specific issues, I worked individually with the new CEO, emphasizing above-board, open, and honest approaches to leadership and involving the full group in decision making. He was never able to regain the trust of some, and there were a few resignations. However, he never again used deceptive or destructive tactics (we kept in touch for several years), and his company grew and flourished under his leadership.

He let on to me after I'd worked with him for almost a year that his wife remarked how much I had changed him for the better. This shocked me, because changing him had never been my intent. I do think, however, that he had been experiencing personal uncertainty about whether the ends justified the means, and I helped steer him gently toward a more principled, less Machiavellian style of leadership.

• *Ask people to think long term.* This helps people think beyond their narrow self-interest to what kind of legacy they're leaving behind. We might ask participants what story they'd like to tell in ten years about the role they played in solving this problem or what they'd like to see the next generation do with respect to this issue.

Former President Carter tells a story of mediating the Camp David accords. At the last minute, the negotiations had reached an impasse when the Israelis objected to Carter's promise to produce an official letter restating the United States's long-held position on Jerusalem. Negotiators were packing to leave. Carter had come up with an idea for altering the text in the hope of making it acceptable to the Israelis. Lower-level Israeli negotiators thought the situation was hopeless, that there could be no acceptable wording. Before presenting the text to Israeli Prime Minister Menachem Begin, Carter gave him a set of autographed pictures, addressed personally to each of Begin's grandchildren. Begin read each name aloud, and his eyes welled up as he told Carter about each child. Shortly after, Begin accepted the revised letter, clearing the way for finalization of the Camp David accords that are still in effect today.[7] Perhaps the thought of his grandchildren's future helped Begin overcome his entrenched position to help make peace.

We often can promote people's sense of belonging to the group and the broader community and to feel some sense of duty to contribute positively to that community. Love, faith and hope, gratitude, truthfulness, and community are among the ways we can help fortify people's own spiritual strength and tap the spiritual capacity in group members to transcend their worst human tendencies and reach their higher human potential. All of these depend heavily on our own spiritual capacity.

Your Own Spiritual Capacity

As should now be clear, your own spiritual capacity is key to drawing on the spiritual strength of groups. You promote love in the group by offering genuine love, caring, and compassion. You promote faith and hope by having faith in people's ability to transcend and hope in the possibilities that may result. You promote an attitude of gratitude and abundance by being thankful for your own

blessings. You promote honesty and truthfulness first by exemplify-
ing it. You ignite the desire to contribute to community by helping
provide a sense of community.

No one is perfect at all this. I'm certainly not. I feel that as long
as I keep these goals in the forefront of my mind and strive toward
them continually, I'm headed in the right direction.

Instead of posing fraudulently as a spiritual adviser, I offer some
questions that you may choose to consider in developing your own
spiritual capacity and strength.

- I have suggested love, faith and hope, gratitude, truthfulness,
  and community as important spiritual themes. Do you think
  this is the right list? What would you drop, change, or add?
  Which of them would you describe differently than I have? In
  facilitation, how would these manifest themselves differently
  than I've described?

- In what religion were you raised? What about it was spiritually uplifting? What about it was spiritually stultifying? What
  about it did you accept, and what did you reject? What about
  it left you confused or uncertain? (If you belong to a different
  religion now, the same questions apply.)

- If you remain committed to your religion, what do you need
  to do to live it fully? In what ways are you living according to
  your beliefs, and in what ways could you improve? How can
  you take advantage of the resources of this religion to seek
  guidance and strength when you're feeling weak, insecure, or
  self-protective?

- If you do not accept the religion in which you were raised or to
  which you now belong, what would the ideal religion look
  like—one you would believe in, participate in, and practice
  wholeheartedly? What would be its precepts, its rituals? (The
  term "ritual" calls up stereotypes of indigenous tribes dancing
  around a bonfire, but we have many rituals, such as Christmas
  trees and gifts and Easter baskets, not to mention nonreligious

ones such as graduation ceremonies, birthday parties, weddings, and many more.) Who else would be in your spiritual community? How would this religion suggest you live day-to-day?

- If you are an atheist and reject all religion, in what ways are you nurturing your highest and best self? What inspires you to be the best and most giving that you can be? How would you maintain your ability to love even in the face of the most painful loss? What defines your moral values? To what communities do you belong, and how do you contribute to them? In what do you have faith? How do you reaffirm your values and beliefs?

- As a facilitator, how can you be a living example of your beliefs and your faith? Are there moments when your behavior seems at odds with your spiritual self? How can you bring them back in congruence? Do you bring your spirituality with you when you work with groups, or do you feel you have to check it at the door? Why? Do you think spirituality is relevant to facilitation, or do you think this chapter should have been omitted? Why? Do you look at group members (and all the people you work with) as whole human beings, or do you see them merely as potential threats to your authority, as potential obstacles to success, as scary? How can you come to relate to them the way your beliefs or faith would suggest?

I invite you to join me in exploring how we can build our own spirituality and extend it to our work in helping people transcend their baser instincts and relate to each other and their issues in ways that demonstrate the best in human nature. The spiritual capacity can complement the physical, emotional, intellectual, and intuitive capacities in bringing out the best in people, and in helping them to address the most extreme challenges successfully.

In the next chapter, we tie together preparation, facilitation basics, and the five capacities in looking at process design and handling particular challenges in extreme facilitation.

Notes

1. Acquaro, "Out of Madness, a Matriarchy," pp. 58–63.
2. Harwood and Ellis, "U.S. Soldier Hits Back in Torture Storm," pp. 4–5.
3. Kelley, "Early Complaints About Abu Ghraib Ignored, Records Show," p. 24A.
4. My knowledge of world religions is largely attributable to Smith, *The World's Religions*.
5. Curle, *In the Middle*, p. 27.
6. Batson, *The Altruism Question*.
7. Carter, *Keeping Faith*, pp. 398–400.

Chapter Twelve

Putting It All Together

We've covered a lot of ground. We've discussed the concept of the extreme facilitator as architect of a custom process, one tailored to the group and its needs, goals, and culture. We've discussed how the facilitator's inner qualities, including authenticity, confidence, presence, trustworthiness, and calm, are at the core of what it takes to be an extreme facilitator. We've covered the preparatory phases of facilitation—assessment, convening, and contracting. We've overviewed the basics of facilitation—basic stages, interventions, and formats. Then we've taken the five capacities of groups— physical, emotional, intellectual, intuitive, and spiritual—and explored how to maximize these capacities in the group and in oneself, so as to enable the group, and ourselves, to meet the most extreme challenges.

In this chapter, we tie this all together, in two ways. First, we explore process design—the "architectural" work of drawing on all these approaches when creating a custom process. Second, we consider how to handle some specific challenges that facilitators often fear.

Process Design

Earlier chapters of this book covered the preparatory phases of assessment, convening, and contracting. One piece of preparation was omitted: process design. That's because it's difficult to discuss process design without having discussed the raw materials—activities and techniques—which were laid out in Chapters Six through Eleven.

Ongoing Process Design

To some extent, process design occurs throughout a facilitator's engagement with a client group. When conducting assessment, you're beginning to get ideas about what the group needs in the process you design. In convening, you're figuring out who needs to be at the table and in what configuration, so this phase is part of process design. In contracting, you're negotiating expectations about what the group can expect and what they'll need to commit to in order for you to produce those results. This, too, is related to process design.

In particular, the second milestone of contracting—the assessment report—includes your initial proposal about process design—how many meetings will be needed, with what frequency, and what major topics will be addressed in each.

The third milestone of contracting is agreement with the full group about how to proceed, including the purpose, agenda, ground rules, and roles. These are all part of process design. As the meetings take place, you are constantly responding to what you experience in the moment and readjusting the agenda, thereby revising the process design on the spot. After completing one meeting, you design the agenda for the next meeting. In this way process design continues to unfold.

Creating the Agenda

There is a particular span of time when process-design work is in highest gear. This is when you are designing the initial agenda. The agenda for the first meeting is created toward the end of assessment-convening and before the first full-group meeting.

At this point, you have achieved a rich understanding of the group and its needs, goals, and culture. You have identified the stakeholders and have begun to make recommendations about who should be at the table. You're beginning to develop a realistic picture of what this group might be able to achieve. You may have formed a process advisory group and run some ideas by them. Now you are ready to sit down and design either an agenda for the whole process (if the process is a one-shot event such as an annual retreat), or a schedule of meetings accompanied by an agenda for the first meeting.

An agenda needs to include three things for each item:

1. *The topic.* This is the subject matter for discussion. It's what people usually put on agendas.

2. *The activity.* This may not go on the written agenda, but you need to have a plan of how to approach the topic. Will you use open discussion? Rounds? Small-group breakouts? Something more creative?

3. *The outcome.* This is the part that's easy to forget. What is the hoped-for outcome of discussing the topic—a decision, a recommendation, input to a decision maker, greater understanding? Will the item result in a short list of issues, a hundred solution options, a handful of criteria? Will the item result in participants being more inspired, better informed, more coordinated, more at peace with each other? You may or may not put the outcome on the written agenda, but the group should be clear when the topic starts (at the latest) what the outcome should be.

As discussed briefly in Chapter Two (under the section "Tapping and Applying Your Creativity"), coming up with an agenda is a creative process. When I am conducting assessment and convening, my mind gets increasingly jumbled with the myriad issues, the various people's hopes and goals for the facilitation, and perhaps the sea of detailed technical information. There is often a point at which I feel overwhelmed, wondering how I can possibly put together a coherent plan that will solve or improve anything. Then, as I let it all sink in, sleep on it, review my notes, and think ahead to the meetings, an agenda begins to form. In particular, several things start to become clearer in my mind:

1. *Key issues and goals.* Particularly in organizational facilitation, there is often a morass of interwoven issues, but one or a handful of pivotal or overarching issues may begin to float to the top.

2. *Key features of the group culture.* A picture forms of how I will need to handle this group differently from others.

3. *Process ideas.* If I create the conditions for my own creativity as discussed in Chapter Two, ideas start to pop into my head for activities or techniques to use. I begin to imagine the meeting unfolding. I jot my ideas down, look at what else needs to be accomplished, and fill in the gaps until I can put together a complete agenda.

When you try this creative process of agenda design, you will draw on the many techniques and activities discussed throughout this book, along with others you may have experienced, read about, or used before. You may use some of these as is, or they may help you come up with new ideas.

The agenda development process is less linear and tidy than the way most instructional manuals teach how to do something. I can't honestly lay the process out in a neat sequence of steps. That's the nature of creativity. It may not work for you exactly the way it works for me. You may feel as though you're groping around aimlessly for a while. You may need to ask others for advice. (Don't forget your process advisory group, if you have one—they might have good ideas.) If you're more extroverted than I, your ideas might emerge more through discussion with others than through silent reflection. Regardless, this aspect of facilitation is for me the most magical and fun, and it continues as you conduct the process and make changes in the moment.

An Illustration of Process Design

An example will help illustrate one way the agenda design process can unfold. I was working with a group of physicians that was in considerable turmoil. They had numerous internal issues to grapple with, which came out in one-on-one interviews with all twenty or so of them.

Key Issues

Some key issues that were repeated over and over again during assessment were physicians failing to live up to performance expectations—coming in late, leaving unfinished work for others to do, being "unavailable" when one of them was overworked and needed help. Because these physicians were all partners in the firm, it was not simply a matter of a supervisor doling out rewards and punishments. Part of the problem was lack of clarity or consistency of expectations; the other was that there was no mechanism for holding each other accountable.

My colleague and I discussed which task we should start with: clarifying the expectations or developing an accountability mechanism. (The physicians had phrased this latter issue as "physician discipline" and we reframed that to "accountability"—they were accustomed to almost complete autonomy and did not relish the thought of anyone "disciplining" them.) While logically one needs to set expectations before discussing how to hold people accountable to them, we also knew that most of the physicians were skeptical of the whole facilitated process. (As is often the case, we were brought in by a creative, eccentric individual who was not typical of his organization.) Therefore, we wanted to leave the first meeting with a tangible product. As a result, we decided to focus first on developing an accountability mechanism.

Group Culture

There were a few things that distinguished this group's culture. First, it was an extremely task-oriented culture. The physicians were not accustomed to long meetings and were not looking forward to them. Because of their work schedules, we had to meet in the evenings, from 5:00 to 9:00 P.M. They were tired by this point; most of them began work at 7:00 or 7:30 A.M. We had to keep the meetings active, with every segment of the meeting producing a clear result. We drew heavily on the principles in Chapter Seven on maintaining physical energy.

Second, this group was not emotionally expressive in the least. There were lots of emotional issues—anger at some physicians for shirking their duties, confusion about expectations, grief over the loss of the warm, family-like atmosphere as the firm had grown over the years. None of these were on the surface in the group meetings—however, we learned about them in the individual interviews. We would have to provide safe ways to uncover issues without requiring much self-disclosure.

Process Ideas

As my colleague and I discussed what to do with this first meeting, some pictures began to form. First, we needed to come up with a logical approach for designing an accountability mechanism that would respond to the actual complaints and concerns. This was in effect a problem-solving effort. We needed to draw on the approaches in Chapter Nine ("The Intellectual Capacity") and run a kind of problem-solving sequence to put this approach together. We would also need to draw upon the group's creativity (Chapter Ten, "The Intuitive Capacity") to help devise a new approach where none existed before.

The Agenda

Having discussed these goals for the first meeting with my colleague, I came up with a draft agenda and worked with my colleague to refine it. Following is what we wrote on the agenda distributed to participants, with a description of each item.

5:00–5:20 Discuss preliminary matters

- Review overall purpose and schedule of meetings
- Review purpose and agenda for this meeting (focus: physician accountability)

- Clarify expectations of CDR
- Agree on procedural guidelines

During this item, we quickly went through a number of contracting issues. Note that to do this all in twenty minutes (or less, with a late start) is fast and reflected the task-oriented nature of this group. Everything we presented here had already received the approval of a process advisory committee, which maximized the likelihood of acceptance by the full group.

Using a laptop computer and LCD projector, we projected a schedule of meetings with the topic for each. It showed that this meeting would focus on an accountability mechanism. We projected a purpose for the entire facilitated process, which was to "Establish structures and procedures to resolve difficult issues—such as accountability, compensation, and strategy—and to develop better teamwork and communication." We also projected the proposed agenda for this meeting, explaining that we felt it would be more productive to develop an accountability mechanism before working to clarify expectations. We sought and obtained the group members' agreement on this point. We also passed out a sheet of standard ground rules (this was before I developed my more customized approach to ground rules explained in Chapter Five, "Contracting").

We did not do introductions of any kind. We had met all of the participants through interviews, they all knew each other intimately, and we felt that this task-oriented group would want to get right down to business.

5:20–5:45 Discuss overall objectives and outcomes

During the next item we completed contracting through a start-up question (see Chapter Six, under "Basic Stages," the subsection "Opening and Setting the Tone"). We asked each participant to state what outcomes he or she hoped would come from the entire facilitated process. We discussed which of these outcomes would be realistic to expect and which would not, and obtained the group's agreement.

5:45–6:05 Identify issues/problems people want the physician accountability mechanism to address

For this next item, we distributed large sticky notes and invited participants to write down the kinds of "offenses" they wanted an accountability mechanism to address. We had them post these on the wall (thereby getting participants out of their chairs and moving). We then asked what themes emerged from this exercise.

6:05–6:30 Survey current approaches/responses for addressing accountability issues and assess their effectiveness

During this item, we asked the group how these kinds of offenses had been handled up until that point, and we captured these in notes on the computer (which was still attached to the LCD projector so that all could see our notes). The responses were fascinating, and ranged from "frustration" and "backbiting and gossip" to "section director talks to the physician in question, and resolves it informally." We had planned also to ask the group to generate pros and cons of each approach, but when the time came in the actual meeting, this seemed like overprocessing for this task-oriented group. It was obvious which of the approaches were healthy and which were pathological.

6:30–6:45 Develop a list of principles/goals and objectives to guide the design of the physician accountability mechanism/structure

We then asked the group for principles or objectives to guide the development of the accountability mechanism. Again, the responses were fascinating. Some examples: "Mechanism should provide opportunity for problem solving, not just punishment," "Physician in question should know specifics of complaints and be able to respond/explain," and "Mechanism needs options between informal conversation and drastic consequences."

7:00–7:45 Brainstorm: identify ideas for building a better physician accountability structure (small-group work)

At this point, we had identified problems the mechanism was meant to respond to, approaches that were currently in use (both healthy and unhealthy), and principles that should guide the new mechanism. We were ready to let the group members put their creativity to work. We had them break into smaller groups to brainstorm about ideas and come up with some proposals.

It was only during the meeting that we determined how to break up into groups—though we did think of some possibilities in advance. We suggested that one group work on initial, informal approaches and that another group work on a more formal approach for issues that were not successfully resolved in the informal stage. There had also been some discussion of performance reviews—these had been initiated but were not taking place in a consistent schedule or form. We suggested that one group discuss how to refine performance reviews as one more approach to maintaining accountability.

Were we to do this part of the meeting again, we might have introduced some of the methods in Chapter Ten ("The Intuitive Capacity") to increase creativity. For example, we might have elicited a story or two of successful experiences of holding one another accountable. We might have done a quick, simplified visualization exercise in which participants would imagine themselves being held to expectations in a constructive way when they had fallen short. We might even have asked them to role play an informal conversation between a section director and a physician over an alleged infraction.

7:45–8:30   Present and discuss suggestions for a more effective accountability mechanism

8:30–9:00   Reach agreements and decide upon next steps

During these next agenda items, the small groups reported their
results, and the full group discussed these and reached agreements.
The small groups did succeed in coming up with a skeleton of an
accountability mechanism. When they got stuck about who would
sit on a decision-making panel in the formal phase of the mechanism, I gently asked whether it might make sense to compose a
peer panel including one colleague selected by the physician who
committed the alleged misdeed, another selected by the section
director, and a third selected by the first two (this idea was inspired
by the way some arbitration panels are selected). They immediately
adopted this idea. In this case, my creativity substituted for theirs,
and it worked out fine, but they might have come up with something better using their own creativity.

We captured all these ideas in a draft accountability document
and inserted some questions that remained to be clarified in the
next meeting. The first half of the next meeting was devoted to
finalizing the details of this mechanism, and the second half to a
discussion of expectations.

I should add something about the spiritual capacity, even
though this was not an explicit part of the process design. My colleague and I felt that many of these doctors were, in my colleague's
words, "wounded souls" (though none would describe themselves
as such). They also were feeling hopeless—they wanted to stay
with the firm because of its stellar reputation, but they couldn't see
a way out of their troubles and conflicts. The caring, compassion,
and hope we brought them were, I believe, key ingredients in the
success of the endeavor.

This case is just one example of process design. Each case is, of
course, very different. However, the same general approach applies:
conduct the assessment and convening; conduct contracting to
determine what would be realistic for the group to achieve; look for

key issues and features of the group culture, and begin to think of process approaches; and put them together. In doing so, you draw on a wide range of techniques and activities to come up with a unique sequence of topics and activities to help the particular group reach its goals. You remain flexible throughout, and adapt the design as you go along.

Specific Challenges

We've now covered all the phases of extreme facilitation. When I teach facilitation, however, class participants often hunger for a substantial training component on handling "difficult people" or "negative behavior." Of course, this entire book has been about facilitating in difficult circumstances, but it may be useful to focus on some particular kinds of trouble spots.

Difficult Situations

For a while I was puzzled by my trainees' need to address these so-called difficult situations. Why don't I recall having very many of them? Why do others think there's so much more of this scary material to deal with than I do? I realized there are two answers.

First, dealing with such problems requires about 95 percent prevention and 5 percent cure. You will experience fewer attacks, instances of rudeness, or processes falling apart if you do all the things already discussed in this book:

- Approach facilitation as an architect of a custom process to fit the particular group and its culture and goals
- Conduct a thorough assessment
- Identify all the stakeholders and convene the right participants
- Contract carefully with the client and the group to agree on mutual expectations

- Create a setting and a process that maximize physical energy
- Welcome and channel emotions effectively
- Develop and execute a logical process for managing complex information and solving technical problems
- Creatively devise activities to draw on participants' intuition
- Access participants' spiritual capacity—for love, faith, hope, gratitude, truthfulness, and community
- Cultivate your self—your authenticity, confidence, presence, trustworthiness, and calm, as well as your five capacities: physical, emotional, intellectual, intuitive, and spiritual

In short, if you work to understand in depth the group and situation and yourself in relation to it, design the process accordingly, and engage all the participants' capacities—and your own—to overcome the most extreme challenges, things will go well more often than not.

A colleague of mine told me of facilitating a meeting that went very poorly. It was supposed to be an internal meeting, a kind of focus group for staff of an agency that was sponsoring a public-policy stakeholder group and a public-involvement process. Somehow, however, some members of the public caught wind of this meeting and invited themselves. The agency staff apparently felt they had to accommodate them.

Moreover, the goal of this meeting was not clear—the term "focus group," strictly speaking, actually refers to a research method, but the term is often misused. Finally, my colleague was invited to run the meeting without being given the opportunity to conduct assessment, convening (hence the unexpected hodgepodge of internal and external people), contracting, or process design. The agenda was already in place. The agency officials just wanted him to play traffic cop. The meeting went very poorly and my colleague got eaten alive by participants. We could discuss at length how to handle the attacks he faced, but it would be beside the point. He was set up for failure.

Again, dealing with "difficult people" is 95 percent prevention.

There is a second reason I can't remember facing so many "difficult situations." I have, but I often don't frame them that way in my mind. Perhaps because most of my work has been in high-conflict or highly complex situations, I tend to see a lot of difficulties as routine. More important, I tend to see them as not being entirely about me. I certainly seek to understand and accept my own responsibility when things go wrong, but I also try to understand the "difficult" person's behavior in its context. It often has nothing to do with the facilitator. This point will be illustrated in different ways as we explore each of a variety of difficult situations and behaviors.

Difficulties will arise, and some people will seem simply impossible to handle. We can address these situations effectively if we apply the same principles that are woven throughout this book: try to understand in depth first, try to work by agreement with the group, welcome the difficult situation, and creatively design an approach to manage it—drawing on the many techniques and approaches described in this book and encountered elsewhere in your experience. This won't turn every lion into a pussycat or make difficult situations easy. Instead, it will help the group make the best of these difficulties—to see what can be learned from them, to honestly confront the reality of its challenges, to build understanding as much as possible, and to achieve its tasks as far as possible.

Dominating Individuals

A common concern is how to cope when one person or a few people dominate the discussion. Here is an example of behavior that some see as "difficult" but I see as ordinary. Some people just talk more. Perhaps they're full of themselves and have big egos, but perhaps not. Perhaps they're higher up in the hierarchy and don't fear others' reactions. Perhaps they're more confident or articulate. Perhaps we're focusing on the wrong problem and the real problem is that others don't talk enough.

Sometimes it's simply that some people are more interested in the issue at hand or have a more central role. In this case, uneven participation is not pathological at all. For example, I worked once with a department within an international lending institution. This department had its own informal group of external advisers with whom it conducted strategic planning. Some of the advisers had been more intimately connected with the group over the years, so they had more to say. It was fine.

In another case, I facilitated among representatives of several government agencies working to resolve a dispute over a contaminated site. Although there were four agencies at the table, two of them were most directly engaged in the dispute. It made sense that their representatives did more of the talking. The other two were there mainly because they had to sign off on the final agreement, and they didn't have as much to say.

Let's just assume for a moment, however, that you've concluded that it is indeed problematic that some people are dominating, and they are preventing others from expressing important views. There are many different ways to cope with this:

- *Rounds*. Pose a question and ask everyone to respond to it in turn.

- *State an observation*. Point out that some participants have been speaking more than others.

- *Make space for the quieter participants to respond*. You could ask generally if there is anyone who wants to comment who has not done so. Alternatively, if it doesn't seem too high-pressure, invite some of the quieter participants by name if they have any thoughts they'd like to express.

- *Use small-group breakouts*. These allow people who might feel bashful about speaking in front of the entire group to express their views in a more comfortable setting.

- *Confront the individuals who are dominating*. Notice that this is just one choice among many. If someone's behavior is chronically interfering, it may be time to lovingly raise the subject directly, perhaps during a break. Make sure also to be receptive to this person's views of why he or she is behaving that way or how the process is going for him or her generally.

Let's move on now to some tougher challenges.

Undermining the Facilitator

Novice facilitators often worry about "maintaining their authority." Again, this is to some extent in the eye of the beholder. First of all, what authority does the facilitator have? The whole concept of facilitation is that the facilitator has little authority at all, and instead is in a role created to serve the group.

Paradoxically, then, the best way to maintain your authority is to assume you have none to take away. Instead of worrying about your authority, worry about the group and its needs—and the needs of the individual who seems to be trying to undermine you.

Once I was facilitating a large consensus-building process, and we were at the point of developing draft consensus language. I was using a computer and LCD projector, so I could make changes as the group discussed and agreed on them. This process can be messy—sometimes you make changes that someone has proposed, then erase them as others object, then put them back in but with some word changes, and so on.

At one point a participant asked me to go back to an earlier version of a particular phrase, even though the current version said almost the same thing. What's more, the current version contained improved language that had achieved broader agreement than the earlier version. I began to explain this, but he snapped back, "Go back to the earlier language!" I didn't like being snapped at, and I felt anger rising up in me. But mindful (belatedly) that I was there to serve, I restrained my own anger, and hit "undo changes" to go back to the language he wanted to see. It turned out that he just wanted to see it. "Thank you," he said sternly, "now we can go back to where we were."

Was he trying to undermine my authority? A better way to look at it was that I had undermined his authority, or rather assumed too much authority for myself. I shouldn't have refused to comply with his request in the first place. If I thought others in the group might object, I could have asked others if it would be OK to go back to the earlier language, at which point he might have clarified that he just wanted to see it to compare the versions. We never would have gotten in a tussle.

During a simulated facilitation in a training I conducted, I saw the facilitator set out the agenda and ground rules as if they were law. "Here are the ground rules we will follow," she said, and "Here's our agenda." Her tone was firm. The trainees who were playing the roles of participants soon started to chafe under her authoritarian style and began to challenge her: "Excuse me, I believe my hand was up first." "I don't think that's what we should be talking about now." (They probably would have challenged her even more forcefully had they been real-life participants rather than role players.)

You must remember—you're not in charge of groups like a boss; you're there to help them. You must offer your process guidance—from the purpose and agenda to every activity you set up and every intervention you make—as a proposal. This doesn't necessarily have to be explicit; you don't always have to say, "This is just a suggested agenda and I'm open to your changes." But it should at least be implied in your tone and choice of words: "Here's the agenda I propose" instead of "Here's your agenda." In this way, you paradoxically maintain control by giving it away.

Hidden Agendas

Facilitated sessions are often rife with actual or perceived "hidden agendas," and this is often a source of great concern for new facilitators (or experienced ones new to extreme situations).

It helps to examine exactly what a hidden agenda is: it is simply an interest that remains unarticulated, because it might seem unacceptable. Hidden agendas are often about individual self-interests that lie outside the interests one's avowed role is intended to serve.

The question is to what extent those interests conflict. The more nefarious "hidden agendas" are ones that conflict severely with the interests one is supposed to serve. For example, imagine a mayor is seeing to it that the city is awarding large contracts to a company owned by the mayor's nephew. The mayor's hidden agenda is to do favors for his nephew, while in his role as mayor he's supposed to serve the public interest—which includes open competition for government contracts. This is a fairly serious conflict of interests, and a serious hidden agenda.

Many hidden agendas, though, are much less sinister. They may still be individual interests—often related to the individual's career ambitions—but they don't necessarily conflict with the interests the person is supposed to be serving.

For example, I once worked with the legal department of a large company to help develop and implement an alternative dispute resolution (ADR) process for workplace complaints and disputes. As is common, the attorneys had a separate reporting line from the operational personnel who were their "clients."

The legal department had a hard time gaining acceptance for the ADR process. It was used a few times, but it didn't catch on widely. I repeatedly urged the attorneys to enlist the support of the director of operations, as he was the person with the power to ensure that the ADR process was written into standard procedures and to put the weight of the executive management behind this new way of approaching disputes.

Each time I suggested this, it seemed to fall flat. Finally, one of the attorneys shot back at me, "Do you know how hard this team has worked on this?" I was puzzled, but after asking a couple of follow-up questions, I figured out that the reason they didn't want to involve the director of operations was because they thought he would take credit for it. I tested this: "So you're concerned you won't get proper credit for all the work you've put in on this effort." He replied, "I *know* we won't get credit for it, and what's more, it'll get screwed up" by the operations people altering the process.

Here is an example of a hidden agenda that's not so sinister, yet it prevented this team from doing something that would have benefited their project. The hidden agenda was simply to get credit for this substantial project (as well as to have the integrity of the project maintained). Getting credit and recognition for something is the kind of career-related self-interest that people may not want to confess to, yet there's nothing particularly wrong with it.

I coached the legal team on bringing up the issue with the director of operations. I urged them to state plainly that they were looking for his support for the project and also his recognition that the ADR initiative was the legal department's product. I suggested they ask the operations director if they could play an ongoing consultative role as the ADR process was incorporated into standard personnel policies and procedures. They followed this advice, and by and large, it worked out as hoped.

Most of the hidden agendas I've become aware of in my facilitation career have been of this more benign kind. Certainly, there are crooks out there who are embezzling funds, succumbing to nepotism, cooking the books, and conducting other unethical behavior. We should never collude in maintaining these kinds of hidden agendas. Most of the time, though, all we need to do is surface the hidden agenda and *normalize* it—frame it simply as an interest, an individual one perhaps, but not an illegitimate one. It may or may not need to be shared with the group.

If members are suspecting another group member has a hidden agenda, it is helpful to ask what they think that hidden agenda is. The answer may come back, "Well, she's got political ambitions" or "He's looking to get promoted to vice president." Then we can ask, "And what impact will that have on our process here?" If there is a significant potential impact, it may merit some discussion with the person who allegedly has the hidden agenda. Often, though, once the suspecting person articulates what the possible hidden agenda is, he realizes it's not so horrible. Maybe someone is pontificating a bit in meetings because she might later run for office—so what?

In one case involving the possible development of a convention center, one developer expressed concern that another group member, a city councilwoman, was prepared to sue if she didn't get the outcome she was seeking from the facilitated process. In fact, she had already stated this during a full-group meeting! This agenda wasn't hidden at all. I reminded the developer of this, and I treated it as no big problem—after all, she was simply doing what she felt she needed to further the interests of her constituents. This was another case of normalizing a "hidden" agenda.

Clashing Cultures

In Chapter Three ("Assessment"), we examined group culture and how the approach to facilitation can be customized to it. This didn't address the question of cultural differences *within* a group. What happens if there are sharply different cultures, and they begin to clash?

I described earlier (in Chapter Four, "Convening") a facilitation I did to help a municipality select a slate of health-insurance plans for its employees. The participants included representatives of the police, fire, and municipal-employees unions as well as several non-union employees. The first couple of meetings had awkward beginnings. The police and firefighter representatives were sitting in their seats, hands folded on the table, several minutes before the scheduled start time. The municipal employees' union representatives and the non-union employees wandered in between five and fifteen minutes after the scheduled start time, often still chatting with each other as they entered the room.

Most everyone says they value punctuality, but what "on time" means varies a great deal across cultures—even occupational cultures, as this case illustrates. Police officers and firefighters depend for their job success on being precise, punctual, and task-oriented. In office work, little is lost when meetings start a few minutes late—it takes up people's time, but the time can be used for relationship-building, which is also important for doing one's job well. (Cultural views toward time and punctuality are often related to the task-process-relationship orientation.)

I had to do something, because I could sense that the police and firefighters were perturbed by the others' lateness. I intervened first by stating an observation (see Chapter Six, the section on basic interventions): "What it means to start on time depends a lot on culture, and I see that some of you have a culture where that means being ready to start precisely at 2:00, and others of you seem to have a culture that says that you typically get down to business at about 2:10 or 2:15." The trick is to make such observations non-judgmentally. (I succeeded in this, partly because my occupational culture is more like the latter group's!)

I then suggested that it might be more respectful of those who had made the effort to get there early if everyone could try to be ready to start the meeting right at 2:00. They all agreed, and future meetings began at 2:03 or 2:04—a reasonable compromise I suppose.

Another way I could have handled this would have been to ask, after stating the observation, "What would be an appropriate, realistic goal for this group in terms of punctuality?" and wait for suggestions, rather than making the suggestion myself. This might have been more respectful to the different cultures, but of course it would have taken more time.

If this cultural difference had risen to the level of conflict, which it could have, it would also have been helpful to point out the judgments that people can make about each other based on cultural differences. The 2:00-sharp people might look at the others as lazy, irresponsible, or disrespectful. The 2:15-ish people might respond to this by viewing the 2:00-sharp crowd as rigid, uptight, or condescending. By pointing out these side effects of cultural differences, you can help head off negative judgments and help people see their differences just as differences, not as moral failures.

There are cultural differences in all groups, and much of the time they don't matter at all. However, if a cultural difference is standing in the way of healthy group functioning, you simply can name the difference and either ask the group how to proceed or suggest a way to proceed.

The amount of time to spend on this is a judgment call—for example, if this same friction is a chronic problem, and if one of the group's goals in the facilitation is to learn to work together better, the cultural difference might merit an in-depth discussion. If, instead, the group has just come together for a specific, short-term task, you might just take the more expedient path of suggesting a way forward as I did with the punctuality issue. The main point, though, is that the most powerful thing you can do is to name the difference, to state the unstated. You don't have to know how to "manage" every cultural difference, but you can use your awareness of group behavior to heighten the group's awareness and facilitate its process of resolving the difference to the degree needed.

Angry Outbursts

Angry outbursts are not unusual in extreme facilitation. There essentially are two methods for helping cool down an angry person. One is empathic listening (see Chapter Eight, "Empathic Listening," under the section "Responding to Emotions"). The other is taking a break (see "Calling a Break" under the same section). Empathic listening not only reduces the emotional intensity but also helps utilize the person's anger by finding its source, naming it, and allowing the group to address the underlying issues if appropriate.

A dilemma occurs if the outburst is off the topic or the person is otherwise disrupting the group procedurally. For instance, in the facilitated process about whether and how to build a convention center (see the section "Putting It All Together" in Chapter Eight), meetings were open to the public, and the standard procedure was to set aside a few minutes at the beginning and end of each meeting for comments by observers. Otherwise, the discussion was limited to people at the table.

In the middle of one presentation by a technical expert, an observer from the national advocacy group dedicated to preserving local neighborhoods piped up and lambasted the expert for excluding key information from the handout he was discussing. The missing information concerned some of the negative effects of the proposed development on neighboring residential areas.

What to do now? On the one hand, focusing attention on the angry individual in such a situation helps calm him or her down. On the other hand, the group members will feel their process is being derailed, and will be counting on the facilitator to get it back on track—in other words, to steer attention away from the irate person and back to the group's task. In this situation, my colleague who was facilitating listened to the outburst and asked a minimal clarification question, then said firmly that there would be more opportunity to discuss her points during the public comment period, and the group needed to get back on track. Even in the short time this took, however, three participants got up in frustration, as if to say, "This is a waste of time—I'll use my time better by refilling my coffee cup."

Whether to attend to the angry speaker in such a situation or to remain strict about staying on track and ignore the angry person depends somewhat on the group's reaction. If people seem irritated by the intrusion, that's a signal that they want you to take firm control (by saying something like, "Thank you, but we'll entertain observer comments at 4:30"). If people seem unbothered and even interested in the comment, then you too can show more flexibility.

You may have noticed an interesting twist to this story. The angry observer was a representative of a national advocacy group that felt it was unfairly excluded from participating in the consensus process. The underlying problem here was arguably a convening mistake, not just an emotional issue. This advocacy group met at least one of the criteria of "who is a stakeholder" (see the section "Identifying Stakeholders" in Chapter Four). Some of the observer's emotional intensity no doubt arose from ongoing frustration at being excluded. My hunch is that had she been at the table, she would still have been scratchy but probably more inclined to play by the rules. This illustrates how "troublemakers" can sometimes be less trouble if they're inside the process rather than outside of it.

Altercation Between Two Participants

Let's take the angry outburst issue one step further. Suppose one participant directs an angry outburst at someone specific, and that person responds with equal or greater vitriol. You now have a fight on your hands.

As was mentioned in Chapter Eight (in the subsection "What Not to Do" of the section "Responding to Emotions"), you can simply use the same approach as with an angry individual—just repeat it with both. You may have to go back and forth between the two of them to ensure both their points of view are given equal airing.

The extent to which you devote energy to the two antagonists depends on the extent to which the substance of their argument is relevant to the topic at hand. If it is relevant, you can go beyond empathic listening and use reframing (see Chapter Six) to ascertain what are the interests or goals of both individuals that underlie the anger. Then you can frame the issue by posing the question of how to meet interests of both (see the subsection "Defining the Issue" under the section "Managing Complex Issues" in Chapter Nine).

For example, I facilitated a negotiated rulemaking process about limiting the environmental damage of numerous chemical products used in households and small businesses. At one point, an environmental advocate argued, "The agency has to have records of what chemicals are used at what establishments." A representative of a small-business association countered, "That's crazy! I can see Big Brother is alive and well." Offended, the first shot back, "Well I can see your only concern is for your profits!"

I used active listening with both. Through my exchanges with both of them, I learned that the environmentalist wanted the record keeping so that safety checks could be done and spills could be responded to quickly and with the right cleanup techniques. The small-business advocate was worried about the burdensome paperwork requirements that would be imposed on small businesses already struggling to keep up with a range of regulatory requirements. The tension cooled. Clearly this issue was at the heart of what we were all there to accomplish.

I then posed the question, "How can we ensure compliance with safety standards and quick responses to spills while keeping paperwork requirements to a minimum?" This is an example of framing an issue by incorporating both sets of interests into a question. The group came up with new suggestions such as safety education programs for small businesses.

In contrast to this scenario, if the altercation is not related to the group's task, it merits less of the facilitator's attention and the group's time. Still, it has to be dealt with. Suppose, for example, that two individuals in an organizational strategic planning retreat have some interpersonal conflict unrelated to the planning issues. They trade hostile barbs that detract attention from the matters at hand and sour the atmosphere for everyone else.

Your goal is to close the curtain on this distracting sideshow without alienating the two participants. This could be done in many ways. One is simply to ignore it and focus attention on others who are engaged in the substantive discussion. Another is to say something explicit, such as, "Let's return our focus to the mission statement." You might get more direct, perhaps with humor: "Children!" (As with all uses of humor, success depends on your rapport with the group, its culture and openness to kidding, and your ability to deliver the humor with warmth rather than condescension.) Or you might confront them directly during a break: "The tension between the two of you is getting in the way of the group's work. What can we do about this?"

If the group (including the two who are at odds) are going to work together long-term, it might be worthwhile to help resolve the interpersonal conflict to minimize its future damage to the whole group. You might encourage them to discuss the issue calmly with each other, or ask them privately if they'd like your help working out their tension.

Physical Aggression

There's a difference between anger and aggression. Handling anger is part of a facilitator's role and expertise. Handling physical violence is not. If someone starts a fistfight, throws furniture around, or brandishes a weapon, you're not obligated to continue a dialogue with them or to try to control their behavior. You have to focus on keeping yourself safe and getting security or law enforcement personnel on the scene as quickly as possible.

Fortunately, facilitated processes don't tend to create the conditions for violence to break out. People at the table in a facilitated dialogue or decision-making process typically feel their voice is legitimized and their needs are being taken into account. Anger and frustration occur, but they rarely escalate to physical aggression. Still, things can go wrong.

Public meetings (ones open to the general public rather than only to invited stakeholders or members of intact groups) are the most volatile forums for facilitators. Participants in public meetings have no investment in the group's success; they haven't had the validating experience of being identified as "stakeholders," and they are in an ideal setting for grandstanding. I've witnessed many angry speeches at public meetings, but no violence to date. Still, for extremely contentious issues, it might be worthwhile to inform police in advance of the gathering and have their phone number handy.

Basic Principles

You will undoubtedly face more challenges than the ones I have identified and explored here. You don't need to have a formula for each of them. Instead, you can rely on the principles that are woven through the specific challenges just discussed:

- *Ask if there's really a problem.* Maybe the bad thing is not really bad. The hidden agenda, the "dominating" behavior, and so forth may be fine. You might ask yourself or, if uncertain, you might ask the group.

- *Name it.* If there is a problem, identify what you observe.

- *Put it to the group.* You don't have to be a genius with the perfect answer to every inappropriate behavior or unnerving incident. Instead, you can ask the group members how they'd like you to handle such things.

- *Keep the focus on the needs of the individual and the group.* Most likely, the "difficult" person is not out to make your life difficult—he's there to meet whatever interests and needs he has, or to relieve the emotions he's experiencing. Rather than focusing on defending or protecting yourself, focus on how to meet the needs of the group and the individuals in it.

A Closing Thought

This book has offered my views and experiences on how to bring our skills, creativity, and compassion to bear in helping groups achieve their goals under the most difficult circumstances. Facilitation is the practice of helping groups reach their highest potential. Bringing out the best in others has to start with bringing out the best in ourselves.

Human beings are a peculiar species. We are clearly social; cooperation with others is necessary to our survival. Yet our needs conflict often with those of others. Sometimes we want nothing more than to be left alone to do what we want to do without thinking about anyone else. It can be a burden to have to worry about the needs of others. Yet many of our finest achievements as human beings are collective ones.

In those endeavors when we can achieve our individual goals at the same time that we are participating in a group accomplishment, it is sublime. Some of our greatest accomplishments involve both in-dividual ingenuity and the cooperative work of a group. In science, individual ideas get put to the test, often with group effort, and the scientific community as a whole exchanges and digests this informa-tion and produces breakthroughs and progress. In the arts, individual artists compose, draw, sculpt, paint, choreograph, or improvise, but groups of artists often work together, and the artistic community as a whole spawns innovations and new ways of creating beauty. In the best organizations, the individual worker takes pride in contributing one small piece to the organization's overall mission, and through the coordinated efforts of many individuals, the organization as a whole makes strides and accomplishments. In a democracy, at its best, there is a collective balancing of the rights and needs of individuals and the rights and needs of the broader society.

The true challenge of the facilitator is to help draw out the best in individuals and in groups, and to help balance the needs of one against the other when they conflict. To do this, we have to start by putting forth the best in ourselves. Through some mechanism that remains mysterious to me—but has been proven to me over and over—we enhance others' capacities when we build them first in ourselves. In our finest moments, we can look at each of the indi-viduals in a group and know their shortcomings but build on and play to their strengths. We can look at a group as a whole and see both the sobering reality of the troubles it faces now and also the goodness and the remarkable achievements that are possible. In this way we become catalysts for positive change.

Bibliography

Acquaro, K. "Out of Madness, a Matriarchy." *Mother Jones,* 2003, *28*(1), 58–63.

Batson, C. D. *The Altruism Question: Toward a Social-Psychological Answer.* Hillsdale, N.J.: Lawrence Erlbaum, 1991.

Blake, R. R., and Mouton, J. S. *Solving Costly Organizational Conflicts.* San Francisco: Jossey-Bass, 1984.

Boulding, E. *Building a Global Civic Culture: Education for an Interdependent World.* Syracuse, N.Y.: Syracuse University Press, 1990.

Buckingham, M., and Clifton, D. O. *Now, Discover Your Strengths.* New York: Simon & Schuster, 2001.

Bush, R.A.B., and Folger, J. P. *The Promise of Mediation: Responding to Conflict Through Empowerment and Recognition.* San Francisco: Jossey-Bass, 1994.

Carpenter, S. L., and Kennedy, W.J.D. *Managing Public Disputes* (2nd ed.). San Francisco: Jossey-Bass, 1991.

Carter, J. *Keeping Faith: Memoirs of a President.* New York: Bantam Books, 1982.

Collins, J. *Good to Great: Why Some Companies Make the Leap . . . and Others Don't.* New York: HarperCollins, 2001.

Cormick, G., Dale, N., Emond, P., Sigurdson, S., and Stuart, B. *Building Consensus for a Sustainable Future: Putting Principles into Practice.* Ottawa: National Roundtable on the Environment and the Economy, 1996.

Crum, T. F. *The Magic of Conflict: Turning a Life of Work into a Work of Art.* New York: Simon & Schuster, 1988.

Curle, A. *In the Middle: Non-Official Mediation in Violent Situations.* Leamington Spa, U.K.: Berg, 1986.

Doyle, M., and Straus, D. *How to Make Meetings Work!* (2nd ed.). New York: Berkley Publishing Group, 1993 [1976].

Edwards, B. *The New Drawing on the Right Side of the Brain: A Course in Enhancing Creativity and Artistic Confidence.* (Rev. ed.). New York: Tarcher/Putnam, 1999.

Fisher, R., and Ury, W. *Getting to Yes: Negotiating Agreement Without Giving In* (2nd ed.). New York: Penguin, 1983.

Goleman, D. *Emotional Intelligence.* New York: Bantam, 1995.

Gordon, T. *Group-Centered Leadership: A Way of Releasing the Creative Power of Groups*. Boston: Houghton-Mifflin, 1955.

Harwood, A., and Ellis, M. "U.S. Soldier Hits Back in Torture Storm." *The Mirror*, May 13, 2004, pp. 4–5.

Hofstede, G. *Culture's Consequences: International Differences in Work-Related Values*. Beverly Hills: Sage, 1984.

Interaction Associates. *Essential Facilitation: Core Skills for Guiding Groups* (2nd ed.). San Francisco: Interaction Associates, 1997.

Kelley, M. "Early Complaints About Abu Ghraib Ignored, Records Show." *Rocky Mountain News*, June 12, 2004, p. 24A.

Lederach, J. P. *Preparing for Peace: Conflict Transformation Across Cultures*. Syracuse: Syracuse University Press, 1995.

Mayer, B. S. *The Dynamics of Conflict Resolution: A Practitioner's Guide*. San Francisco: Jossey-Bass, 2000.

Moore, C. W. *The Mediation Process: Practical Strategies for Resolving Conflict*. (3rd ed.). San Francisco: Jossey-Bass, 2003.

Rees, F. *The Facilitator Excellence Handbook: Helping People Work Creatively and Productively Together*. San Francisco: Jossey-Bass/Pfeiffer, 1998.

Rosenberg, M. B. *Nonviolent Communication: A Language of Compassion*. Encinitas, Calif.: PuddleDancer Press, 1999.

Rothman, J. "Action Evaluation and Conflict Resolution Training: Theory, Method and Case Study." *International Negotiation*, 1997, *2*, 451–470.

Schwarz, R. M. *The Skilled Facilitator: Practical Wisdom for Developing Effective Groups*. San Francisco: Jossey-Bass, 1994.

Silvester, M. N. "Writing Fiction: A Beginner's Guide—Part 8: Form and Structure." [http://teenwriting.about.com/library/weekly/aa111102h.htm]. 2004.

Smith, H. *The World's Religions: Our Great Wisdom Traditions*. San Francisco: HarperSanFrancisco, 1991. First published 1958 as *The Religions of Man*.

Tavris, C. *Anger: The Misunderstood Emotion* (rev. ed.). New York: Simon & Schuster, 1989.

Thatcher, R., and Kelley, M. "Slaying Suspect Surrenders." *Austin American-Statesman*, July 14, 1999, p. A1.

U.S. Environmental Protection Agency, Office of Pollution Prevention and Toxics. *Constructive Engagement Resource Guide: Practical Advice for Dialogue Among Facilities, Workers, Communities and Regulators*. Washington, D.C.: U.S. Environmental Protection Agency, 1999.

Watkins, J. M., and Mohr, B. J. *Appreciative Inquiry: Change at the Speed of Imagination*. San Francisco: Jossey-Bass/Pfeiffer, 2001.

About the Author

Suzanne Ghais has facilitated a wide variety of group processes in the organizational and public-policy arenas. She has worked with large and small corporations, government agencies at all levels, industry and business associations, educational and health care institutions, and nonprofit organizations from large advocacy groups to local volunteer committees. She has also trained thousands of people in a variety of skills including facilitation, mediation, arbitration, negotiation, conflict resolution, and communication. She began a career in conflict resolution in 1990 and earned a Master of Science degree in conflict analysis and resolution from George Mason University in 1996. The same year, she began work at CDR Associates as a facilitator, mediator, trainer, researcher, and writer. Ms. Ghais is a member of the Association for Conflict Resolution and the International Association of Facilitators.

Index